Creole Recitations

Creole Recitations

JOHN JACOB THOMAS AND COLONIAL FORMATION IN THE LATE NINETEENTH-CENTURY CARIBBEAN

Faith Smith

New World Studies

A. James Arnold, editor

University of Virginia Press

Charlottesville and London

University of Virginia Press
© 2002 by the Rector and Visitors of the University of Virginia
All rights reserved
Printed in the United States of America on acid-free paper
First published 2002

9 8 7 6 5 4 3 2 1

Library of Congress Cataloging-in-Publication Data
Smith, Faith, 1964–
    Creole recitations : John Jacob Thomas and colonial formation in the
late nineteenth-century Caribbean / Faith Smith.
        p. cm. — (New world studies)
Includes bibliographical references and index.
    ISBN 0-8139-2142-2 (cloth : alk paper) — ISBN 0-8139-2143-0 (pbk : alk paper)
    1. Thomas, J. J. (John Jacob) 2. Scholars—Trinidad—Biography.
3. Creole dialects—Caribbean Area. 4. Blacks—Race identity—Caribbean
Area. 5. Black nationalism—Caribbean Area. 6. Trinidad—Biography.
I. Title. II. Series.
    CT388.T48 S55 2002
    972.983'03'092—dc21

For Winifred Josephine and Ashley Alexander

Contents

Preface

THE FIRST part of my title evokes images of the colonial classroom: Jamaica Kincaid's protagonist in *Lucy* being smothered by Wordsworth's daffodils (18) and Patrick Chamoiseau's young student struggling to reconcile the French of the schoolroom with the Creole speech of his home. Twentieth-century Caribbean literature and music are replete with examples of the mindless recitals of the colonial classroom—Sparrow's *Dan Is the Man in the Van* comes to mind here:

> . . . But in MY days in
> school they teach me like a fool THE
> THINGS THEY TEACH ME A SHOULDA
> BEEN A BLOCK-HEADED MULE
> Pussy has finish his work long ago
> An now he restin and ting. . . .
>   (Brathwaite, *Roots,* 280, his emphasis)

Yet recitations by generations of schoolchildren of verse such as Henry Wadsworth Longfellow's are often represented as more than just an assault on the vowels and postures or an insult to the intelligence of the region's children:

> The heights of great men reached and kept
> Were not attained by sudden flight;
> But they while their companions slept
> Were toiling upward in the night.

Just as Beenie Man uses Longfellow to assure his rivals that he worked hard to achieve his superior ranking and that he will not compromise his principles, "toiling upward in the night" pays tribute to the intellectual labor of generations of Black male schoolmasters struggling to displace the image of cane cutting, which the colonial economy and metropolitan visitors deemed the proper occupation of Black bodies.

John Jacob Thomas, the subject of my study, toils through the night in the late 1860s, teaching himself modern and ancient languages in rural ward schools in Couva, Savonetta, and Cedros, in central and southwestern Trinidad, after instructing his young students in the three R's during the day. These late-night labors in rural Trinidad as well as in the Trinidad Public Library in Port of Spain transform him in the eyes of his peers from a good primary-school teacher into a scholar praised for his 1869 text *The Theory and Practice of Creole Grammar,* his lecture before the Philological Society in London in 1873, and his vindication of Caribbean people and people of the Black diaspora in his 1889 *Froudacity: West Indian Fables by J. A. Froude.*

Indeed Thomas's whole life is a kind of vindication, as he delivers lectures in Port of Spain and San Fernando and writes letters to newspapers. In January 1884, as the new headmaster of the San Fernando High School, he delivers an address to a well-attended event at the Baptist Tabernacle titled "Teaching as It Is and Ought to Be." On the first day of the term he tells students and their parents that he is a strict disciplinarian but hates the "rod" and hopes that parents will share disciplinary responsibilities. Two weeks later he defends himself against the charge by the local French priest that the "*soi-disant* High School" and his installment as head are the result of a "freemason conspiracy." Identifying himself as a freemason, Thomas laments "the old talk about secular education alienating the recipients of it from the Holy Catholic Church," a perspective that "leaves the student as void of Science as he is full of Theology." "I, who am born of the people," Thomas tells the priest, "and who belong to them, have better opportunities of knowing their feelings and their needs than any outsider, however sincere he may be in striving for their welfare."[1]

A year later Thomas resigns from the position to protest the San Fernando Borough Council's refusal to remove the Scottish headmistress of the Girls High School, from whose cruelty, as well as lack of deportment and dress sense, he says his own children and others suffer. In July 1888, as he leaves the Caribbean for England to seek publication of the "Froudacity" manuscript, he accepts the thanks of students he has been tutoring in St. George's, Grenada's capital, praising the "correct style" of the letters they have addressed to him in Spanish.[2]

The ponderous reference to grammar in responding to a student's letter of thanks, the delineation of outsider and insider in his objections to French priests and Scottish schoolteachers, the reference to physical appearance in his criticism of a female teacher, and the casting of Catholicism as anti-populist and antimodern by the man who marries Mary Ann Jane Regis in the Port of Spain Roman Catholic Cathedral in 1876[3]—I am interested in such labored vindications.

Thomas offers his own account of his life in the 25 October 1884 issue of the *San Fernando Gazette*, calling it "What has Been, Is, and Might have Been, Being Records of a Student and Official Life in Trinidad," a "prologue" to a forthcoming publication. Like so many of his other proposed publications, this one is never published, but in the article he sets out his own conception of an "exceptional" career in "the fierce light of public attention." He promises to "speak plainly" of the encouraging as well as unjust criticism of his work, his rise from humble circumstances, the "high personages" who have supported him, the people who have attacked him for "refusing to act according to promptings foreign to my nature," his ideas about teaching.

Thomas says that his proposed "Autobiography" will employ no "artifice" or "fine writing" and will be divided according to the "epochs" of his life: 1841–44, birth and childhood; 1844–58, school days; 1858–67, days as a student and teacher; 1867–1879, official career; and 1877–83, illness and tribulations. He thus proposes to give his own account of a life spent almost entirely under public scrutiny. Depending on which of his peers is telling the story, Thomas's "official career"—placing first in the new competitive civil service exams and leaving teaching for a position as a third locker clerk in the receiver general's office, with subsequent appointments as clerk of the peace in Cedros and Caroni, secretary to the council of Queen's Royal College, and secretary to the board of education—either demonstrates the liberalism of the colonial authorities or is the inadequate response to complaints that civil service appointments are reserved for White men.

"Illness" no doubt refers to the rheumatism and partial blindness that prompted his early retirement with a pension in 1879, but "tribulations" could refer to any number of things. If published as proposed in the early 1880s, such a narrative would have omitted his decision to leave Trinidad to go and live in Grenada sometime in the late 1880s, and the year in England poring over books in the British Library as he prepared a revised edition of the *Creole Grammar* and tried to raise funds to publish *Froudacity*. He died of phthisis in King's College Hospital, London, on 20 September 1889, weeks after the publication of *Froudacity*, leaving his widow and three children.

As one of the better-known figures of the last decades of the nineteenth-century anglophone Caribbean, Thomas has been thoroughly assessed by many commentators. They celebrate his audacity in responding, as a "self-taught" man, to a prominent Victorian intellectual, note his defense of the Creole language and Black diasporic perspectives long before twentieth-century proponents, and marvel at his extreme faith both in British institutions and in the capacity of Whites to share power with Blacks and Coloreds in the Caribbean (Anthony; Benn; Brereton, "John Jacob Thomas"; Barros; Campbell, "John Jacob Thomas"; Cudjoe, "The Audacity of It All"; Harris; James, "West Indian Intellectual"; G. Lewis; R. Lewis; Rohlehr, "Froudacity"; F. Smith, "John Jacob Thomas"; F. Smith, "Man"; Wood, "John Jacob Thomas").

But what follows is neither a biography nor an assessment. As I pore over his *récits,* the stories that he and others tell about nation, class, and race, I am interested in re-citations, in resituating my own contexts. I am after a messier, richer texture of literary and cultural production in both the late nineteenth century and the twentieth. Kincaid's statement that she never aspired to be a writer because she never knew they existed (Cudjoe, "Jamaica Kincaid," 218) raises questions for me about the precise ways in which newer Caribbean writers are connected to earlier generations of writers. With what institutions of education and publication, for instance, has Kincaid been linked, relative to writers such as George Lamming, and what are the stories of generation, class, and gender that we can tell about such linkages? (see Edmondson). Selwyn Cudjoe's celebration of the "audacity" with which Thomas and other men responded to metropolitan figures makes me want to see whether the peripheral relationship to metropolitan affairs that makes their achievements laudable mystifies their prominence relative to others—middle-class women, working-class men and women—who do not have the same degree of access to significant public institutions. His linking Thomas and the Colored solictor general of Trinidad in Thomas's time, Michel Maxwell Philip, as Black vindicators makes sense given that both smarted at being passed over for positions given to less-qualified expatriate Whites. At the same time, there are significant differences: Philip organized a ball for White and Colored Creoles in 1876 from which dark-skinned people reportedly were excluded (Brereton, *Race Relations,* 98, 103).

Rupert Lewis's noting Thomas's awkward fit in the course on modern political thought at the University of the West Indies—since Thomas, like John Stuart Mill and Harriet Taylor, was a liberal polemicist, though this, according to Lewis cannot fully account for him—raises questions for me about classification. "Victorian liberal polemicist" should surely be one of the ways in which Thomas is contextualized, and yet it does not fully describe him. How can Thomas be made sense of in the postcolonial university curriculum?

Wilson Harris's critique of *Froudacity* as symptomatic of the dead end in which Thomas and other Caribbean intellectuals have been locked takes issue with C. L. R. James's contention that Thomas "overwhelms" Froude. Just as Froude represents Whites' ownership of property in the Caribbean as fortuitous, Thomas's juxtaposition of *good* governors and administrators, who underscore the rightness of the law, and *bad* governors, who make of the law a bad instrument, commits him, according to Harris, to "fortuitous idols on the side of heaven or on the side of hell" (7). Property (for Froude) and the law (for Thomas) are represented as essentially good. Thomas, Harris insists, was a child of the nineteenth century who "could not supply a figurative meaning beyond the condition he deplored." He and Froude thus "consolidated an intellectual censorship of significant vestiges of the subconscious imagination"—limbo, vodun, Carib bush-baby omens—"which they needed to explore if they were to begin to apprehend a figurative meaning beyond the real or apparently real world" (8).[4] What, I want to ask, is at stake for Thomas in his discussion of good governors and bad ones? Might his very livelihood depend on the whims of individual colonial governors in a way that late-twentieth-century commentators depend on institutions such as the university rather than the state as such? If Thomas and Froude both censor vodun, do they do so in the same way or with similar consequences? In what terms do other readers of the period respond to Froude's text or to travel narratives generally?

I use Thomas to get a clearer sense of how situations familiar to me in the twentieth century—the complicated blend of desire and repudiation that Caribbean ideologues have shown toward England and English writers, the gendering of national and racial discourses, the evidently natural association of Creole languages with "folk" or working-class "authenticity"—might appear from the vantage point of the latter half of the nineteenth century.

What is the significance, for instance, of the word so often used in descriptions of Thomas—*self-taught*—or of C. L. R. James's description in his introduction to the 1969 edition of *Froudacity*, "the Trinidad schoolmaster without European or university education of any kind?" ("West Indian Intellectual," 27). What did *self-taught* mean in a British colony in the mid-nineteenth century? "The schoolmaster has been sufficiently long abroad," or some version of this phrase, permeates the pages of late-nineteenth-century newspapers in Trinidad, often during pre-Lenten

Carnival celebrations. It registers impatience with the persistence of obeah, all-night drumming sessions, or illiteracy in English—anything perceived to hinder the advent of modernity. The "schoolmaster abroad" is the antidote to backwardness, the sign of hope that the remnants of slavery's perceived negative legacies will be obliterated. Yet Thomas's *Creole Grammar* shows him to be in disagreement with the conviction of many local and foreign commentators who predicted that Creole speech was destined to die out as well. What should be kept, and what discarded, in the march toward progress?

In the past decade a nostalgia for the good old days of male school-teachers such as Thomas has been coupled with a characterization of the current preponderance of women in the Caribbean classroom as a patholog-ical stifling of male possibility (Miller, *Men at Risk* and *Marginalization*). I am interested in how *self-taught* and *schoolmaster* mark and re-mark the idealization of the Black male figure celebrated as the cornerstone of anglophone Caribbean societies, the center of every small village, the master of "good English," the teacher who enters the professions when this becomes possible, and the rightful candidate to assume the leadership of nationalist struggles when the time comes. James romanticizes the men who "have made the Caribbean what it is today. [They] taught you every-thing you needed to know: reading, writing, arithmetic, proper behav-iour, good manners, how you were to wear your clothes—everything" ("Discovering Literature," 239–40). "Everything you needed to know"— who? and for what? Is there a separate cataloguing of the things one might need to know provided by women of the same class, or by working-class or non-Black men and women? Furthermore, in precisely what sense would Thomas and others of the 1870s and 1880s have provided James with a critical vocabulary for the modes of life that he and others were beginning to interpret in the mid-1930s: is James being *dutiful* here?

The "black English country gentleman" who is the persona's grandfather in Kamau Brathwaite's "Ancestors" (*Arrivants,* 239). James's grandfather, going to church every Sunday in the "broiling" sun in his "frock-coat, striped trousers and top-hat, with his walking-stick in hand, surrounded by his family, the underwear of the women crackling with starch," the "armour" of "lower middle-class respectability" keeping the "mass of poverty, dirt, ignorance and vice" at bay (*Beyond a Boundary,* 17–18). Naipaul's B. Wordsworth: "Black Wordsworth. White Wordsworth was my brother" (*Miguel Street,* 40). In these presentations of a respectable Black lower middle class by the region's canonical writers there is a strong sense of incongruity. All that clothing in the boiling sun. The English so

good "it didn't sound natural" (*Miguel Street,* 39), the kind of sentiment
that had riled Thomas and others almost a century earlier. But besides the
incongruity, the loss and nostalgia after the demise of these men is palpable
in each narrative. We might say that the period from the late 1950s to the
late 1960s, when these texts are written, is a moment of celebration of these
figures, though they are also ironized for their pretentious Englishness by
Naipaul ("Flag on the Island"). Thomas's extant texts are republished by a
diasporic Caribbean community resident in England. As some Caribbean
nations are experiencing their new independent status, at a heady moment
for Black nationalism in the late 1960s, and during the struggle to assert
the rights of Black immigrants at the seat of the empire the intellectual
abilities of the Black man, past and present, are being rehearsed. Thomas
is at once a late-nineteenth-century pan-Africanist precursor of Marcus
Garvey, a Caribbean anti-imperialist who is an important nodal point in a
tradition stretching "from Toussaint L'Ouverture to Fidel Castro," and a
worthy competitor of White Victorian intellectuals.[5] A recent Caribbean
guidebook says of Thomas: "For a largely self-educated black West Indian
of that era to take on one of the foremost British academic figures of the
day was no mean thing. His courage in doing so has been amply rewarded
by the oblivion which soon befell Froude's book, compared with the fame
that has accrued to *Froudacity* ever since" (Dyde, 159).

The significance of Thomas's nonacademic formation, the way in which
Froude remains an important standard even as he is supposedly being
vanquished, and the way in which *educated, black, West Indian,* and
male fold into each other naturally are all interesting to me. But I also find
interesting Naipaul's investment in the travel narratives of Froude and
others (*Middle Passage*). How does the Victorian travel narrative position
the region's working classes, Indian and Black, relative to each other?
How do Indians figure in the elaboration of national, "Creole" discourses
by Thomas and others?

I want to immerse Thomas in a network of institutions and recitations
in an effort to unearth these things. Rather than presenting a complete life,
then, I begin in the middle of an event, moving forward, backward, or in
circles. Thomas's relationship to institutions such as the metropolitan
university, Queen's Royal College, or the San Fernando Borough School is
clarified with reference to Black political reformers of the early twentieth
century such as C. P. David, Thomas's pupil at the Borough School, who
was present at his deathbed in London, as well as those Coloreds and
Whites whose cultural production preceded or coincided with his own in
the 1870s and 1880s. These include Jean-Baptiste Phillipe, the slave-owner

physician who petitioned for the rights of free people of color in his 1824
Free Mulatto, Michel Maxwell Philip, whose 1854 novel *Emmanuel
Appadocca* portrayed a Colored protagonist's revenge on his White father,
the White physician Louis de Verteuil, who wrote a comprehensive study
of Trinidad's natural resources, and P. G. L. Borde, the White writer of a
two-volume history of Trinidad.

When Thomas objects to "fine writing" and "artifice" in his proposed
autobiography, then, I am curious about how this might be linked to his
access, or lack thereof, to particular institutions and curricula, given the
access to grammar schools and universities that some of his peers had. But
Thomas also helps to pinpoint a regional network of nineteenth-century
figures and contexts: Haitian intellectuals such as Hannibal Price, Louis
Janvier and Anténor Firmin, whose vindication of Black people locally
and globally privileged bourgeois French culture; Black and White French-
speaking Creole activists in Louisiana in the mid-nineteenth century; the
Afro-Cuban mutual aid societies, newspapers, and organizations that
sponsored libraries and lecture series and forged complicated alliances
with White Cubans in the repudiation of colonialism; pan-Africanists
such as St. Thomas–born Edward Blyden; North Americans such as
Frances E. Harper and Alexander Crummell; and later figures such as
Trinidadian H. Sylvester Williams, the Jamaican-born pan-Africanist
Theophilus Scholes, who wrote *Glimpses of the Ages, or the Superior and
Inferior Races So-Called, Discussed in the Light of Science and History,*
and the Guyanese Norman Cameron, author of *The Evolution of the
Negro* (Firmin; Plummer; Dash, *Literature and Ideology;* Bell; Howard,
Helg; Bryan, "Black Perspectives"; Brereton, "Historiography," 5).

Thomas can also be positioned in relation to the Venezuelan Andrés
Bello and other Latin American intellectuals who negotiated between "the
blatant neocolonialist greed of the Europeans they so admired" and the
"tremors and volcanic eruptions from below," the "subordinated indigenous, mestizo, and African majorities, many of whom had fought in the
wars of independence" (Pratt, 175). Their novels and other texts encoded
national, White Creole identities by documenting the evils of slavery but
"narratively closing off the possibility of slave rebellion as a legitimate
option in the struggle to end them" (Márquez, 297). Doris Sommer draws
our attention to the ways in which the writing of history and fiction were
closely tied to nation building in the Latin American context. "Can there
be a national life without a national literature?" asked José Martí, despairing over the lack of cultural autonomy in Mexico and celebrating its man-
ifestation in the Dominican Republic, in the form of Manuel de Jesús

Galván's 1882 *Enriquillo* (Sommer 9–10). In such texts, as Sommer shows, the heterosexual marriage plot is used to show that love rather than force secures and maintains hierarchies of power.

When the journalist Philip Rostant chides Thomas in 1884 for frittering away his obvious talent on satirical verse instead of a historical novel, he can be interpreted as participating in a discussion about what discourses are suitable to a modern Trinidad. The ordered rhyming couplet of the neoclassicists, charged with personal invective, must give way, presumably, to the narrative expansiveness of a novel documenting the characteristics of the nation. Though Rostant elsewhere expresses his distaste for Émile Zola—the nationalist novel cannot be *indecent,* after all—he suggests a preoccupation with form that is outside the scope of the present study, one that links Philip's 1854 *Emmanuel Appadocca* to Rostant's displeasure in the late 1880s, to novels such as Robert Archer Tracy's 1919 *Sword of Nemesis* and Valerie Belgrave's *Ti Marie.* Thomas does not write a novel, but his letters to the editor and his books are his contributions to nationalist discourses.

Thomas's links to a Black lower middle class increasingly visible in Trinidad's public arena toward the end of the century, to Trinidadian society, and to the eastern Caribbean and his interests in a francophone trajectory stretching from the southeastern Caribbean to Louisiana, in Victorian intellectual life, and in an African diasporic community, place him in many different contexts. Barry Higman distinguishes between a "Black stream" of late-nineteenth-century historians in the Caribbean who were born in the West Indies, wrote their texts after traveling outside of the region, and were global and diasporic in perspective and a White stream of gentleman historians who were relatively parochial, tended to be made up of expatriate Englishmen who had resided for a long time in the Caribbean, and pursued interests in the natural sciences and literature. The latter stream was typified by James Rodway, of British Guiana, and N. Darnell Davis, of Grenada and British Guiana, while Thomas and Blyden would be examples of the former (Higman, 56; Brereton, "Historiography"; Goveia).

While Higman's distinction is very useful, it glosses over the difference between Blyden, who does not return to the Caribbean, and Thomas and Davis, who are born in the Caribbean and reside there for most of their lives. If Whites such as Davis are parochial, it is in the context of having the resources to travel outside of the region whenever they choose to do so. The challenge here is to see how Thomas's discourses gesture "in multiple directions at once," to quote Elsa Barkley Brown (Bair 121).

In the past decade we have been encouraged to replace a limited conception of intellectuals and literary canons that ties them rigidly to nationalist and racial agendas with a conception of what Carole Boyce Davies calls "migratory subjectivities," which privileges border crossing (Appiah; Gilroy, *There Ain't No Black;* Gilroy, *Black Atlantic;* Gilroy, "Cultural Studies"; Davies). Here, specifying location and context are essential to disrupting seamless, blanket pronouncements of blackness, as is noting how subjects borrow from many traditions. With reference to contextualizing Thomas, Gilroy's work helpfully undermines Englishness, critiquing its claims to superiority and stressing the "black in the Union Jack" that is concealed by idealized representations of the British Isles, from the beginning of the Enlightenment to our Merchant-Ivory present. In this regard, Gilroy reminds us of the Black British identities that are "English," "Irish," "Scottish," "Welsh," no matter how tenuously, with whom visitors to England such as Thomas must sometimes have had contact. Besides critiquing an Englishness that would deny these identities, Gilroy also questions an African American stranglehold on blackness in popular music and in literary and intellectual histories by stressing the place of Europe in the formation of intellectuals from the United States.

However, the notion that diasporic and Atlantic paradigms should be used to dislodge nationalist narratives risks occluding the specific context of British colonial subjects such as Thomas, since undermining English and American national hegemonies is not quite the same thing as undermining Trinidadian ones. This is not because colonial Trinidad promises Thomas and others an unquestioned share of the fruits of modernity. Indeed, he and others struggle for limited franchise reform in a crown colony system of colonial government administered by an English governor, an executive council made up of English officials appointed by the governor, and a legislative council made up of appointed officials and two nominated "Unofficials." In principle, the crown colony system protected colonial subjects from oppressive landowning interests, and in practice it gave the British colonial administration more control than did the assembly systems with elected representatives in colonies such as Barbados. Despite significant tensions between expatriate government officials and nominated "Unofficials" resident in Trinidad, the latter were drawn from the planter-merchant constituency, particularly sugar interests, and shared the worldview of the expatriate community in important respects (Brereton, *Race Relations,* 24–33).

The elaboration of a diasporic context that uncritically renders all nationalisms equally essentialist and hegemonic can further marginalize the nationalist and anti-imperialist struggles, no matter how limited, of Thomas and others. "Britain" and "America" are demystified in Gilroy's account, but by virtue of being the only spaces under discussion they are also again privileged. In this sense, a diasporic context can help to further diminish the unremarked local space of Thomas's Trinidad (Edwards; Barnes). This is why it is so important to activate all of Thomas's perspectives simultaneously and to see how his diasporic discourses not only are a way for him to pursue a global Black nationhood without a state but help him to specify his local, national context. A diasporic context might usefully question national narratives, as Gilroy enjoins, but it can also *consolidate* them, as Thomas and others insert "Negro" discourses into what constitutes "Trinidadianness."

As an instance of this tension between the diasporic and the local, Sandra Pouchet-Pacquet takes issue with what she sees as the denial of the claims that Black Caribbean subjects can have on the space of the Caribbean in the following statement by Sylvia Wynter: "For the African in the New World became a Negro. And the Negro is the world's first uprooted race. He is the only race who is not tied to a land mass. The African belongs to Africa. The European to Europe. The 'negro' has no such territorial cradle" (Wynter, 34; Pouchet-Paquet, "Heartbeat," 132). "Not tied to a land mass" is inadequate to comprehend Mary Prince's attempt to escape enslavement while in England with her Caribbean owners in the early 1830s and then her attempt to return to her family in the Caribbean. For Pouchet Paquet, Prince "reveals a profound identification with the West Indies as a territorial cradle" (132).

Wynter, of course, means to indicate the liberatory registers of not being tied to Old World orthodoxies. Because Africans brought to America could not count on recovering their cultural forms intact, they led the way in forging hemispheric American modes: "a new cultural creation" (34). The loss of one range of specificities leads to the creation of another. Along the same lines, Sterling Stuckey notes: "During the process of becoming a single people, Yorubas, Akans, Ibos, Angolans and others were present on slave ships to America and experienced a common horror. . . . As such, slave ships were the first real incubators of slave unity across the cultural lines, cruelly revealing irreducible lines from one ethnic group to the other, fostering resistance thousands of miles before the shores of the new land appeared on the horizon" (1). As newly enslaved people leave the African continent, ethnicities and allegiances to local spaces are blurred and refigured during the period of slavery.

When can we imagine such allegiances being activated in relation to the Caribbean? Are Black subjects destined to be regarded as forever loosened from such ties, as in Anthony Trollope's statement in 1859: "But how strange is the race of Creole negroes—of negroes, that is, born out of Africa! They have no country of their own, yet have they not hitherto any country of their adoption; for, whether as slaves in Cuba, or as free labourers in the British isles, they are in each case a servile people in a foreign land" (55)? "Having no country of their own" nullifies the claims of Thomas and others to the right to participate in the political life of their colonies, to own land, or to demand fair wages. Their being "servile" and "foreign" consigns them to a particular relationship to others in their respective territories, destined to be outsiders.

IN HIS 1932 *Reminiscences of Old Trinidad* Lionel Osborne Innis recalls the female town crier on Trinidad's streets in the mid- to late nineteenth century, attired in traditional Creole clothing, what he terms "Martinique dress": chemise, *jupe,* foulard, "zano cylendre in her ears, grain d'or round her neck, and stiff canlandey headkerchief." Three or four of these criers would be hired to announce the particulars of a family "having a dead": "Ladies and gentlemen, the funeral will take place this afternoon at the Cathedral. The deceased used to sell plantains at the market. His mother sells accras and floats in front of Mauvais Temps rumshop" (Besson, 67). Because newspapers appeared only weekly, Innis notes, these criers were crucial to the dissemination of information within the community. Speaking in Creole, they addressed a Creole-speaking community: "Patois was the almost universal language of the people and no one could get on without it; and it seems a pity to think it is dying out. Jacob Thomas, a Government school-master, years ago, made a grammar of the Patois, but there are very few copies of it extant now. At the time, I did not think it deserved the dignity of a grammar, as it was only bad French and bound to die out, as the younger generation were being educated in English, and my prediction has come true."

Innis presents a powerful portrait of a world marked by cohesion as well as by its difference from his present. The quaintly dressed town criers are superseded by more newspapers, as well as by the English language. That Creole is "dying out" is "a pity," but it is inevitable in the face of a willed modernity. He offers this account, at once nostalgic and practical, just before a period considered to mark the birth of "modern" literature as well as politics in the anglophone Caribbean. As I will show, Thomas and others struggled to distinguish between the "jumby stories" of the premodern past and the modern narratives that would usher in Trinidad's future. Reflecting both creolized African folkways and plantation regimes, jumby stories were quaint if properly contained and dangerous if regarded as truth.

Though Thomas cannot take for granted that he is the social equal of many, if not most, of the persons with whom he participates in bringing Trinidad into the modern age, I refer to him as an *elite* in what follows, meaning simply anyone above the level of those considered to be part of the lower classes. The term thus embraces Thomas, who was of working-class origins, Louis de Verteuil, the most prominent member of the White francophone Creoles, and Victorian intellectuals. This usage is deeply problematic, to be sure, but it allows me to group together all those who participated in the public dissemination of "respectable" discourses or those who belonged in the same social groups as persons who did. There are many classes of elites in the period under consideration, but all are at least lower-middle-class and educated, differentiated from the disreputable masses but also from the "poor but respectable" members of the lower classes such as Thomas's parents.[6] Their words are taken seriously, and they are written about and quoted in the newspapers.

I focus on newspapers because they are an important source of nation-alists' discussions in the late nineteenth century. Thomas has as much access to them as his wealthy compatriots. Focusing on newspapers gives me a broader field than Thomas's extant texts but also limits me to the selective interests of those associated with this genre, for example, the economic interests represented by advertisements for Holloways Pills and other products. I isolate articles and words that contemporary readers would have linked to yesterday's explosion or last year's ball, incidents perhaps never reported. It may be that in cases where I assume that an excerpt of Creole speech or a letter to the editor with grammatical errors was clearly intended to suggest to an elite readership that the correspondent did not have a good command of the English language, contemporary readers of those papers in the 1870s and 1880s understood the writers of such passages to be elite members of society who were deliberately using such discourse.

This may well be the case with a letter to the editor in the 15 August 1883 edition of the *Trinidad Chronicle:* "You better look out or I are pro-mis to give you a good thrashing the very first time I see you with my hors whip which is not the first time you deserves it. You d —— demerara muddle head brut [you] better stop them dirty artikles. Yours truly, The Avenger." Below the signature of this letter is an octagonal drawing inscribed "Your Koffen." Since it is headlined "An Interesting Letter," I assume that the editor draws his well-read and well-spoken readers' attention to its grammatical peculiarities, but the writer may very well be a gentleman mimicking a member of the working class who is trying to perform the role of a gentleman in a context known by the readers of the newspaper.

If Benedict Anderson is right to identify the newspaper as central to the beginning of modern conceptions of citizenship because of how it facilitated the experience of the simultaneity, or "meanwhileness," of time, it is important to keep in mind that this medium did not embrace all of its readers in quite the same way. When "Dolly" was congratulated for "Only a Country Lass," a story published in the Trinidad paper *Public Opinion* on 14 October 1887, it was clear that many of her readers knew who she was. Dolly and other women of her class presumably read these papers, contributed letters and other items, and joined their male counterparts in imagining various versions of Trinidad's future. However, just as Innis's past is powerfully embodied in a woman dressed in francophone attire, or just as some Colored men aligned themselves publicly with other men of African descent by identifying with "my mother's race," women were imagined in specific, gendered ways in relation to Trinidad. Relying on a medium that powerfully invoked this gendered rhetoric privileges the men who owned and edited these papers, to the detriment of not only women such as Dolly but also the majority of Trinidad's inhabitants imagined as marginal.

In highlighting the words of Thomas and others in such newspapers, then, I am not attending to the 166 "descendants of Africa" who petition the San Fernando Borough Council in 1867, such as Rose Turner ("Ever since I was a child, I have never seen Trinidad so hard for the poor black people to get a living as now") and Thomas Richardson ("Those employers of a clearer hue will prefer to have the coolie labourers, because they can beat them as they like, whereas they cannot beat the Creole labourers in that manner" [Brereton, *Race Relations,* 148–49]). Nor Ramdin, the San Fernando shopkeeper who testifies that he explained the police regulations to people who came into his shop at the inquest to investigate the brutal killings by the police force of Hosay participants in 1884.[7] It is not their voices I attend to here but the discussions of gentlemen about submissiveness or about why Ramdin, twenty-seven years resident in Trinidad when he testifies in 1884, is never considered "Creole."

Recitations are a tedious business: don't recount the details of the plot, I tell my students. Yet I have reproduced the narratives of Thomas and his contemporaries, sometimes word for word, because I am interested precisely in their narration. A colleague once objected to my reference to "*the representation of* Indian men as wife murderers" in my discussion of nineteenth-century narratives. My reference to "representation" seemed to use rhetoric to displace the material reality of the many women who were killed by their partners during this period. Far from diluting the political and historical import of these murders, I would argue, "the representation of" alerts me to the ways in which language constructs rather than represents reality. Not only are Indian men represented as hardworking cane cutters and submissive house servants in the same breath as they are reported to have killed their sexual partners but the Victorian travel writers who relate these *récits* never refer at such moments to wife murderers at "home" in England. These connections made and not made have the effect of making powerful, naturalized correspondences for readers. It is Thomas's and others' rhetorical negotiations that interest me here.

Acknowledgments

I WANT to thank my editor, Cathie Brettschneider, who believed in this project long before I did. I thank Julius Scott, Eve Sedgewick, and Susan Thorne for their questions and encouragement, as well as Kenneth Surin, Toril Moi, and Jacqueline Looney, who, more than they could possibly know, helped me to survive the dissertation stage of this project. Susan Staves, Fionnguala Sweeney, Maureen Warner-Lewis, and Belinda Edmondson went over portions of the dissertation or manuscript with a fine-toothed comb, and I want to thank them for their generosity. Gordon Rohlehr, Jeffrey Green, John La Rose, and Monica Sherwoood will hardly remember now how they helped me. Natasha Barnes's advice provided much-needed focus. Scholars on whose work I draw here, including Catherine Hall, Bridget Brereton, Maureen Warner-Lewis, Carl Campbell, Michel DeGraff, and Gerard Besson generously shared their time and expertise with me. Winifred Smith, Marjorie Salvodon, and Canon Ancil Ramsay provided invaluable translation assistance. I am grateful for the support of Molly Krakauer, Lisa Pannella, Theresa D. Cedrone, Lianne Finney, and Jennifer Cook. Mrs. Joyce Thomas has been an inspiration. For their patience and persistence I thank Joanne Allen and David Sewell.

No less than four department chairs and two deans supported my requests for leave and conference funding. An Advanced International Fellowship from the Graduate School of Duke University, a Latin American Studies Jane's Award, Mazer Awards, conference travel grants, and a Bernstein-Marcus Fellowship from Brandeis University supported me in the writing of this book. A Brandeis University Mazer Award allowed me to use the cover art; I am grateful to Chris Cozier for his generosity. An Andrew Mellon Foundation fellowship allowed me to use the Huntington Library. The Black Atlantic Seminars of the Rutgers University Center for Historical Analysis provided me with a collegial atmosphere in which to air my work, as did meetings of the Associations of African Literature, American Literature, Caribbean Historians, Caribbean Studies, and Caribbean Women Writers and Scholars, the C. L. R. James Society, and the Mid-Atlantic Conference on British Studies. Audiences at the "Contextualizing the Caribbean" and "Re-thinking Caribbean Culture" conferences also gave me valuable feedback, as did colleagues at the Tulane African Diaspora Studies and the University of Rochester Black Studies Speaker Series. I continue to draw sustenance from members of the Small Axe Collective.

For their invaluable assistance I am indebted to librarians of the Interlibrary Loan Departments of Duke and Brandeis Universities, the West Indian and Special Collections at the University of the West Indies at St. Augustine and at Mona, the Manuscript and Newspaper Collections of the British Library, the Public Records Office at Kew, the Huntington, John Carter Brown, and Houghton Libraries, and the Barbados, Grenada, and Trinidad Government Archives. I wish to thank in particular Sandra Barnes and Kathleen Helenese Paul, at the Main Library of the University of the West Indies at St. Augustine.

I have been extremely fortunate in having a community of colleagues, friends, and family members, not named here, who have helped me to put my work in its proper perspective. Brandeis colleagues in English and American literature, African and Afro-American studies, and Latin American studies took me out to dinner and kept my spirits up during particularly stressful periods. On Pine, Riverside, Carver, and Constantinople Streets, Quail Point Drive, and Wyldewood, Sequoia, and Seven Oaks Roads; Tantine Trace, Waterhall Terrace, and Hololo Mount Road; in Gamle, Lac Superieure and at Thornton Heath; at Margaret, Mammee River, Ritchie, Worthington Terrace, and Parkin Close, many friends and family members consoled and encouraged me and indulged my sweet tooth. Here in the Boston area, Porter Road, Pleasant Avenue, Maynard and Abbey, Dana, Chestnut, Queensberry, Mount Vernon, and Watson Streets have become second homes to me. My friends at Smart Street supported me unstintingly. First one, then two, and now three residents of Stephen Street laugh at all of my jokes. Finally, I hope that present and former residents of 20 South Monterey know how much their support has meant to me.

Creole Recitations

Introduction

Keywords

LOCATED IN the southeastern Caribbean, close to the Venezuelan coast, and with a population of just over one hundred thousand, John Jacob Thomas's mid-nineteenth-century Trinidad was a complex array of constituencies straining against the supposedly stable, distinct, knowable classifications of classes, religions, ethnicities, and races.[1] *Panyols* (from *espagnols*) were the descendants of the few remaining indigenous *Amerindians,* or Warahouns, who migrated back and forth between the South American mainland and Trinidad's southern coast, and rural loggers and cocoa laborers whose ranks were continuously swelled by migrants from Venezuela (see Moodie-Kubalsingh). This group tended to be racially mixed—Amerindian, African, and European—and did not include those exiled, upper-class Venezuelans who were part of the dominant White Catholic group.

Most of the rest of the society was classified as *European, African* or *East Indian.* As Daniel Segal has pointed out, these were understood as three distinct racial groups, identifiable "in terms of an ancestral territory, that is, a delimited area belonging to and occupied by its own 'race' [from] which they were said to have 'originated'" (82).[2] *Persons of color, Colored,* or *mixed-blood* usually referred to members of the society who had both African and European ancestry. This ancestry was understood as being readable on the body, with a corresponding social categorization that ranged from working class to wealthy plantation owner. Individual Coloreds were thus similar to many Blacks and many Whites socially, but as a group they were often assumed to be distinct from either group.

Onto these general categorizations was superimposed a range of specificities that might be comfortably absorbed within the larger framework or stand out incongruously: Black, White, French, English, Yoruba; Barbadian, Negro, Hindu, Chinese, Scotch; Asiatic, Madeiran, Presbyterian,

American, Catholic, Mohammedan; heathenish, respectable, violent, sensitive, urban, squatter; cold, alien, English and warm, volatile French; "heathen" Indians and Chinese who nevertheless originated from valid cultures and civilizations; Negroes adaptable to whatever the rest of the world had to stamp on them.

Creole, African, and other terms hover over the period examined here either because they are embedded in discourses of the period or because they reflect inclinations in my present. I use *Caribbean* rather than Thomas's *West Indian,* for instance, in keeping with current perceptions of the latter term as narrowly anglophone. I use *Black* to refer generally to people of African descent, whereas Thomas and his contemporaries are more likely to use *Negro* and *African* and to distinguish these from *Colored* or *mixed-race* constituencies.[3] At the risk of keeping alive what are often deemed fictions of racial difference, I capitalize *Black, Colored, White,* and *Creole* to give them the same quasi-national, even civilizational, resonance as *Indian, African,* or *European.*

These and other terms are appealed to in ways that are both dynamic and conservatively static, and the "inquiry into a vocabulary" of a particular culture and society is a recognition that they are crucial to struggles for power in specific social circumstances (R. Williams, 15). This is the case in Thomas's time but also in mine. The national and diasporic institutions associated with Trinidad's state and individual citizens—the Carnival Commission, the Sanatan Dharma Maha Sabha, Paria, Calaloux, and New Beacon presses—currently compete for ownership of many of the terms discussed here. I examine Thomas's period from the vantage point of the university and from the perspective of the early twenty-first century, or perhaps more specifically, the post-postindependence period. This convergence of contexts produces readings that are more likely than not to question nationalist narratives, though in the sense of taking them for granted rather than of dismissing them. In addition, such readings tend to be provisional and to stress anxieties rather than the assertions of power that characterize more urgent agendas.

Thomas and his contemporaries responded to the contexts that gave these terms resonance, and with each utterance they brought into being definitions that helped them to structure their realities and iron out contradictions. Complacencies as well as anxieties attended the usage of these terms in the late nineteenth century, as commentators tested the extent to which *Negro* could be linked to *distinguished,* or *respectable* dislodged from *White.*

As much prescriptive as descriptive, and implying linguistic, phenotypic, nationalistic, or other resonances, *Creole*'s earliest usage in the hemisphere is generally identified as taking the form *criollos* in the hispanophone Caribbean, referring to Whites descended from European-born settlers but born in and claiming an attachment to the Americas. However, Maureen Warner-Lewis traces an even earlier usage to "Africans in Brazil [who wished] to designate their own children born and socialised in the Brazilian slave régime and therefore culturally alien from their parents," and she has also proposed a Kongo origin for *criollo:* "nkuulolo meaning 'alien person' or 'outsider'" ("Trinidad Yoruba," 50, 60 n. 1).

In both senses *Creole* has the register of "outsider who is cut off from the Old World (European or African)" or "insider" from the perspective of those born in or otherwise identifying themselves with the Americas. *Creole Negroes,* for instance, were distinguished from newly arrived, "unseasoned" Africans, who were designated *saltwater, bozal,* or *guinea.* Creoles who were Whites felt themselves to be judged and found wanting in relation to Europe. They were possessive of and proud of the space of the Americas, in which they sometimes dominated socially but at other times could not because of the hegemony of European officials. *Creole* carries both a negative connotation of lack, with regard to sullying some essential racial or Old World purity, and a related, positive characteristic of mixture, in the sense of combining—phenotypically, linguistically, culturally—the "best" of two essentially different groups.[4]

The self-evident connotation of essential authenticity in the term is suggested by the Martinican authors of *Eloge de la créolité:* "Creole, our first language, we the Caribbeans, the Guyanese, the Mascarins, is the initial means of communication of our deep self, or our collective unconscious, of our common genius, and it remains the river of our alluvial Creoleness" (Bernabé, Chamoiseau, and Confiant 899).

A less rhapsodic account is offered by Maryse Condé, who questions the "simplistic" opposition between French as a language of colonization and Creole as a "mother tongue" of resistance. Creole was "the language of unity and compromise [between] slaves from different origins and masters rather than the core of resistance," writes Condé (95). Impatient with claims that the mere presence of Creole language "guarantees the authenticity of Antillean writing" (95), Condé suggests that Creole's connection to explicit sex in the work of some Martinican writers serves to exoticize Caribbean cultures for a French reading public.

In a similarly dispassionate tone Nigel Bolland takes issue with the notion that creolization is the product of the cultures of (European) master and (African) slave, "as if these are individuals who have an existence independent of each other, rather than social roles that are mutually constituted and defined by their relationship" (64). Rather than examining *Europe* or *Africa* as if they represented unified homogenous entities that were then introduced into the Caribbean context in an undifferentiated manner—British colonialism as an "outside influence" or various religious practices examined as if they had the same meaning in all of the African societies in which they originated—we should examine such processes in the context of the social structures and relations of power within a particular society, since individuals or groups do not act in a vacuum.

"Creolization," Bolland insists, "is not a homogenizing process, but rather a process of *contention* between people who are members of social formations and carriers of cultures, a process in which their own ethnicity is continually re-examined and redefined in terms of the relevant oppositions between different social formations at various historical moments" (72). *Creole* is something that is struggled over and "marked by situation" rather than "atemporal," though it might be *appealed* to as timeless and self-evident (Trouillot, "Culture on the Edges").

In Thomas's time, when thousands of "outsiders" threaten to destabilize who "we" are, or ought to have been, *Creole* is as much a statement of regulation as anything else. But since a term such as *French Creole* both distinguishes francophones from other Creoles, such as Dutch Creoles, and overstates *French* because of the implied *French* in *Creole,* to the detriment of African Caribbean registers, Thomas also seeks to correct such disparities. That "Indians" from Asia are represented during this period as essentially incapable of being bound by the term, for example, is less interesting from the perspective of empirical observation (see, they can't speak this and they don't eat that) than the willingness of all commentators to reiterate this incapability. This reiteration, I argue, guarantees their inability to be embraced by the term: a Corsican newcomer was granted the Creole status that an "East Indian" who had resided in Trinidad since the 1840s could not have. In any case, very few people in Trinidad in the 1870s and 1880s could claim to have had ancestors living there for a century or more. *Creole* designates insider versus outsider in relation to complex and not necessarily consistent notions of nationalism, ethnicity, respectability, and authenticity, as well as to phenotype and complexion.

African is often, but not always, synonymous with *Negro* in this period and may or may not also include wealthy Coloreds. It refers to persons of African descent in the region, a constituency whose capacity for "civilization" four decades after the abolition of slavery is the subject of much discussion. Members of this group may be rural laborers, urban clerks, or small landholders. They engage in any number of legal or illegal trades in the major urban centers of Port of Spain in the northeast and San Fernando in the southeast. Or they wait for almost negligible opportunities to acquire limited places in the civil service or to begin legal or medical study abroad. They earn wages on sugar or cocoa estates and supplement their incomes by selling produce grown on small plots.

Generally, in the accounts written by elite observers of the period, "Negroes" are vulgar performers of unseemly songs and dances during the annual Carnival celebrations or at all-night wakes. The accolades that Thomas receives for his accomplishments stress the difference between his attributes and the "known" characteristics of this general constituency. He and others argue from a variety of perspectives that thousands of "Negroes" from the eastern Caribbean or from western Africa who are brought in during this period to supplement the agricultural work force are in danger of disturbing the cultural equilibrium established during slavery, an equilibrium consisting of "Negroes," "Coloreds," and "Whites" bound together by a francophone Creole ethos.

Francophone Creole Black people are distinct from anglophone Creoles from the eastern Caribbean, such as the Barbadians, who arrive by the thousands, attracted by the higher wages in Trinidad (Johnson). They are also more or less distinct from the "Merikins," or "Americans," who live in some of Trinidad's southern districts, descendants of the United States–born soldiers granted land by the British for fighting on their side during the American Revolutionary War (Laurence, "Settlement"; Adderly; Trotman, 26). *Negroes* born in the Caribbean and those born in Africa experience creolization in various ways. Many brought to Trinidad as slaves before the 1830s from French colonies, such as Martinique, or from colonies that were culturally francophone, such as Grenada, came from nearly a dozen ethnic groups in western and central Africa (Trotman, 26).

By the 1870s they have a different relationship to "Creole" status than the more than ten thousand newly arrived indentured immigrants brought to Trinidad from the late 1830s to the late 1860s, some of whom are taken from slave ships bound for Brazil and Cuba and resettled in Sierra Leone. This reminds us that African ethnicities within the African continent are undergoing upheaval throughout the nineteenth century and that a term such as *Yoruba* has a different meaning in the mid-nineteenth century than it did in the mid-eighteenth. *African*, then, is sometimes specific to non-Creoles, who perhaps speak Yoruba or Congo and make their home in Trinidad after the 1840s, but making clean distinctions between *Creole* and *African* is problematic.

When Thomas describes his parents as "African" or says that he has been "familiar since early childhood" with Africans (*Froudacity,* 142), he is most likely identifying himself as a child of African-born parents and thus of persons born in Africa and brought to Trinidad either directly or from elsewhere in the Caribbean.[5] His parents may have been brought to the Caribbean during slavery or as indentured immigrants in the late 1830s (he was born in 1841). But his "familiarity" may also mean that he lived in close proximity to people who had been born in Africa. Some of his letters to newspapers in the 1870s are from New Town, a section of Port of Spain where many Yorubas settled.

Thomas's invocation of *African* is also to be read as his claiming for himself and other Caribbean persons an explicitly Negro dimension of "Creole" and "Trinidadian" identity. Thomas may also be indicating his phenotype. When newspapers of the day state that Thomas is "a pure African and looks it," they are telling their readers that he is dark-skinned or "unmixed," with no evidence of "European blood" readable in his features. Here, "mixture" is connected to "amounts" of "European"/White and "African"/Black biological features. Yet "European," "White," "African," and "Black" are all complex categories in Trinidad at this time, and thus the phrase "pure African," though obviously understood by Thomas and his readers, is so fraught with displacements and re-routings within the African continent and throughout the diaspora that it approaches the oxymoronic.

French delineates a francophone ethos that embraces the francophone Creole Blacks just referred to, as well as their White and Colored counterparts. *French* often indicates those Whites who regard themselves as the custodians of a francophone, Roman Catholic heritage that is under threat from the encroachments of a hostile, hegemonic, and coarse "English Party" comprising colonial authorities, merchants, or planters born in England, Scotland, or Ireland. However, Whites born in Trinidad of English parents are Creoles as well, and some Irish persons are identified as French because of their Roman Catholic status. When planters from French colonies, such as Martinique, or from colonies that were culturally francophone, such as Grenada, entered Trinidad in large numbers from the 1780s at the invitation of the Spanish Governor, *French* quickly subsumed *Spanish,* though it was not synonymous with it. Persons descended from the aristocrats who fled the effects of the French and Haitian revolutions in other parts of the Caribbean sometimes intermarried with descendants of officers of the Spanish empire. Upper-class persons who fled revolutionary upheaval in Venezuela were often planters who had fled Saint Domingue generations earlier. *French* in its elite White registers therefore sometimes means broadly "non-anglophone" and may include Irish, Corsican, and German settlers who are not Protestant or who marry Catholics. The term never embraces Madeirans, who, as indentured laborers, lack the requisite social status to be classified as White.

French also means "Coloreds." Many of the planters entering Trinidad from the late eighteenth century are Colored. Wealthy plantation owners who dominate the Naparimas, in southern Trinidad, create their own distinguished society and are proud of their role in "civilizing" Trinidad. They smart at the racially determined social restrictions that render them inferior to the "English" Whites, who hold political sway, and to the "French" Whites, who are often blood relations. As Bridget Brereton has shown so vividly, the sacred prefix *de* in the names of these families could easily become a site of struggle. Membership in the White French Creole elite was predicated upon the absence of "Negro blood," and those children of White men and Black or Colored women who insisted on taking the complete name of their fathers—for example, *de Verteuil* instead of *Verteuil,* which was thought proper to mark their "illegitimacy"—caused much consternation (see Brereton, *Race Relations,* 40, and "White Elite," 54).

Just as there were Negroes who owned significant amounts of land, there were Coloreds whose only capital was intellectual. Moreover, given the rigid stratification of the society according to race, propertied Coloreds felt themselves to be discriminated against by the colonial government. Thus Coloreds and Negroes contrasted themselves to the "more favored classes" of Whites, and as the century drew to a close younger members of both groups banded together in explicitly racial terms.

French Creole links Trinidad to a wider francophone context during this period and is deeply tied to a plantation matrix. This strong sense of a world shared by and familiar to White, Colored, and Black pervades narratives of the period as well as twentieth-century accounts. It is often closely tied to the bodies of women, such as the elderly Black woman in "Creole" headdress, feared for her knowledge of herbs, who tells folktales to her young White charges on the back veranda of a planter's home. Though she is represented as a self-sufficient cultural institution, a certain paternalism and nostalgia underlie such recollections, and the fixity of social relations is never questioned. Recently Antonio Benítez-Rojo has resuscitated a similar image: at the height of the threat of nuclear war between the United States and the Soviet Union in the 1960s, as Cubans waited fearfully, "two old black women passed 'in a certain kind of way' beneath my balcony. . . . there was a certain kind of ancient and golden powder between their gnarled legs, a scent of basil and mint in their dress, a symbolic, ritual wisdom in their gesture and their gay chatter. I knew then at once that there would be no apocalypse."[6] Such women are idealized as antinuclear and anti- or premodern: mammies who will save us from the apocalypse.

As francophone White and Colored sugar planters lose ground to English Creole and resident proprietors, as well as to British companies, in the mid-nineteenth century, some are able to recover by switching to cocoa. By the last decades of the century their resentment of the Anglicization and anti-Catholic policies of the colonial authorities has given way to "a period of rapprochement between the major factions of the white community" (Brereton, "White Elite," 47). Louis de Verteuil and J. V. de Boissière, two prominent members of this group, hold seats in the Legislative Council from the 1860s, for example. Alliances that lessen somewhat the overt tensions between anglophone and francophone Whites also, by the same token, facilitate the further weakening of the cultural superiority of francophone residents. As the century closes, younger members of these families speak English instead of French at home or attend Stonyhurst and other Catholic institutions in England rather than schools in France. French priests are replaced by Irish clergy, and Mass is no longer said in French.

English indicates British dominance in a crown colony system of government controlled by a governor who appoints members of the Legislative and Executive Councils. With no elected officials, Trinidad thus lacks the tradition of local assemblies in British colonial territories such as Barbados, and much of the political fervor of the 1870s and 1880s is related to demands for franchise reform by elites. Though politically dominant, English authorities cannot take for granted the superiority of either Protestantism or the English language in a colony that has only been a part of the British Empire since the late eighteenth century. By casting the Catholic French as a marginal or even "foreign" special interest the colonial authorities justify the lack of state funding for Roman Catholic personnel and schools.

English in this period refers to nonresident, Protestant Whites but also Caribbean-born Whites. Creoles such as Charles Warner, attorney general for several decades prior to the 1870s and the "main instigator and idealogue" of Anglicization policies, are lauded by Froude, who makes a point of visiting the aging Warner during his visit to the Caribbean in 1886 (Brereton, *Race Relations*, 46; Froude, *English*, 84–85). But for this "chief and representative" of "the oldest of West Indian families," Froude notes, "Trinidad would have been a wilderness, savage as when Columbus found the Caribs there." Some British newcomers marry into Roman Catholic families and thus become identified with the "French." In a colony where so many economic avenues were closed to non-Whites, the enterprising shop clerk who was newly arrived from Scotland could become the wealthy merchant who lavishly celebrated Robert Burns's birthday. Scottish clerks and Irish policemen remind us that the term *English* threatens to simplify the complexity implied by *British Isles:* many Whites who come to the Caribbean during this period are in fact British-but-not-English.

Finally, *English* sometimes corresponds with *Englishness.* Most "respectable" persons of this period acknowledge the superiority of the British colonial machinery, as well as the canonical texts and norms of gentility thought to constitute Britain's gift to the world, though of course the French arrogantly questioned the superiority, if not the dominance, of the colonial authorities. In this sense Englishness denotes the literal presence of the colonial administration: the Colonial Office in London, the upper echelons of the police force, the governor. It also implies the "surrogate Englishman" of the British canonical text, as Gauri Viswanathan has identified it: "In effect, the strategy of locating authority in English texts all but effaced the often sordid history of colonialist expropriation, material exploitation, and class and race oppression behind European world dominance. Making the Englishman known to the natives through the products of his mental labour removed him from the plane of ongoing colonialist activity. . . . The English literary text functioned as a surrogate Englishman in his highest and most perfect state" ("Currying Favor," 103).

For non-Whites, particularly those without economic property, such as Thomas, Englishness is a crucial marker of social status and intellectual capability: it is the very foundation of their prestige. While francophone Whites lament the dominance of anglophone traditions, their prestige does not inhere in the mastery of canonical texts alone or even at all. When Thomas critiques Englishness, it is for its crassness, as well as its failure to recognize the validity of francophone cultural modes. When he berates Froude in the late 1880s, it is for failing to measure up to the noble standards set by William Wilberforce and other "great" Englishmen.

In delineating Thomas's relationship to Englishness, one might stress his famous response to Froude's book *The English in the West Indies.*

Comparisons of Thomas's "fame" and Froude's "oblivion" suggest that one way of reading this period is in terms of their ideological battle. Froude has been described as "one of the greatest intellectuals of his time, ranking with Macaulay, John Richard Green, and other famous writers of the day," and it is sometimes even assumed that he already held the distinguished Regius Professorship of Modern History at Oxford when he published *The English in the West Indies*.[7] Besides perhaps indicating Thomas's own prestige in daring to respond to a figure of such weight, such accolades also tend to mystify the authority of those to whom they are applied. They become "great men" whom it then becomes an honor to praise or challenge. It would be absurd to deny the impact a text such as *The English in the West Indies* had on British colonial policy, as well as its contribution to the prevailing metropolitan image of a Caribbean inhabited by lazy Negroes and a well-meaning but beleaguered plantocracy. Without denying the prestige of Froude or any of the other Victorian intellectuals with whom Thomas was identified, however, it is important to recognize that "there is nothing mysterious or natural about authority. . . . [It] can, indeed must, be analyzed" (Said, *Orientalism*, 19–20).

But Thomas is no more defined solely in terms of his response to Froude than Froude is defined in terms of his text on the Caribbean. Their texts are part of a larger dialogue. Intellectual formation in nineteenth-century Britain cannot be fully understood outside of the context of the relationship between Britain and the rest of the world, particularly those places designated as part of the British Empire. Happily, it has become increasingly difficult to continue to argue otherwise, although this has been a long time coming, not least of all, perhaps, because even colonial and postcolonial intellectuals have sometimes seemed to insist on their own marginality. V. S. Naipaul's infamous pronouncement that "history is built around achievement and creation; and nothing was created in the West Indies" comes readily to mind, but C. L. R. James's reflection on his childhood also implies that the real events occur in the metropolitan center: "So there I was, *way out in the West Indies*, before I was ten, playing games and running races like other little boys" (Naipaul, *Middle Passage*, 29; James, *Beyond a Boundary*, 27, emphasis added).

While it has not been difficult to demonstrate the impact "Englishness" has had on many Caribbean intellectuals, issues of race and empire are often seen as merely peripheral to British or English ideologies. Viswanathan has taken British cultural critics to task for their failure to theorize adequately the relationship between nationalism and imperialism ("Raymond Williams"). She takes exception to the tendency to explain events or ideas in England, for example, in purely "national" terms, whereas comparable developments in the colonial arena are assumed to be "English" developments simply transported to another setting. Thus the imperial dimension can only be explained in terms of the metropolis: national-local phenomena such as elite hegemony over the English working classes are used by such intellectuals to account for British hegemony over colonized peoples. Discussions of "Englishness" thus assume its formation within the geographical boundaries of England and then proceed to consider the ways in which this fully formed identity was exported whole into the colonial sphere.

Viswanathan's own work has pointed the way out of this mind-set, showing how British colonies were used as "a test-site for secular experiments in education," which were then introduced into the metropolis.[8] She suggests that English culture should be examined "first and foremost in its imperial aspect" before looking at how that aspect is "itself constitutive of 'national' culture."[9]

Victorian travel writing should thus be seen in the context of "the imperial metropolis [understanding] itself as determining the periphery . . . [but blinding] itself to the ways in which the periphery determines the metropolis—beginning perhaps with the latter's obsessive need to present and re-present its peripheries and its others continually to itself" (Pratt, 6). Thus, Froude's travelogue on the Caribbean, as well as Charles Kingsley's 1871 *At Last*, receive attention in this study. At the same time, one can just as easily stay at "home" when considering one's "peripheries," and midcentury critiques of liberal ideologies associated with "Exeter Hall philanthropy" or the "dismal science" of free trade are both "national" and "imperial" in their resonances.

In an essay entitled "The Niger Expedition," published in 1841, Charles Dickens sneered at the "weird old women who [went] about, and exceedingly roundabout," on the Exeter Hall platform (46). Exeter Hall was the venue of antislavery meetings in the years prior to and just after the abolition of slavery in the 1830s and 1840s and again during the American Civil War and was therefore a symbol of the misplaced philanthropy that Dickens and others condemned. Such activities, as they saw it, only encouraged social chaos. Noteworthy in this quotation is the gendered characterization of such activity. Abolitionist and missionary activity were two public domains in which women participated, and whether Dickens's sneers are directed here at women specifically or at male politicians who, by "softening" under the pressure for reform, are casting aside the tough, manly actions worthy of "real men," his words can be seen as a condemnation of liberalism as unwholesome and feminine. The abolition of slavery was of particular concern at midcentury and was the subject of an influential essay by Thomas Carlyle in the 1850s.

Carlyle's exhortations on action and heroism were understood by his readers to have direct bearing on England's political life. Writers derived prestige from speaking out with authority and influencing the political sphere. At midcentury it seemed to Carlyle that the liberal policies of those who held political power encouraged the "anarchy" of the "hordes," both locally and abroad. Free trade, legislation instituting reforms in prisons and factories, laws pertaining to abolition, and the treatment of formerly enslaved constituencies were heatedly debated from the 1840s. So even as the metaphors and iconography of abolitionism—the juxtaposition of slavery and freedom in Brontë's *Jane Eyre,* for instance, or Wedgewood's kneeling slave—fired the imagination of the public, Carlyle and others felt that harsh measures rather than reform were required for anarchic and chaotic times.

Carlyle hovers over the period of this study, then, even when he is not directly invoked and even though he is not alive for most of it. He is linked to Froude and to Kingsley through personal acquaintance, but more significantly, he normalizes certain readings of the Caribbean. In passages such as the following, the "New World" is cleansed of any significant lives and cultures other than European ones:

> England, looking on her Colonies, can say, "Here are lands and seas, spice-lands, corn-lands, timber-lands, overarched by zodiacs and stars, clasped by many-sounding seas—wide spaces of the Maker's building, fit for the cradle yet of mighty nations, and their Sciences and Heroisms. Fertile continents still inhabited by wild beasts are mine, into which all the distressed populations of Europe might pour themselves, and make at once an Old World and a New World human" (*Latterday Pamphlets,* 27).

Non-Europeans are consigned to oblivion, or at least to a position at the receiving end of metropolitan supervision, and both the violence at the heart of this "oblivion" and the survival strategies in the face of European onslaughts are ignored.

Carlyle's reference to the "New World" as a receptacle for the "distressed populations of Europe" underscores the point that commentaries on "colonial" matters were linked to concerns about working-class populations "at home," who might be siphoned off to the Caribbean, Australia, and other locations. In more specific ways Carlyle cleared discursive ground

for subsequent commentators on the state of the postemancipation Carib-
bean by representing the region as overrun by lazy, Black pumpkin eaters
who needed to be taken in hand. His essay "Occasional Discourse on the
Negro Question," first published in 1849 and republished in 1853 as
"Occasional Discourse on the Nigger Question," has been identified
as significant for its willingness to "come out" on the question of "anti-
Negro" opinion and for its influence on the public discourse on this issue
(C. Hall, *White, Male, and Middle Class;* Holt). The article, which blasted
"Exeter-Hall Philanthropy and the Dismal Science" (308), offered for
public consumption lazy pumpkin eaters who were being cosseted by the
misguided policies of British reformers. Defenders of the interests of these
pumpkin eaters were responsible for the anarchy "at home" as well.
Catherine Hall sees the essay "as an extremely significant moment in the
movement of public opinion away from anti-slavery as the respectable
orthodoxy and towards more overt forms of racism" (*White, Male, and
Middle Class,* 275). Thomas Holt points out that although intellectuals
such as John Stuart Mill would have winced at what they would have
considered its vulgar racism, they would have been inclined to agree that
the refusal of Black people in the Caribbean to work in the interests of the
sugar economy was problematic. Holt contends that the extreme nature of
Carlyle's tone in this essay would have cleared the way for more moderate
but quite similar views: "It is conceivable that publication of Carlyle's
extreme rhetoric shifted the terms for *public* discourse on race and public
policy" (283, Holt's emphasis).

To put Thomas and these Victorians in the same conversation is important, but it should not obscure their differing social positions. They share
an intellectual arena as well as ideas regarding the importance of "respectability" and "civilization," but this does not mean that Thomas can take
for granted that he is their social equal nor even his social equality with
many Creole elites in Trinidad.

As we shall see, Thomas has enormous respect for *the fairer sex,* women
of his social constituency—middle-class Blacks and Coloreds—whom he
considers partners with him and other men of this group in the vindication of people of African descent and in the elevation of the cultural tone
of the society. That they are largely absent from the newspapers of the day
does not mean that they do not attend the events being described in its
pages, that they do not participate in the discussion of the ideas discussed
therein, or that they are not part of the reading audience of these papers.
However, if participation in the public arena confers and confirms prestige, their absence is significant.

Elite women are expected to have intellectual interests in order to add grace to the character of their society. Their "womanly" virtues are considered to be the basis of the moral character of their homes and of the society. For women of Thomas's group this included the rearing of children who would continue the work of rehabilitating the race in Trinidad and in the African diaspora more generally. But their identity as virtuous mothers is by no means the only reason for Thomas's interest in them. When Thomas berates Grenadians for the absence of women at lectures, he indicates their role as a sort of leavening presence: they add "grace" to such events, and to society generally, stimulating intellectual inquiry and confirming its importance.

Ironically, Thomas's admonition of Grenadians in the 1880s echoes an English visitor to that territory in the 1840s: "Gentlemen of Grenada and the Grenadines as far as Cariacou [*sic*], where are your wives? . . . [Y]ou will say that there are just forty ladies in the island! It may be so, but show them, gentlemen, to the world, and but to silence the moralities of Englishmen and Barbadians. Of Grenada alone can I say that I never saw a single lady all the while I was on it" (Coleridge, 99). By "ladies," of course, Henry Coleridge means White women who are not of "easy virtue." White women's absence underscores, even causes, White male degeneracy. That the latter drink excessively, do not read, and have sexual liaisons and children with Black and Brown women is due to the absence of White women.

When Patrick Keenan, sent from Ireland by the Colonial Office to review Trinidad's educational system in the late 1860s, declares that the preponderance of Black male teachers is a "moral" problem that can be solved by importing White female teachers, he echoes these sentiments. Thomas's outrage at the conduct of a Scottish headmistress of the San Fernando Girls School in the mid-1880s combines resentment at the supplanting of qualified Creole talent with inefficient outsiders with assumptions about the specific responsibilities of female teachers. Thomas's social group smarts at its representation in Victorian travel narratives as absurd mimics of "authentic" White ladies and gentlemen but shares with elite Victorians the notion that women *as women* are crucial to the moral and cultural health of the nation and race.

I know of one woman in Thomas's group, broadly defined. She is Emilie Maresse-Paul, a member of a prominent Colored francophone Creole family. In a letter to the editor of the *San Fernando Gazette* after the period of this study she protests the proposal to abolish the limited free places to Queen's Royal College, seeing in it the maintenance of the privilege of "the sons of rich or well-to-do families."[10] Maresse-Paul published two anticlerical pamphlets, *The Clericals and the Education Question* and *La nécessité des enterrements civils, et l'impertinence du clergé Dominicain.*[11] While I know nothing about her intellectual formation—she may have been educated in Europe or at an institution such as St. Joseph's Convent, or she may have been tutored privately—I assume that Thomas is as honored by her support of his response to Father Violette as he is by the support of the elite men who share the public arena with him.[12]

If I know little of the authority that such women wield as intellectuals, I know that at least in a symbolic sense they are crucial to the rhetoric of these men. When Thomas and others condemn the laboring classes for their crudeness, Maresse-Paul and others provide the implicit or explicit standard of morality that throws such vulgarity into relief. Women such as Sarah Smith underscore the importance of "respectable" women. In October 1876 it is reported that she is charged with "approaching the complainant," John Jacob Thomas, "in a menacing manner, and was bound in her own recognizance, conditioned to keep the peace for three calendar months, under a penalty of five pounds." She in turn charged Thomas with "threatening, in Edward Street, on Tuesday (3rd inst), to kick and beat her."[13]

Because of the nature and location of this incident, I assume that Sarah Smith is a member of the working class, and I am curious about her ability to bring a cross-action suit against a gentleman. That many editorials of the period focus on "disreputable" women may mean that there are, empirically speaking, more incidents involving women. It may also mean that women's "unruliness" is more shocking and thus more noteworthy because of prevailing notions about women's virtue and domesticity. *Women's* unruliness has implications for the nation or colony as a whole since women are considered to be key to its moral health. This is so both for Thomas's group and for metropolitan visitors.

Visitors to the region expressed their shock at the seeming equality of Black Creole men and women. Charles Kingsley's travelogue notes that "Negro women are, without doubt, on a more thorough footing of equality with the men than the women of any white race," locating the reason for this in the absence of "difference between the sexes in mere physical strength and courage" and the "light labour," which makes it unnecessary for the "Negro woman . . . to marry and make herself the slave of a man." In Port of Spain he is "shocked" by their "masculine figures, their ungainly gestures, their loud and sudden laughter," and in reminding the reader that "this is a seaport town" he notes that the sexual "licence" that this implies is "aggravated by the superabundant animal vigour and the perfect independence of the younger women. It is a painful subject" (*At Last*, 1:50–51, 138–39).

Since according to genteel standards the "proper" relationship between the sexes is women's physical and economic subservience to their husbands—even if Kingsley is willing to concede that they are thereby "slaves" to them—women who confidently and independently assert themselves in the public domain instead of circumspectly occupying the domestic realm are "masculine." "Independent" women violate norms of femininity and presumably the larger fabric of society, which is held together by such norms. Though Kingsley finds such gendered arrangements "painful," they are nevertheless normal in the context of the "inferior" societies he is visiting. "No schemes for civilizing the Negro" that ignore these arrangements, he warns, "will have any deep or permanent good effect" (*At Last*, 1:51).

Even though Thomas and others who respond to metropolitan commentaries such as this sometimes make no specific reference to gender, I imagine that the outrage that they feel about being classified with persons such as the women who shock Kingsley has gendered implications. A key objection to such travelogues during the period is that they fail to focus on the "intermediate" classes, considered to be central to the region's progress. The focus on the laboring classes allows Kingsley and others to argue that Caribbean societies will regress into barbarism unless they are administered by Whites. Thomas and others resent this focus because they know that Kingsley does not lump himself with the laboring classes in his own society. They agree with him that such classes are objectionable, but they object to his refusal to portray elite Creole Black constituencies. Since middle-class modes of gentility are key to respectability, and since the "good woman" who has a particular relationship to "respectable" domestic life is central to such modes, their objection to his portrayal of "shocking" women may also be an objection to the independence and equality that they embody.

Given the historical experience of slavery, which in some senses "equalized" the status of Black men and women relative to bourgeois norms, it can be argued that Thomas and others do not have a stake in Kingsley's assumption that the equality of the sexes is reprehensible. In *Froudacity* Thomas approves of the "Ethiopic women of North America," who move "shoulder to shoulder" with their male counterparts (192). However, I insist that this equality is in tension with notions of women's special virtues and spheres. The rejection of Kingsley's slights about the

"Negro race," a rejection that is explicit, may include an implicit desire to assert the "normality" of the respectable, intermediate classes by establishing that women are, in fact, most properly to be thought of as *supporting* men, by being good wives and mothers in the private arena—intellectually vigorous but having their own sphere nonetheless. That there are loud and "ungainly" women who are equal to men or, as in other accounts, are perceived to be "hardworking," whereas Black men are "lazy," may imply that men are not up to the task of being men; such accounts "unman" them. Independent women, in this equation, imply lazy or otherwise pathological men. The explicit (classed) repudiation of Kingsley's focus on persons whom Thomas agreed were vulgar, then, may include the implicit (gendered) rejection of suggestions of masculine inadequacies.

"Is noise whole day," Earl Lovelace's paean to the restless energies of Laventille's dispossessed, introduces *noise*, another keyword (9). Kamau Brathwaite's "shak-shak, shekesheke, wood block, gong gong, the cheng-cheng of the steel band, [the] decorative energy [investing] the nation performance, unnecessary but without which not enough," constitute the late-twentieth-century celebration of the sounds that plague the respectable classes in late-nineteenth-century Trinidad (*History of the Voice*, 301–2). Elites complain constantly about the noise that disturbs their sleep at night, and a significant range of ethnicities, occupations, and religions is obscured by the designation, as are the relationships that elites themselves have to "noisy" practices.

When middle- and upper-class francophone Creoles protest the Music Ordinance in the 1880s, they are objecting to the Protestant state's failure to recognize the distinction between "good" music and dances, on the one hand, and the "indecent" ones performed by immigrants from other Caribbean territories, on the other. The "jacket-men" who go to calypso yards at nights are elite men who value these spaces (Rohlehr, *Calypso and Society;* Warner, 109). Thomas must disapprove of obeah practices as much as any other "respectable person," and yet it is the disapproval of someone "in the know," to judge by his references in *Theory and Practice of Creole Grammar* to persons who have been "harmed" or tied" or who "handle grasses" (118–19). Upper-class commentators often take pride in bearing the marks or wearing the attire of the working-class other. Lechmere Guppy, the White Creole scientist, displays the tattoos that Maoris marked on his back during his sojourn in New Zealand in the 1850s (Bridges). Governor Arthur Hamilton Gordon's wife proudly displays the bangles that she purchases from Indian immigrant women.[14]

"Noise" includes drum dances; stick fighting and the Kalinda songs and dances that accompany it; whe whe gambling, associated with Chinese immigrants; Islamic prayers; obeah work; Shango-Baptist ceremonies; Hindu prayer flags; and two annual events, pre-Lenten Carnival and Hosay (also known as Hosein or Muhurram). The energy involved in constructing tassa drums or conducting all-night wakes represents an insistence on honoring old and new traditions in a society that prefers nonelites to engage solely in activities that will benefit the economy, namely, working for sugar and cocoa producers. In this sense "noise" also includes the many activities in which Black people are engaged and that allow them to earn incomes that supplement estate labor or eliminate the need for the latter altogether.

Coalers, then, are "noisy" since they are Black men and women who work independently of the wage labor system. So are the higglers or hucksters who take agricultural produce from rural areas to sell in town markets. In fact, the provision grounds or market gardens that enabled Black people to grow the crops that fed them during slavery and thereby enabled plantation owners to save money were the foundation of the system of crop production and markets that helped to diversify the slavery and postemancipation economy. These crops were grown by and for Black people and were the basis of their ability to ask for higher wages when they chose to work part-time for the planters. Thus Kingsley's reference to "light labor" in a passage quoted above, implying that work that is not done for wages is no work at all. Carlyle's lazy pumpkin eater, who benefits from a prelapsarian landscape yielding pumpkins that do not have to be planted or harvested, works on his or her own provision grounds instead of for planters.

While Black movements cannot be reliably monitored, those of Indian laborers can and must be since they are the antidote to Black flight from the plantations. The two groups are defined in relation to each other during this period. "Jamettes," the single Black women who dominate Trinidad's urban spaces and seem to encapsulate all the transgressive energies of the nonelite, are contrasted to their male counterparts and to middle-class women, as we have seen, but also to Indian women, who are considered to be docile.

Yet, the actual or potential independence of Indian women causes just as much anxiety as that of their Black counterparts. Female immigrants, who are mostly single, are imported in low numbers, an indication that planters did not want a permanent community of Indians—women being conceptualized as key to the permanence of any community, as well as to the maintenance of certain standards, in this case those of caste. A small number of single women violates patriarchal norms at all levels. Insistence on paying Indian women lower wages goes hand in hand with the logic that they should have male partners: they ought not to head their own households.[15] The comments of Sarah Morton, the wife of a Canadian Presbyterian missionary, in a period after that covered by this study assert the "right-thinking" views of elites on households headed by women and on sexual autonomy:

> The loose actions and prevailing practices in respect of marriage here are quite shocking to the newcomer. I said to an East Indian woman whom I knew to be the widow of a Brahmin, "You have no relations in Trinidad, I believe?"
>
> "No Madame," she replied, "only myself and two children; when the last immigrant ship came I took a 'papa.' I will keep him as long as he treats me well. If he does not treat me well I shall send him off at once; that's the right way, is it not?"[16]

Rhoda Reddock notes that such behavior is viewed during the period as "downright immoral" or indicative of women's passive victimization, as they are "seduced and enticed away from one man to another" (43). Women who assert the right to choose and to change sexual partners are abused and/or killed: "Owning a wife had become a social and economic necessity and controlling her an issue of life and death" (42). Thus, as Reddock and Tejaswini Niranjana point out, the pressure to import a higher number of female immigrants conflicts with the need to find "docile" women and morally suitable ones—"the right kind of women" (Reddock, 28).

Thousands of immigrants enter Trinidad from India during this period, mainly from northern Indian territories of the United Provinces, the Central Provinces, Oudh, Orissa, and Bihar but also from Bengal, the North West Provinces, and the south. Mostly Hindu, from artisanal, agricultural, as well as upper castes, they are also Muslim and Christian (Reddock, 27; Tinker; Laurence, *Question of Labour;* Brereton, "Experience of Indenture-ship"; Parmasad). We shall see how both metropolitan elites and Creoles such as Thomas, who knows Hindi, assert the right to keep Indians in their presumed place based on the "facts" about their "origins" and "char-acter." But nationalists, including Mahatma Gandhi, also measure Indians in the Caribbean according to "authentic" notions of "Indianness," partic-ularly at the turn of the century, after the period of this study. They seek to construct the modern middle-class Indian as free of both Western deca-dence and the coarseness of the working-class subject. Niranjana points out that Caribbean indentureds present a conceptual problem since they represent a modern subjectivity that supplements the middle-class subject in India but without the latter's jurisdiction—an "illegitimate" modernity, as she puts it. Indians in Trinidad are posited as "debased," having lost their authenticity. Indian nationalists are unwilling to take account of their modernity in the new, diasporic space. The eventual success in abolishing the system of indenture in the early twentieth century entails discourses of rescue from degradation, particularly for women, who are posited as having been disconnected from an originary virtue in India.[17]

Cross-referencing is another important keyword, then. As we have seen, Indians are crucial to definitions of the identities of both Black Creoles in the Caribbean and middle-class Indian subjects in India. When Trinidadian elites assert Black respectability, this is sometimes secured by belittling Indians, while commentaries in travelogues on Indians' exotic bangles and veils are linked directly to the vulgarity and lack of "culture" of Black Creoles. Since for this period "Indian workers [are] the medium through which sugar planters [reassert] their control over Afro-Caribbean workers," various elite constituencies, for differing reasons, pit one group against the other (Kale, 76).

Just as antislavery discourses are revived for the abolition of Indian indentureship or of widow burning, *nigger* enters public discourse in Victorian England after the Indian "Mutiny" or Great Revolt, making it available for Carlyle, who used it for Black Caribbean people in the 1850s (Reddock, 27; Rodney, 39; C. Hall, *White, Male, and Middle Class,* 275). A lamentation by Froude to a friend reminds us that the Irish, Blacks, Indians, and White females are linked in discourses of the time, even if not in exact correspondence: "Once upon a time we did grand things out there, as we did in other places. Now all is going to the Devil. All our white people there flung overboard like the Protestants in Ireland, and the islands becoming nigger warrens" (qtd. in Dunn, 2:554; see also Lebow). In this sense the "noise" of Caribbean subjects might be used to invoke the noise of demonstrations in London's Hyde Park, or "light labor" in the Caribbean context might be contrasted with harsh factory conditions in the British Isles. Noisemakers are deported from one part of the empire to another: from India to Trinidad, or from England to Australia.

Mutiny is another keyword for this period. Events in Cawnpore and Lucknow in 1857, the so-called Indian Mutiny, are a reminder to imperial authorities of their constant vulnerability in the face of the savage regressions of their subjects. Charles Dickens writes to an acquaintance in October 1857, "I wish I were Commander in Chief in India. . . . I should do my utmost to exterminate the Race upon the stain of the late cruelties rested . . . to blot it out of mankind and raze it off the face of the Earth."[18] As J. C. Jha has shown, Trinidad's elite society reacted with fear to events in India in the aftermath of 1857, particularly because some participants in the rebellion were shipped to Trinidad: "Indian labourers who had so far been treated as meek, docile and trustworthy creatures by the white planters were now on occasion looked upon with suspicion." Quoting Donald Wood, Jha states that Cawnpore "had joined Haiti in creating a terror among white and coloured planters and other rich men."[19] Decades later, Indians are represented as the docile foil for Black intractability. "Mutinies" acquire a mythology that exceeds actual events and persists as a reminder of the essential savagery of the lower classes and non-White constituencies, as well as the limits of elite authority. Like Lucknow and Cawnpore in 1857, *Morant Bay* is another index of savagery, and we shall see how debates around Edward Eyre's brutal handling of events in eastern Jamaica in 1865–66 helped to cast Victorian intellectuals as liberal or conservative (C. Hall, *White, Male, and Middle Class;* Heuman).

Haiti represents the biggest "mutiny" of all, and its revolutionary over-throw of slavery at the end of the eighteenth century, as well as its engage-ment of France, Spain, and England in a twelve-year war, continues to cast a shadow over the later nineteenth century. This is in part because of the émigrés who settle all over the Caribbean, creating a sort of Saint Domingue diaspora. In examining the conceptual space from which a his-tory of the Haitian Revolution can be written, Michel-Rolph Trouillot uses Pierre Bourdieu's notion of the "unthinkable": "that which one can-not conceive within the range of possible alternatives, that which perverts all answers because it defies the terms under which the questions were phrased. In that sense, the Haitian Revolution was unthinkable in its time: it challenged the very framework within which proponents and opponents had examined slavery and colonialism in the Americas" ("From Planter's Journals to Academia," 85). Africans were thought to be incapable of acting "decisively," not because of actual empirical evidence, but because of the colonists' conceptual arrangement of the world into West and non-West, savage and civilized. "The Haitian Revolution thus entered history with the peculiar characteristic of being unthinkable even as it happened." For "colonial slaveowner and metropolitan leftist alike, the Haitian Rev-olution was inconceivable" (85).

When Haiti is invoked by Victorian travel writers to imply the possibil-ity of Black "reversion," Thomas and his peers offer Trinidad, Grenada, or Liberia as "civilized" substitutes, leaving the definition of *savagery* or *civilization* unprobed. Vodun, obeah, and other forms are "savage" because cultural viability is "unthinkable" outside bourgeois European contexts. It is as important for some constituencies to insist on Haiti's "barbarism" in order to discount its achievements and to justify the denial of political power to other Caribbean territories as it is for other constituencies to establish themselves in opposition to its example.

1 "Writing Was Easy to Him"
Education, Labor, Distinction

ON 24 DECEMBER 1887 a letter from John Jacob Thomas appeared in Grenada's *Chronicle and Gazette.* Thomas used the occasion of a lecture by William Galway Donovan, a young Colored Grenadian journalist who edited the *Grenada People,* to consider the role of "advantages" or "compensating privileges" for Black and Colored men in the Caribbean. In the week preceding Thomas's letter Donovan had given a lecture entitled "Grenada and Its Resources" at York House in St. George's, an event presided over by Governor Sendall. Thomas began his letter by expressing dismay at what he considered to be the "scanty attendance" at the lecture, "knowing something of the spirit which activates the community both in my native land and elsewhere, when a leading public character of the status of Mr. Donovan is to make a public address."

"But when I expressed my disappointment," Thomas continued, "my Grenadian friends said the attendance was 'a very good one for a lecture in Grenada!' Bumper houses, they said, were in Grenada reserved for buffoonery or tricks of legerdemain, while he who comes before the public requesting to be heard on useful, enlightening subjects usually finds his to be *vox clamantis in deserto.* This, certes, is a woeful intellectual state for a community to be in." Like John the Baptist crying in the wilderness, Thomas suggested, those interested in devoting an evening to "useful, enlightening subjects" were competing with trivial and dexterous conjurors for the soul of the Grenadian public.

Thomas noted in particular the absence of women. Referring to Lady Sendall, the governor's wife, he asked, "Is Mrs. Sendall, then (who, by the way, is NOT a Grenadian) the only lady in your island who can deem it worthy [of] the high mission of her sex, to encourage and stimulate worthy effort, to grace with her presence the arena of intellectual exercitation? To this question, which I also wonderingly put, a similarly unsatisfactory answer was given, to the effect that 'ladies don't attend lectures in Grenada!!'"[1]

In the remainder of the article Thomas examined the possibilities available to Donovan, "your brilliant young countryman," and others like him compared with those available to elite White men. Noting with satisfaction that Sendall, "with the keen insight of a well-trained intellect," had reminded the audience that "the utmost admiration" was due to someone who could acquit himself "in a manner that would have done credit to those who had enjoyed a hundred-fold more advantages than had ever fallen to Mr. Donovan's lot," Thomas compared Donovan with two journalists, both deceased, with whom he had been "more or less intimate" in Trinidad. The first, Otto Wenkstern, editor of the *Trinidad Chronicle* in the 1860s, had angered the planter constituency with his support for Governor Gordon. (The *Chronicle*'s press published Thomas's *Creole Grammar* early in 1869, a few months before Wenkstern succumbed to yellow fever.)

Thomas outlined for his Grenadian readers Wenkstern's distinguished career: "a member of the German aristocracy" who possessed "all the thorough culture common to his order," English private secretary at the Prussian Embassy in London under Baron Brunow, and then subeditor of the London *Times*. For Thomas, Wenkstern's writing, "of a marvellous lucidity and polish," "bristled with antithesis and point, when he so willed, but in dealing with questions involving grave issues, he could stir the heart with his pathos, and impress the mind with the sublimity of his conceptions." But this brilliance had to be viewed in the context of his "advantages":

> He had leisure, affluence, and all the requisites for perfecting the higher life of man—in woeful contrast to the beginning and actual career of your countryman in homage to whose merits I trace these hasty lines. Yet, of the two men, I prefer Donovan. If he be put to the test, *conviction* which I believe to be the secret of his influence and the impelling force of his inner life, will be found all-pervading in his breast. With Wenkstern it was far otherwise. He wrote because writing was easy to him, and he wrote well because he could not do otherwise. In fact, the polished stylist planned, while the untrained young athlete of Galway Donovan *feels,* the sentences that are addressed to public appreciation, the one being concerned more about his diction, while the other is eaten up with zeal for his people's and his country's cause. Wenkstern was often cynical, generally playfully sarcastic; Donovan is usually sober and serious, and not without frequent ebullitions of scathing indignation. (Thomas's emphasis)

Wenkstern, then, is distinguished because he cannot help it, and notwith-standing his ability to "stir the heart with his pathos," he begins to seem shallow by comparison with Donovan. The polish of his writing, a function of his "affluence," becomes an indication of his obsession with diction to the detriment of "zeal." By the end of the passage Wenkstern is confirmed as the "polished stylist" whose cynicism distances him from a genuine com-mitment to the issues of the day. By contrast, Donovan's "conviction" is visceral in its intensity: his breast, his inner life, his very being, is "eaten up" by it. He can afford neither impeccable diction nor playful sarcasm. While the expression of "scathing indignation" in public discourse would by one kind of reckoning compromise the ability to appear considered, sedate, and objective, Thomas here seems to eschew these qualities as the province of leisured elites. Figures like Donovan, and perhaps Thomas himself by extension, do not inherit this capacity for ease and ironic dis-tance and have no time to pursue the art of acquiring them. They are a different breed.

Thomas pressed his point home by comparing Donovan with another editor, William Herbert, "with whom I was on terms of the closest friend-ship." Herbert, a Colored Barbadian, had angered the authorities as editor of Trinidad's *Telegraph,* the *Trinidad Free Press,* and the *Trinidad Colonist.* Thomas noted that in "personal history and individual character" Herbert more closely resembled Donovan than did Wenkstern, though here, too, there were significant differences. Though Herbert had lacked the "advan-tage of anything but the barest rudiments of book-learning," as a young man in Barbados he had enjoyed the "more than compensating privilege" of working with Samuel Jackman Prescod, who had died in 1871. He edited the Barbados *Liberal* and was the first Colored member of the Barbados House of Assembly (Vaughan; Hoyos, 135). Prescod, Thomas pointed out, had also mentored "two other eminent men," Conrad Reeves, the chief justice of Barbados, and William Brathwaite, the late proprietor of the Demerara *Creole.* Reeves, born a slave in 1826, had received his education at Roach's Seminary in Bridgetown, paid for by the sister of his White physician father. He was thus trained in the classics, after which he apprenticed at Prescod's *Liberal,* one of Barbados's many newspapers. He eventually won a scholarship provided by Barbados's literary and debating societies to read law in England, embarking on a legendary par-liamentary and legal career on his return (Hutchinson).

"Constant intercourse" with these "exceptional men," Thomas noted, was worth "half the scholastic training in the world" so far as a "political education" was concerned, and an intellect as "quick" and "omnivorous" as Herbert's "could not fail, with aids like those, to emancipate as well as to triumphantly assert itself." Despite similarities in career and the "self-same fearless and sometimes impudent outspokenness in behalf of what is thought the right," Grenada's Donovan, "the young political struggler," had been "denied, from youth up to this moment, every chance of compensating privileges" such as Herbert enjoyed in later life. "Impudent" here might be a reference to Donovan's imprisonment for six months in 1884 for accusing an expatriate judge of incompetence.[2] Donovan, Thomas concluded, would be remembered in the "history of colonial politics, as an achiever of great and permanent results under conditions that would have daunted less resolute and more mercenary souls into discouragement and despair."

While Thomas never gets to a discussion of Donovan's lecture in his letter, then, he maps out a blueprint for successful Black and Colored men in the public sphere in the southeastern Caribbean, indicating that considerations of length prevent him from pursuing "comparisons to Dominica, Barbados and other countries." Such men are, or ought to be, supported by women who are as intellectually engaged if not always as visible. They need the governor's seal of approval, provided he is a "well-trained intellect" such as Sendall, who is urbane enough to include someone like Donovan in his intellectual community. The "constant intercourse" of like-minded figures is also important since they affirm one another's efforts. Lacking "advantages," Herbert enjoyed the "compensating privileges" of an "omnivorous" intellect and "constant intercourse" with men whose company secured him the equivalent of the formal education to which he did not have access. He could thus "triumphantly assert" himself in Barbados and then in Trinidad, earning "comforts and encouragements without number to sweeten his toil": the addresses and positions that both confirmed and secured his prestige—for example, Herbert was the mayor of Port of Spain—just as Thomas's letter to the Grenadian public was doing for Donovan.

Such "encouragements" were owed to such men by their communities. "Resolute" and therefore not "mercenary," they entered public life without the expectation that they would become wealthy. Such men became brilliant journalists and judges when these fields were opened to non-Whites, and if they earned comparatively little money in these posts, they acquired other kinds of capital. All were "exceptional" men who surpassed social limitations and pursued their causes with courage, earnestness, and zeal, functioning best in societies that nurtured them by attending their lectures and being politically engaged.

Thomas closed the letter by expressing dismay that Donovan was "expected not only to *do*, but to suffer also, whilst battling on behalf of his country" and stating his hope that the praise Donovan's lecture had received from the governor would "induce those whom it concerns to cherish him *now*, while he is alive and young, and not wait to honour his memory with a useless and perhaps costly apotheosis." What are these struggles worth to you? Thomas seemed to be asking his Grenadian readers. Would this young man (Donovan was about thirty-one at this point) have to wait in vain for *his* "compensating privileges"? Did Thomas, forty-seven and suffering from disappointment and chronic illness, have an inkling that he himself would be dead in less than two years?

Given the lack of "ease" and "natural" advantages enjoyed by men such as Wenkstern, what "unnatural" things would take their place, and by what means would this lack of "ease" be transformed into a superior virtue? Since lack of property is represented as disinterest in it and as evidence of one's commitment to noble causes, what is the relationship between economic and intellectual capital? Did Reeves's access to a classical education bring more "advantages"? Herbert, Prescod, Reeves, and Donovan had White fathers, but Thomas makes no reference to the significance of "mixed" ancestry and complexion in relation to their success in public life.

It is clear from Thomas's letter that journalism was an important institution, providing a base from which to enter other spheres of public life, as well as giving the men connected with it the power to control public opinion and to determine what was serious and what constituted "buffoonery" (see Brereton, "Liberal Press"; Cave; and Thomas-Bailey). It was a forum for elevating and deflating men in public life. In Barbados, where there was a long tradition of assembly government, lower-class Whites made political alliances with Coloreds and Blacks that were reflected in journalistic as well as parliamentary arenas. In Trinidad, where many Creole Whites and all Blacks and Coloreds were excluded from political participation, newspapers were a critical means of criticizing the ruling authorities in broad, anti-Protestant and multiracial terms. But newspaper ownership and editorship, as an important forum for securing "family honor" among the French Creoles who dominated the profession, also reflected inter- and intraethnic rivalries.

The 1884 assault of Joseph de la Sauvagère, of the *Trinidad Review* and *Pixy*, in the streets of Port of Spain by the son and nephew of Philip Rostant, the editor of the *Public Opinion*, demonstrated that disagreements about government policy could be moved from the editorial pages to the streets.[3] On another level, the street incident represented the playing out in public of an intraethnic feud between well-known White French families. The details of the events are intriguing, even humorous: the "small stick" sent by one of de la Sauvagère's printers that enables him to ward off his assailants and Rostant's public whipping a week later by de la Sauvagère's brother-in-law. Readers knew the larger, extratextual contexts that framed such events, just as some of them knew the personalities behind the pen names on letters to the editor.

As Philip Rostant aligned Whites, Coloreds, and Blacks against crown colony government, using the skills he had acquired from working on Daniel O'Connell's campaign in Ireland to organize a massive 1886 reform meeting and petition drive, he used his editorship of a number of papers and then his own *Public Opinion* to assert himself as one the leading voices in the fight for political reform.[4] As a member of a prominent landowning family he believed in the sanctity of property and opposed universal suffrage, as did his supporters. His status as the leader of radical reform would be challenged by Black and Colored men *as Black and Colored men* in the late 1880s. The struggle to assert race as equal to or more significant than religious or other lines of solidarity would increasingly be reflected on the pages of these newspapers, revealing fissures in "Creole," "Catholic," and other lines of solidarity.

While many papers reflected White French Creole ownership—the longstanding, pro-planter *Port of Spain Gazette,* owned and edited during this period by T. R. N. Laughlin, an Irish French Creole, *Star of the West,* and the *Venezalano,* which served the exiled Venezuelan community—others reflected Colored and Black proprietorship. The editor of the *San Fernando Gazette* was Samuel Carter, a Colored journalist from Tobago who had apprenticed under Herbert at Wenkstern's *Chronicle* and founded the *New Era* with Joseph Lewis in 1869. The *New Era* would be one of the chief venues of Black and Colored advocacy until it folded in 1891, and many of Thomas's letters were published in it. By the mid-1870s Carter had left Lewis to take up ownership of the *San Fernando Gazette,* begun in 1850 under the ownership of a Colored journalist from Carriacou, Alexander Murray. Carter's paper reflected the importance of San Fernando's Colored and Black middle class in the latter half of the century.

Published weekly or biweekly, these papers reprinted news items from papers in the Caribbean, South America, the United States and Europe, as well as advertising, shipping, and agricultural news. Their presses also printed handbills, labels, and other materials. The papers could be read free in the local and international offices of its advertisers; the *San Fernando*

Gazette could be read at the offices of Hendy and Company in Russell Square, London, for example, as well as at Winchell and Crompton in New Haven, Connecticut. These papers depended heavily on the mail steamer that brought periodicals from Europe every few weeks and docked in many territories in the region. News of Thomas's death in 1889, for instance, reached Trinidad at the same time that the announcement of the publication of *Froudacity* did.

Though not a journalist per se, Thomas was "on intimate terms" with many journalists. His entire public life was recorded in the pages of the newspapers, with his own commentaries helping to frame his own public image, as well as the issues of the day. He assisted in making newspapers a powerful site for the performance of Black and Colored prestige: the *New Era* and the *San Fernando Gazette* published many of his letters and carefully noted his promotions as well as his indignities.

In 1874 Thomas was "unlawfully" arrested by a policeman. "Although aware, from what we had seen and heard, that persons of the class to whom Mr. Thomas belongs were often ill-treated by the policemen, yet we scarcely believed it possible that a person of Mr. Thomas's respectability and official position could have been treated this way," complained "Sambo" in a letter to the *New Era* on 27 April 1874. When the police chief, L. M. Fraser, an Englishman who had married into a French Creole family, merely gave the policeman a minor penalty, Thomas complained to the governor, who went over the head of the police chief and dismissed the constable. For "Sambo" this indicated that the governor would not show "fellow-feeling with the skin-arrogance" demonstrated by a policeman who had "dared to insult the respectable coloured people of this colony in the person of Mr. J. J. Thomas." In a letter published on 4 May "Sambo" noted that it would be a herculean task "to clean the Augean stables from which the nigger-oppressing heroes come out" but said that the dismissal of the policeman was a step in the right direction.

On the one hand, Thomas had to suffer the ignominy of public arrest and the snub of the police chief. On the other hand, the incident proved that Thomas had the ear of the governor, as well as the support of editors and letter writers who could influence public opinion in his favor and frame the incident in terms of racial discrimination.

As we have seen, he was also "on intimate terms" with papers identified with the governor's party, such as the *Chronicle*. He edited the short-lived *Trinidad Monthly Magazine* in 1871, as well as the *Trinidad Review*, owned by de la Sauvagère, in the mid-1880s—"on its first appearance," according to his obituary.[5] Looking through the articles of the *Trinidad*

Review, it is difficult to know which pieces to attribute to Thomas, which suggests both the disembodied nature of authorship in that context and perhaps the similarity in viewpoints of like-minded gentlemen. The editorial of 16 August 1883 proposes that the reading books used in primary schools should be inexpensive as well as relevant to local conditions: "What, for example, can a mere child in these colonies conceive of *snow, hail,* and *oaktree, acorns, giraffes,* and such like outlandish things?" While this seems to be consistent with Thomas's views, did he also write the editorial in the same issue charging Exeter Hall with "exaggerated outpourings" of love and concern for indentured Indian immigrants or the 23 August piece declaring that "avarice" was the "master-passion" of "orientals"? Given his usual public support of and by prominent Black and Colored men, could the 13 September piece criticizing Michel Maxwell Philip for blindly supporting the governor really be his? Considering his views on the isolation of Cedros (see chapter 3), did he write the celebratory piece in the 20 September issue in anticipation of the Cedros horse races? Is it Thomas who laments the difficulty of hunting lap meat and other game in the 27 September issue?

When a letter critical of de la Sauvagère appeared in the *Trinidad Review* in October 1884, it was attributed to Thomas, and he wrote to the *San Fernando Gazette* saying that he was used to slander: "You [presumably Carter], I, and Mr. De la Sauvagère can smile at this malice. You, because you know the identity of your correspondent. Me and Mr. De la Sauvagère because our intercourse has been too intimate and harmonious to permit, at least, that he should believe me infamous."[6] Here Thomas identified himself as knowing personally both Colored and White editors.

After his death someone suggested that Thomas had not written the 1883 Yuletime address in the *Trinidad Review* and characterized Thomas's writing as "inelegant, laboured and heavy." Defending Thomas, Edgar Maresse-Smith, a prominent Colored solicitor and nephew of Emilie Maresse-Paul, declared:

> To speak truly, J. J. Thomas's style is not of the milk and water kind which some people (and, possibly, our reviewer) are pleased to qualify as "elegant." His was not the pen which "laboured" over a phrase and chiseled it until it became disfigured. So strong was the flow of ideas in him that he had no time to take up particular ones and pet them. His thoughts appeared to his readers in native grace, denuded of all the useless and far-fetched comments with which certain writers are wont to deck theirs.[7]

Not only was there uncertainty about Thomas's association with this periodical, therefore, but his own distinction between "writing easily" and writing with zeal was being used posthumously both to slander and to defend him.

When Thomas probed the social contexts for "writing easily" in his reference to Wenkstern's "advantages," he was suggesting that rather than being a function of "natural" superiority, writing easily must be explained in relation to specific social circumstances. In referring to "less resolute and more mercenary souls" than Donovan, he was implying a certain relationship between money and "zeal." Did Rostant and de la Sauvagère lose social prestige when their families attacked each other in the streets, or was their status rooted in arenas besides journalism? When Thomas was arrested, or when he was "menaced" by Sarah Smith in the streets, was his public status similarly affected, or more so, given his lack of family connections? That is, if journalism was an important forum for establishing and contesting the prestige of gentlemen, was it the sole forum?

Following Thomas's example in the comparison between Donovan and Wenkstern, I want to situate him and others relative to the acquisition of different kinds of capital. When he was praised for his achievements, was he vulnerable to charges of bribery? Could his and others' use of race in public discourse be cast as special pleading? Gerard Besson surmises that Thomas was probably a member of the Lodge United Brethren. The lodge records, should they ever become public, will be an important means of understanding how Thomas and other men imagined themselves as free citizens across social divisions.[8] Freemasonry, an important arena for the assessment of male prestige, is not yet available to us, but the important context of education is: how did Thomas's acquisition of an education funded by the state give him "compensating privileges" but guarantee "laboured" and "heavy" writing? Was "native grace" and lack of "elegance," to return to Maresse-Smith's letter, always a virtue, in opposition to morally suspicious or frivolous scholars, or could it be cast as insecurity and mimicry, a substitute for innate intelligence?

To PURSUE these matters of exertion, prestige, and advantages in relation to Thomas, I turn briefly to Pierre Bourdieu's account of capital. The model he provides for giving "thick descriptions" of "all the practices (prefaces, footnotes, dedications, earnings, sales quarrels, silences) that [are] part of the struggle for cultural power and prestige" is a useful one (Harries, 473). He locates the institutional contexts of prestige, specifying the role of economic resources and questioning the appeal to "natural" characteristics. I am well aware that his discussions arise out of the very specific contexts of Algeria in the 1950s and France from the 1950s to 1980s. If we keep Bourdieu's contexts and limitations in mind, his analyses can provide a useful paradigm for understanding Thomas's relationship to education and prestige.

Mastering "the capital of instruments of expression," Bourdieu notes, including the classics, grammars, and dictionaries, confers on "those who engage in it a power over language and thereby over the ordinary users of language, as well as over their capital." Having acquired this power, those deemed "authoritative" must constantly "compete within the field of specialized production for the monopolistic power to impose the legitimate mode of expression." Such competition "tends constantly to produce and reproduce the game and its stakes by reproducing, primarily in those who are directly involved, but not in them alone, the practical recognition of legitimacy." Bourdieu notes that "the game is over when people start wondering if the cake is worth the candle" (Bourdieu, *Language*, 57–58).

For Bourdieu, the dominant sector represents itself as self-evident, producing the means to continue reproducing the status quo. Mechanisms of consecration in the educational and intellectual arenas operate according to a set of unarticulated rules that censor speech and thus regulate what is allowed to be uttered or what can be excluded as nonsense. These rules, specific to each field, Bourdieu terms the *habitus*. For playing according to the rules of the game individuals are rewarded with educational capital, though those with other kinds of capital are not dependent on educational capital. Educational qualifications provide a person with "social magic," conferring legitimacy and thus the right to speak. In producing the means of its own reproduction and censoring potential challengers the process enacts "symbolic violence." Education is one of the critical sites in the development of a habitus. The existence of "miraculés"—successful persons from disadvantaged groups—in every educational system functions to perpetuate the myth that everyone has a chance to succeed.

The opposition "between the 'scholastic' (or 'pedantic') and the *mondain*, the effortlessly elegant, is at the heart of debates over taste and culture in every age" (*Distinction*, 69). There is nothing "natural" about culture, even though the "taste" for certain artistic or musical works, for books, or for food is more often than not represented as natural. While the knowledge of a particular work of art might mark one as being "in the know," a self-conscious appreciation of it marks one as "pedantic," as opposed to having a long, "natural" relationship to it outside of the educational system.

Acquiring one's artistic "eye" in the home as opposed to in the classroom marks one as truly cultured and mystifies the process of acquisition: one knows because one just does.

In her discussion of Simone de Beauvoir's consignment to the category "second only to Sartre" despite her equal if not greater mastery of the intellectual symbols of a superior education, Toril Moi shows how Beauvoir's painstaking elaboration of the process by which she acquired her appreciation of music as a child marks her as vulgar and petite bourgeoise. She admits that she listens to music with "obsessional intensity" and that she "profits" from this: "as in the most formative moments of my childhood, pleasure and knowledge coincided . . . I played my records ten times in succession, analysing every phrase."[9] Crudely showing the "sweat" of culture consigns Beauvoir to the realm of the "undistinguished" since "cultural *anxiety*," as Moi points out, "is the very antithesis of true distinction, which seeks to present itself as easy, relaxed and above all *natural*" (70).

In Bourdieu's discussion this is best shown in the words of the aristocracy itself: "I would have a man know everything and yet, by his manner of speaking, not be convicted of having studied"; or "A gentleman should seek, not so much to be expert in what he undertakes, as to undertake it like a gentleman. This air of ease which comes from a fortunate birth and an excellent habit is one of the amenities of a gentleman; he should set about even the most difficult task with such detachment that is seems to cost him no effort" (*Distinction*, 71, quoting Antoine Gombaud, chevalier de Méré, *De la conversation*). This sort of capital, that is, is defined by its distance from "economic necessity" or "practical urgencies" (53–54). Those who fail to "play the games of culture" without seriousness, who have "inappropriate stakes and interests," who "treat intellectual struggles [as] a simple question of right and wrong, life and death," are "boors" and pedants who have violated the "aesthetic disposition" (55). They lack the characteristics of the "connoisseur," who has "an unconscious mastery [derived] from slow familiarization," "the equivalent of the prolonged contact between disciple and master in a traditional education, i.e. repeated contact with cultural words and cultured people" (66).

To be sure, Bourdieu has been criticized for failing to distinguish between those rules that are specific to a particular historical moment and cultural context and those that transcend time and place, as well as for his insistence that the status quo reproduces itself without acknowledging the possibility of transformation. He shows us how people pursue power, wealth, and distinction but takes for granted that their only motive is the achievement of these.[10] Nevertheless, Bourdieu's account is useful since it gets us beyond a language of disinterest.

Trinidad and other Caribbean territories laid bare the sources of the wealth that enabled bourgeois and aristocratic Europeans to develop leisurely and disinterested notions of "culture." But while the possibility of contemplating the sublime in the intemperate eastern Caribbean, with its history of plantation violence, may have seemed absurd to Europeans (more absurd than, say, in the Lake District), the upper classes of the Caribbean were no more averse than their European counterparts to pursuing the life of the mind in close proximity to the noisy rabble. *Jane Eyre*'s Bertha Mason and *Vanity Fair*'s Rhoda Schwartz notwithstanding, Caribbean heirs and heiresses did not perceive *themselves* to be crass and uncultured, even if metropolitan visitors considered them to be so. The typical representation of the Caribbean planter class as uninterested in cultural and intellectual matters—leaving aside assumptions about what properly constituted "intellectual" and "cultural"—ignores those eastern Caribbean Colored and White planters who prided themselves on their appreciation of books, art, and music. They ordered the latest of these from Paris and London even while producing and disseminating poems, musical airs, and folktales in the French Creole language, which they delighted in speaking. They felt themselves to be bearers of culture in a philistine world of Protestant merchants and vulgar non-Whites.

As Black and Colored persons of urban and rural laboring-class origins such as Thomas began to enter the lower echelons of the middle class beginning in the mid-nineteenth century, they would participate in, and even be perceived to dominate, what counted as the intellectual character of the society. Willing to play the game—convinced that the "cake was worth the candle," to use Bourdieu's terms—their entry tested the extent to which only those with a "natural" relationship to high culture enabled by (even if not acknowledging) economic capital could define what constituted Trinidad's cultural and intellectual life. This did not mean that the newcomers would challenge such definitions. Indeed, "the emergence of the nonwhite middle class was accomplished at the expense of the criminalization of large segments of the black lower class and their East Indian compatriots" (Trotman, 7–8). The willingness of Thomas and others to demonstrate personal discipline and ambition was lauded as proof of what the lower orders could achieve since culture and intellect were not considered to be the "natural" preserve of non-Whites.

Education would be the basis of a new middle class rather than, as heretofore, merely complementing wealth or the "right" race. Until the mid-nineteenth century the middle class was composed of perhaps a few White clerks, wealthy Coloreds who bristled at the racial limits imposed on their social status, and Colored and Black small farmers and artisans who had acquired small wealth. Increasingly, the lower ranks of the middle class would be represented by Black and Colored children of plantation laborers and domestic servants who staked their claim to mobility on educational capital.

Not just education, however, but the type of curriculum one pursued contributed to one's power, access, and prestige. Similarly, the bookish Black man who used the wrong fork might still be considered less "cultured" than the planter with the beautiful first edition of Labat's *Nouveau voyage aux isles de l'Amérique* who swore in public.

As a Black man of the respectable classes in the late nineteenth century Thomas would have been well aware of competing conceptions of Black men as intellectual laborers. The Caribbean-born, Liberia-based educator Edward Blyden used the analogy of "the labours of Sisyphus when Ulysses saw him" to refer to his efforts to raise the intellectual tone of Liberia. Apologizing that "an entire stranger residing on a far-off and barbarous shore, and connected with a race down-trodden and despised, should intrude upon the time and patience of one so distinguished as yourself," he asked William Gladstone, England's chancellor of the exchequer and future prime minister, to send him classical texts, books by Shakespeare, Milton, and Kingsley, his most recent budget (which "has demonstrated to the world that literary men can be able financiers, despite the current opinion to the contrary"), and the "Oxford or Cambridge Examination Papers for 1859" (Blyden, 27–28). More specifically, however, Blyden wanted "a succinct account of the manner in which you pursued your classical studies: what works you read and the order in which they were read. How many lines did you read at a lesson in Virgil? How many in Homer?" If such frankness indicated a lack of "natural" cultivation, it also showed personal discipline and ambition in the face of daunting circumstances and a commitment to the advancement of certain notions of "civilization."

Yet this very frankness about their labor was used against Black men, as in Anthony Trollope's famous characterization:

[The Black man] burns to be regarded as a scholar, puzzles himself with fine words, and addicts himself to religion for the sake of appearance, and delights in aping the little graces of civilization. He despises himself thoroughly, and would probably be content to starve for a month if he could appear as a white man for a day; but yet he delights in signs of respect paid to him, black man as he is, and is always thinking of his own dignity. If you want to win his heart for an hour, call him a gentleman; but if you want to reduce him to a despairing obedience, tell him that he is a filthy nigger, assure him that his father and mother had tails like monkeys, and forbid him to think that he can have a soul like a white man. (56)

This is not Thomas's distinction between a Wenkstern who "plans" and is overly concerned with diction and a Donovan who "feels" since neither man is innately unsuited to the words he uses. The Black man in Trollope's example is obsessed with diction without understanding it. "Burning," "puzzling," and "addicting" here capture the exertion and the absurdity of his efforts. *Black intellectual,* by this account, is an oxymoron. Any labors in this direction are necessarily excessive, imitative of Whites, and only skin-deep. Monkey/nigger and gentleman occupy extreme ends of the intellectual and genealogical ladder. Significantly, the White man, who is commentator, implied reader, and standard against which Blacks are judged, calls the tune. He has the power to control the performance of the other, securing particular responses by knowing exactly what to say.

By such rhetorical gestures middle-class Victorian men erased their own anxieties about intellectual labor. Thomas Carlyle, who helped to define the profession of man of letters as heroic, masculine, and distinct from "effeminate" literature, was anxious about the difference between his father, a stonemason turned small farmer in rural Scotland who earned a livelihood doing manual labor, and the pale, anemic writers he met in London (Christ; C. Hall, *White, Male, and Middle Class,* 264–66). After meeting Samuel Coleridge, who had done so much to distinguish the man of letters from the mere hack, Carlyle would write to his brother in 1824: "He never straightens his knee joints, he stoops with his fat ill shapen shoulders, and in walking he does not tread but shovel and slide— my father would call it *skluiffing*" (Carlyle and Carlyle, 90–91, qtd. in Clarke, 29). As Norma Clarke notes, the father's "rugged, abrupt, unpolished" nature would have been associated by the son with "an instinctive commitment towards the morally true" rather than dependence on the shifting values of speech and persuasion (38).

Here the concern was that writers' exertions were effete and sophistic, distinct as they were from the manliness of manual laborers. Black men in the Americas, innately suited for agricultural labor in Trollope's eyes, absurdly mimicked gentlemen when they "puzzled" over words. Thomas and others understood that some metropolitan visions of the Caribbean had no conceptual space for Black and Colored intellectual workers, not to mention their political aspirations. But Thomas's praise of Donovan and Maresse-Smith's defense of Thomas suggest that they were unconcerned about being cast as pedantic and undistinguished, given the history of being deprived of "advantages." The determination to catch up was cast as zeal, and the investment in fine words for their own sake was represented as idle. But idle too were those members of the working classes who pursued activities cast as transgressive. Indeed, the scholar whose "toiling upward in the night" cast him as undistinguished by one aristocratic reckoning was also marking his distance from the laborers on the Rostant and de la Sauvagère family estates or the coalers in the harbors across the Caribbean. In this regard Thomas's sickly body, which slowed his intellectual output throughout his career, was a powerful external sign both of his commitment to a life of intellectual labor that promised few material compensations and of his distance from the "animal vigor" of those Black male bodies described in the pages of metropolitan travelogues.[11]

Thomas's entry into Trinidadian public life coincided with the institution of a state-funded system of primary education in the early 1850s. The opening up of the educational system by the creation of ward schools (wards were administrative districts within a parish) offered the opportunity for a handful of the children of rural peasants and estate laborers, as well as of the urban-based lower classes, to surpass the expectation that most students at this level of schooling would learn the rudiments of the three R's and have no desire to change their station in life. The education of Indians was ignored by both Protestant and Catholic authorities until the Canadian Presbyterian church made this group a priority beginning in the 1870s.

A secular government system financed by local ward rates (as opposed to the general revenues) thwarted the dominance of Catholic-run schools, though the reading books used were the religious Irish national schoolbooks. Ireland offered the model of a Catholic country where the Protestant authorities wished to fund a nondenominational educational system rather than to give parliamentary funds to the Roman Catholic Church (see Campbell, "Education," 65–78, 287–91; and Akenson).

Carl Campbell's detailed analysis of the educational system of that period reveals the consistent concern that the lower classes should be anglicized but not encouraged to pursue social mobility and that the postprimary education system, which catered to a few Blacks, many middle-class Coloreds, and a few middle-class Whites, should carefully regulate access to social mobility, particularly where Blacks and Coloreds were concerned.

Thus the rules barring "illegitimate" children from attendance, for instance, or the careful regulation of fees to keep out undesirable non-Whites but let in Whites in financially straitened circumstances.

By the time Thomas tied for first place with another student in Governor Harris's annual writing competition for ward schools in 1855 he was about fifteen years old.[12] Since the ward school system and the Boys Model School had come into existence only in the early 1850s, we can assume with Campbell that Thomas probably had attended a denominational school, since those predated the new ward ones, and then entered a ward school when these were established. One of his obituaries mentions early instruction by a Protestant minister.[13] By 1858 Thomas was a student at the Woodbrook government school for trainee teachers, where he would remain until 1860, when he took up his first teaching position, at the Savonetta ward school. The teacher-training school, or normal school, was established in tandem with the Boys and Girls Model Schools (later the Tranquility Boys and Girls Schools), allowing the trainees to hone their teaching skills.

For one dollar a week Coloreds, as well as a few Whites and Blacks, received an education that was more advanced than they could have obtained at the ordinary primary schools and similar in the higher classes to that in the lower forms of the two private, Catholic secondary schools, but "without the classics" (Campbell, *Young Colonials,* 67). It was thus functionally the only nonprivate secondary, or at least postprimary, school, and it prided itself on turning out future planters, overseers, and clerks, some of whom would go on to university abroad. The graduates included, in the year Thomas left, a wheelwright, a printer, and a gold-smith.

We know that as a trainee teacher Thomas would have studied alongside the students at the Boys Model School since the report of the inspector of schools for the year Thomas left notes that the headmaster taught the trainees on Saturdays and Wednesdays and that on other days he taught them alongside the students in the science class of the model school. In this science class, which was the pride of the curriculum, students at the top level read reader 4 of the Irish Readers series and studied natural philosophy, political economy, algebra, and astronomy—this in addition to advanced levels of the subjects taught throughout the school, which were geography, grammar, arithmetic, and writing. Initially there were high hopes for this institution, with inspectors' reports and newspaper editorials noting that its graduates would be able to teach anywhere in the West Indies and "fill any position of life *short of that requiring classical attainments.*"[14]

Although the training school produced students who were then expected to assist with the teaching at the model schools before going out to work in ward schools, this institution did not have the prestige of the model schools. Despite the low number of students (between seven and thirteen for the period when Thomas was associated with it), the headmaster seems not to have had time to teach the students at the model schools or to thoroughly prepare the teacher trainees. Besides studying with the model school science class, the trainees received instruction in "reading, writing from dictation, arithmetic, geometry, grammar and the theory of teaching," though the principles of teaching were not given a central place in the curriculum.[15]

Though the establishment of the Queen's Collegiate School (later Queen's Royal College) in 1859, which began to attract the "better" students who might otherwise have attended one of the model schools, led to a dip in the initial excitement created by the establishment of the Woodbrook complex, Thomas certainly benefited from his time there. Campbell suggests that Thomas may have been supporting himself since he was an unsalaried trainee before 1859, when he became one of six trainees to receive an allowance in exchange for teaching and then, later that year, distinguished himself by becoming assistant master while still a student, which meant an increase in his stipend (Campbell, "John Jacob Thomas"; Wood, "John Jacob Thomas").

The report of Inspector Alexander Anderson for 1859 noted a young "assistant master at Woodbrook, who has been entirely educated under our present system of instruction": "With the exception of classical learning, his attainments are of a high order in all that appertains to the business of a school master; while his conduct has been in general most exemplary and commendable."[16] Here Thomas is under close public scrutiny. The phrase "entirely educated under our system," referring to his attendance at two government-sponsored institutions, a ward school and Woodbrook, indicated that the system was working and, by extension, how farsighted Governor Harris had been to institute it in 1851. Thomas's success proved the system's ability to provide mobility to those who would exert themselves, those members of the unwashed masses who had to prove their capability. Thomas confirmed the validity of the rules of the game. It was important that he was "exemplary and commendable": this was not someone who studied his grammar and then swore in public. Moral conduct underlined his educational achievements.

But the repeated reference to "short of classical attainments" bears thinking about. Not only were Woodbrook's teacher trainees in close proximity to, but not as prestigious as, students at the model schools but they were constantly defined in terms of their lack of the classical curriculum that characterized the state-funded Queen's Collegiate School, established in 1859, and its rival, the St. Mary's College of the Immaculate Conception (CIC), established in 1863.

The establishment of these institutions sustained longstanding religious tensions in Trinidad: Queen's was supposedly open to all nationalities, thus justifying full government funding, and for Catholics "government" meant Protestant-controlled, anglicized, and secular instruction, as well as the unfair advantage of full funding. The two institutions disagreed about the relative importance of a classical or technical education, about the dominance of the Cambridge external exams as opposed to the University of London exams, and about whether the coveted Island Scholarships allowing winners to attend Oxford or Cambridge for three years would be opened up to meet "the colony's need for experts in agriculture and for engineers" (Campbell, *Young Colonials,* 35). Catholics tended to champion curricula stressing agricultural and commercial subjects, and their secondary institution offered the classics along with this commercial emphasis, which, as Campbell notes, meant that it "reached further down into the creole middle class" (28) than the Queen's Collegiate School.

Queen's was the jewel in the crown of Trinidad's system, quickly establishing itself as an assembly line for Creoles who excelled in the Cambridge external examinations. Campbell notes that Queen's was the first school outside of England to participate in these exams (26). Since so few in the British Empire took these exams, Trinidadians delighted in the publication of the results, when they could see that a local candidate had placed favorably in a particular subject in relation to all the candidates who had taken the exam in England and throughout the empire. Essentially, no more than about thirty students were trained by three or four masters, at least one of whom was a graduate of Oxford or Cambridge (though not a clergyman, since the school was secular), in Greek, Latin, French, mathematics, geography, English history, English composition, German, and practical science, with considerable time and effort devoted to the class taking the external examinations. Winners of the Island Scholarships were not required to return to Trinidad. Early winners were all White and, Campbell seems to imply, non-Creole. Beginning in the 1870s Coloreds began to win: "They, more than white boys, would have to come home, and would understand the importance of an independent profession" (27).

Having forbidden its members to attend Queen's, the Catholic Church's establishment of the CIC by the Holy Ghost Fathers from France was critical. A boarding school, cheaper and with a curriculum less focused on the classics, it was supposedly less exclusive. Most of the staff was from France, and most students spoke French or Spanish as a first language.

At various times both schools had rules against admitting students whose parents were not married, which effectively eliminated all except a few Colored families and most Whites. Discussing the proposal for the establishment of Queen's, Charles Warner, a White Creole member of the Legislative Council, noted that the school was not for those whose "position in after life will be below the standard of the education which was offered" nor "for any boy whose parents earned their living by working with their hands."[17] It was not until the early 1870s that a small number of Black and Colored scholarship boys began to be admitted annually to Queen's, and the school's attempt to reduce the number of even these places infuriated the Black and Colored middle class. Even if either of these institutions had existed when Thomas entered Woodbrook in 1858, therefore, as a working-class student he would not have been able to attend them. When he was named secretary to the council of Queen's in 1870, one of the posts he occupied after entering the civil service, he became identified with an institution that he himself could not have attended.

To return to the qualification "with the exception of classical learning," then, the classical curriculum was one way of demarcating a particular kind of education and class position from what Thomas had had access to at Woodbrook. In this sense the designation "self-made" that was applied to Thomas and others underscored their zeal in going beyond the offerings of the institution, but it was also a constant reminder of their lack of access to a certain kind of education in the first place. After Woodbrook, Thomas would labor to master those subjects denied to him by "toiling upward in the night." Throughout his career his letters would be dotted with classical references, a sign of both learning and pedantry.

During the 1870s and 1880s Thomas and other graduates of Woodbrook, such as Louis Tronchin, who would later head the Boys Model School, and Samuel Proctor, who headed the San Fernando Borough School before Thomas took over, addressed the literary and debating societies in Port of Spain and San Fernando. The *Grenada Chronicle and Gazette* of 20 December 1873 reported that Thomas had delivered a lecture before the Trinidad Athenaeum titled "Philology vs. Physiology" in response to Tronchin's essay "Physiology vs. Philology." The newspaper disagreed with Thomas's claim that "the man that grows patriotic, generous, or gentle, from solving mathematical problems, or experiences an enthusiastic love for the moral progress of humanity as the result of such exercises, may be—nay, undoubtedly is—a very extraordinary creature." For this editor, Thomas's claims about the superiority of philology, since "Linguistics did not bring into existence the steam-engine, and its marvellous application to our daily wants," were overstated, and he had erred in treating mathematics as a science rather than "in its loftier position of Physics." Thomas was correct in deeming mathematics superior to the "natural and Physical Sciences," however. As he had noted in his lecture, "Botany, Astronomy, Zoology, Chemistry, and the rest of the Natural and Physical Sciences, all deal with *material* objects," whereas philology and literature were devoted to "the sublime operations and products of the diviner part of man."[18] A September 1887 meeting of the Trinidad Literary Association in Port of Spain discussed the benefits of an "English education," and members were encouraged to avoid "trashy novels." They were reminded that the career of Gladstone, the British prime minister, was proof that a literary education was a fitting preparation for public life. He had studied the classics, and he was the "first financier of the age."[19] Membership in such an organization confirmed their standing as cultured men of the society, men who distinguished between "trash" and elevated discourse.

Such meetings were attended by men such as Thomas, who had *only* educational capital, and by Colored and White men, who had other kinds of capital. Many if not all of the latter had studied in Europe, as had other upper-class Trinidadians. Many of the men who had published distinguished papers and books were European-trained doctors and lawyers from wealthy families who had sugar and cocoa estates. Louis A. A. de Verteuil, an unofficial member of the Legislative Council and a member of one of the most distinguished White families, had received his medical training at the University of Paris. He published a comprehensive study of Trinidad in 1856. Antoine Leotaud, a White obstetrician who had received a gold medal from a Parisian society for a paper on confinement, published a study of Trinidad's birds, *Les oiseaux de la Trinidad* (Brereton, *Race Relations,* 55). The Colored Michel Maxwell Philip, who was the solicitor general during the 1870s and 1880s, had done his secondary schooling in Scotland and then studied law in England, returning to Trinidad in 1855. His novel *Emmanuel Appadocca* was published during his tour of Europe in the early 1850s. His relative Jean-Baptiste Philippe had published *Free Mulatto,* a petition to the British government on behalf of the rights of the free Colored population, before his death in 1829. Philippe's family, based in the Naparimas area of southern Trinidad, owned more land and slaves than anyone else in the Colored community. He qualified as a doctor at the University of Edinburgh, completing a thesis in Latin on hysterical moods (Campbell, "Jean-Baptiste Philippe"; Cudjoe, introduction).

Two leading amateur scientists were Sylvester Devenish, the prominent surveyor who was Irish-born and identified with the White francophone sector, and Lechmere Guppy, identified by birth and marriage with the anglophone and francophone White Creole sectors. Guppy edited the *Trinidad Almanac* with his brother and later founded the Victoria Institute, based on the London Polytechnic. He was well known for his studies of marine life, specimens of which he collected and shared with colleagues in England. He gained fame for "discovering" the "Millions" fish, which he found in the St. Ann's River and sent to the British Museum. The fish was named the "guppy," or *Girardinus guppyi*, in his honor.

Such were the men who assessed Thomas's abilities when he left Woodbrook. As he sought to identify with them as like minds in a sea of perceived philistinism he must have been conscious of his difference from them socially, notwithstanding the interests that drew all of them together as intellectuals and nationalists and some of them as race vindicators. As he struggled, mostly unsuccessfully, to publish his own work, he must have smarted (as others did) at the comparative ease with which Lionel Fraser, the police chief who snubbed him in 1874, published his *History of Trinidad*. The Legislative Council voted two hundred pounds toward the cost of publishing it locally to cover the cost of sending proofs to and from Europe and since "his literary ability and knowledge of the subject were well known." A letter to the editor suggested that Fraser had been granted undue privileges and that given his questionable political beliefs, the manuscript should have been examined by persons with literary and historical competence before the public was made to pay for its publication.[20]

Thomas's performance in the civil service examinations and his publication of the *Creole Grammar* in 1869 transformed him into an intellectual whose career was closely followed by prominent locals and Europeans. As he was moved from post to post in the civil service, he was used to prove the liberalism of the colonial authorities, as well as their reluctance to give Blacks and Coloreds, as well as Creoles more generally, significant posts. The public discussion of his career in the newspapers reflected praise for his achievements, disgust when such praise seemed excessive, resentment that he was not rewarded sufficiently, and the underlying conviction that intellectuals operated in a cultural wilderness.

An editorial in the *Trinidad Chronicle* in June 1871 linked Thomas to Woodbrook specifically. While Trinidad had provided Thomas with the "rudiments of mental training," he had done everything else himself: "All the rest is his own doing. His is that hungering and thirsting after knowledge which would not be satisfied with the bare rations served out at Woodbrook; his also the patient toil and the unremitting efforts which were needed to convert a village schoolmaster into a thinker and philologist—one humble and bold enough to try his prentice hand on one of the most difficult subjects that can well be found." It was public knowledge, then, that Woodbrook could provide only the "bare rudiments." It was not that its graduates had *nothing* but that they did not have *more*. Its meager rations were not sufficient to feed, much less nurture or fatten, the true scholar. Any nurturing beyond Woodbrook was an indication of the "self-made" portion of one's efforts. The village schoolmaster could not be an intellectual without this massive, extra effort.

Thomas, the editorial reminded readers, had begun his "labours" in Cedros, where he was teaching when he began his research for the *Creole Grammar* in 1866. Study in such conditions, "in the midst—if we except a few planters and managers—of a rude, ignorant and illiterate population," was the "pursuit of knowledge under extraordinary difficulties," and thus "he who, in such a place, trains his mind and stores it as Mr. Thomas has done, deserves preeminently the honourable and mis-used title of a *self-made man*." We shall see in chapter 3 that Thomas would have endorsed this assessment of Cedros, though other commentators noted its sugar and coconut estates, the excursionists who traveled there for horse racing, and the twelve-mile Icacos Beach, where an anchor in the sand was reputed to be from one of Columbus's ships (Collens). Comparing the *Creole Grammar* to Antoine Leotaud's book on birds, the editorial noted that "two sterling works are the most a young country like this can be expected to produce in a limited number of years, and—to tell the whole truth—they are all the public, in its present state, can put up with." Only rarely did the "tender stem of Creole Literature, languishing in an as yet wild and barren soil," produce "something ripe and substantial" rather than "watery, sour, or husky fruit."

The same paper had devoted an extensive editorial to Thomas when the *Creole Grammar* first appeared two years earlier, reviewing Thomas's career and encouraging readers to purchase the book.[21] The earlier editorial noted that Trinidad's ward school system had produced "several teachers whose capacities and acquirements would have been deemed incredible and—it admitted possible—*dangerous*—in the good old days before Emancipation—men whose acquisitions now put to shame the efforts of many young men of the more fortunate and favoured races." These men had supplemented their skills with study at home, "not allowing resources acquired at Woodbrook to be checked, either by their narrowed means and opportunities, or by the indifference of those around them."

Thomas's work, which showed "abundant proof of laborious inquiry," had been "read with interest in Europe and America, and received the approval of critics whose notice confers celebrity." These included Frederic J. Furnivall, John Malcolm Ludlow, Max Müller, and N. Trübner, "prominent men in the field of philological study," who had had sent letters of praise as well as "gifts of valuable books." Trinidad's governor, Arthur Hamilton Gordon, the son of a former prime minister of England, had praised Thomas, as had the late Otto Wenkstern, "himself a writer of known and high repute and thus qualified to judge of its merits." Sylvester Devenish and Chief Justice Knox, "than whom no two more competent critics of our *patois* could be found in the colony," had also praised the work. Thomas, the editorial continued, had "closely and critically studied the Greek, Latin, French, Spanish, Italian and Hindostanee languages." He spoke and wrote French and Spanish "with fluency and general correctness," had "translated a great deal of Goldoni, Tasso, Petrarch, Politiano," and other Italian authors, and had produced "a small treatise" on Italian verbs. German "was acquired by him entirely from books" and had so far been "confined" to Schiller and Lessing.

The editorial ended by encouraging the public to purchase the book. Disagreeing with the *New Era*'s suggestion that the *Creole Grammar*'s poor sales were due to the public's lack of appreciation, it noted that the book had many "eager borrowers." But this was not sufficient. Trübner had ordered fifty copies for a European public, but a "patriotic public" in Trinidad had not been as dutiful, and "unfortunately, empty fame is *all* the book is likely to bring for all his pains." Thomas himself was going to be rewarded by the governor with "something more tangible than handsome words," noted the editorial. He would be promoted "to an office more suited to his abilities," giving him more "means and time" for his intellectual pursuits, and the paper hoped that "all others, children of the country, of whatever origin," who "by their own merits" excelled would receive similar reward from the government "when seeking service under it."

By 1869, then, Thomas has mastered the classical languages denied to him at Woodbrook and much more. The details are of interest here. Not only had he learned Italian but he had produced a treatise on its verbs. His German was "entirely from books," perhaps a confession produced by his constant awareness of trying to master these languages in a country where so many upper-class elites, including Germans, had mastered the language. His efforts had earned him the praise of eminent gentlemen locally and abroad. His promotion is framed both as something he had earned and as a "reward" from a liberal governor. We are watching you, the paper seems to caution the governor: not only have we publicized Thomas's proposed promotion but others applying to the notoriously exclusive civil service should receive fair consideration.

The appeal to the public to show "patriotism" anticipates Thomas's remarks to the Grenadian public about Donovan almost two decades later. But it can also be read as self-serving, considering that it was the presses of the same newspaper that had published Thomas's book. By purchasing it, the public would enable Thomas to pay off his debts to the press. Its praise for Thomas, then, cannot be separated from the factor of monetary compensation. As if to press this point, an irate correspondent to the same paper, who signed him- or herself "E," questioned the praise for the book in a letter to the editor in the year following its publication: "The sentiments expressed in that bribed letter, are not only ludicrous, but entirely romantic. Where is the man who will not, after reading it say, or come to the conclusion, that that effusion must either be from the author himself or from one of his worshippers."[22]

A note below the letter scoffed at the suggestion that Thomas could afford to bribe anyone even if he wanted to: "Perhaps—Mr. Thomas being notoriously a very rich man—the bribe was administered to both writer and editor." But the connection had been made. Praise for one's intellectual efforts enhanced one's prestige: but also risked cheapening it. The 1869 editorial referring to Thomas's mastery of languages referred to its source as "unquestionable," implying that it was Thomas himself. That is, Thomas had provided the information that had enabled the newspaper to write a favorable editorial about him. Thomas's advice to another writer a few years later, in a review of his book, suggests both his confidence in aligning himself with prominent gentleman of his day and his perspective on the issue of flattery.

Pierre-Gustave-Louis Borde, a member of one of Trinidad's most distinguished White families, published the first volume of his *Histoire de la Trinidad sous le gouvernement espagnol,* in Paris in 1876. In his preface Borde details the labors facing the historian in Trinidad: "For someone who is unskilled and inexperienced to write a history, be it that of the smallest and most remote corner of the earth, is always a difficult task, but it is one particularly arduous and overwhelming when all the material needed is lacking." "Worms and fires" had destroyed archives and family records, in addition to which "the thread of chronology is continually broken, and the irreparable errors of popular tradition, stop one at every turn."

The only "recourse" in conditions such as these, Borde notes, is to study, "not historical science, which we do not pretend to possess," but "the histories published about America during the 16th, 17th and 18th centuries": rare documents on the Pariagotos Indians, Capuchin friars, and buccaneers, geographies and histories of Venezuela, Martinique, the Orinoco, New Andalusia, and so on. But even locating these entails costly research in Venezuela, Martinique, the United States, in France, England, Spain and in Italy. "Several times we had to apply to private libraries and to foreign archives to obtain copies of important accounts and documents which could be found only in those places. To achieve our end, we have spared neither time, work nor money." Borde notes the assistance of the librarian of "our public library," as well as that of a "Martinican cousin" who had sent a copy of Labat's *Nouveau voyage aux isles de l'Amérique*, persons conducting research on his behalf in the archives of the French navy, and the Spanish consul in Trinidad, who had secured for Borde permission to use the archives in Seville, though so far "circumstances have not permitted us to make use of this privilege" (xxviii–xxxii).

The labor of the committed intellectual, then, is arduous, whether the limited resources of the Woodbrook graduate or the network of international contacts that Borde could count on. In the course of his own career Thomas too lamented the "errors of popular tradition" that both hindered and made necessary the writing of history, in his case the history of the slave trade and of the abolition of slavery. But as we shall see, in writing the *Creole Grammar* "popular tradition" was also an important source of Thomas's intellectual work. In this sense his relationship to "family records" differed from Borde's. Whereas the latter's family history as a White Creole coincided with the written history of the region, Thomas's included oral narratives and a repudiation, though not consistently, of the paternalistic master-slave accounts that typified histories such as Borde's.

Thomas reviewed Borde's work in the *New Era* in October 1876. The following week it was announced that Borde had asked Thomas to translate it into English, though it was not until four years later that Thomas sent the translation, which had been "much interrupted by illness," off to the printer's.[23] Doubtless some readers interpreted the exchange as an instance of flattery getting the ingratiating reviewer everywhere (the

Trinidad Chronicle called his review "very flattering"), though others would have seen it as an instance of two intellectuals acknowledging each other's achievements. In addition, Thomas's multilingual abilities would have given Borde's work another audience.

Thomas noted that friends had encouraged him to review the *Histoire* and that Borde had "pressed for criticism by his countrymen." The "freedom with which we handle its contents," Thomas begins his review, betokens an "admiration too genuine to be debunked by flattery." For Thomas, then, flattery would have been the work of a reviewer who did not exercise the freedom to be critical. He was dissatisfied with Borde's modesty since Borde was "proficient" in a topic that he himself had chosen. Thus Borde's modesty suggested "opinions quite the reverse of what he intends," just as a wealthy man who prefaced his resolve to make a monetary donation with the qualification "though I'm a pauper" would have been insincere. The monetary analogy is notable here since it suggests that Thomas's impatience with modesty extended to material wealth as well as intellectual capabilities. The son of "poor but respectable" parents was telling the son of former slave owners that he should adopt a practical rather than either a deprecating or a celebratory attitude toward his wealth as well as toward the learning it facilitated.

When a "man of the requisite intelligence and preparatory culture," such as Borde, undertook a work, it was assumed that he knew he could do it. Borde was "too much of a *littérateur* not to have sat at the feet of Horace to learn the ethics of authorship." (Here Thomas quotes the original Latin of Horace's *Ars Poetica*: writers should select topics within the scope of their abilities, and consider carefully what load their shoulders were unable to bear.) The discerning scholar did not bite off more than he could chew. Borde's modesty, Thomas declares, recalls Uriah Heep, Charles Dickens's unctuous character in *Great Expectations,* and Thomas cautions him against joining the "mighty array of critics, jealous of their rights," in criticizing himself.

Thomas was displeased with Borde's preface for another reason. It was true that ignorance of history undermined the patriotism that made people identify themselves as Trinidadians rather than as English, French, or Spanish. However, Borde's assertion that "being in the great majority of cases, descendants of French colonists, we have a common origin, a common country, a common religion" was objectionable. "At least one section of true Trinidadians," Thomas declares, "who are more numerous than those who are descended from French Colonists," would be displeased by the "limits" circumscribing Borde's "patriotic union and fraternity."

Thomas, then, takes issue with Borde for devaluing the importance of Black and Colored Trinidadians in the national fabric.[24]

Thomas also disputes Borde's justification of the beginning of the African slave trade. While Borde convincingly vindicated "the great philanthropist" Bartolomé de Las Casas of the charge of advocating African slavery after the genocide of Amerindians, his assertion that African slavery was a "necessity of the period," proved by the fact that European nations followed Spain's example, entailed a "begging of the whole question in favour of mere actuality, while first principles are quietly left out of sight." If a man spent his inheritance and then, driven by hunger and need, demanded his thrifty neighbor's property, finally killing him in the face of resistance, would this robbery and murder be "extenuated" by his "intolerable distress"? Or would he be guilty of both breaking the law and perversely creating the circumstances that made him do so? The Spaniards created the conditions of the "nefarious traffic in Africans," Thomas declares, by their cruel "using up" of the first inhabitants.

Otherwise, Borde's scholarship earned high marks from Thomas. The texts he consulted for his book were "out of the range of ordinary Creole reading," available only by "laborious gleanings throughout the whole conquest of the New World." Borde's style proved Voltaire's dictum that "le style c'est l'homme," for he wrote in the same serene, straightforward, and earnest way in which he "moves among us": free of "epigrammatic tours de force," "windy raptures," "sensational twaddle," and "dandyism." Modesty and plain speech were thus different for Thomas, the one an indication of insincerity, the other an admirably direct style recalling the comparison between Wenkstern and Donovan. Wenkstern's "polished" style was linked for Thomas to his social status as an elite White man, while Borde's similar background did not seem to prevent a tendency to plain speech. Presumably, "windy raptures" were the belabored speech of Trollope's Black men, though for Thomas this would have been anyone who reveled in rhetoric for its own sake. "Windy raptures" would seem, however, to be distinct from both labored rhetoric and plain speech, so that Thomas appears to have been comparing different sets of characteristics at different times. Borde, Thomas concludes, weighed his facts "dispassionately," and his work was an "ornament and acquisition to our native literature." Henceforth educated Trinidadians would not have to "blush" at their ignorance of the past.

Thomas reviewed the second volume of Borde's *Histoire* in the 2 August 1883 issue of the *Trinidad Review,* and his translations of the text also appeared in issues of the journal during that time. "The most eminent critics in Europe," Thomas noted, corroborated his 1876 review of Borde. Such scholarship could only be a "labour of love," given the uncertainty of or desire for reward. Borde had chosen the path of isolation and scholarship despite knowing the difference between "the material prizes that throng the path of men of commerce, and the depreciation and, what is worse, the insolent *condescendence* that fall to the lot of the studious in Trinidad." "The gifted of the world," Thomas declared, "can afford to be poor in the world's goods; for the ineffable ecstasies that mark the pulsations of the truly intellectual life, are the emotions which the world can neither give nor ever take away. The glory of the ideal life is, that it is beyond the pollution of being desired by the sordid."

In pursuing the distinction between intellectuals and philistines, Thomas ignored the fact that it was precisely Borde's status as a "man of commerce" that allowed him to pursue his scholarship since his intellectual labor complemented rather than (as for Thomas) secured his prestige. To characterize Borde as "poor in the world's goods" was to indicate that just like Thomas, Borde would not sell many copies of his books. Thomas thus stressed the factors that drew the two men together as like minds in a wilderness characterized by "ordinary Creole reading," and, returning to the comparison between the *Creole Grammar* and Leotaud's *Oiseaux*, "watery, sour, or husky fruit."

Those who congratulated Thomas on his promotions or complained when he was overlooked emphasized the disparities that Thomas seems intent on downplaying here. There were complaints that Thomas and others who had distinguished themselves since leaving Woodbrook should have been considered for the post of inspector of schools, held by Lechmere Guppy, a White Creole, from 1870. Thomas was briefly secretary to the board of education in the early 1870s, but he was never inspector of schools. He was accused of inciting teachers to protest Guppy's appointment, and he denied it. Four years later, when Guppy was on leave, an editorial commented that since Thomas was the only internationally renowned literary man in Trinidad, it was ridiculous that some people in Trinidad doubted his capacity to act as inspector during Guppy's absence.[25]

The report of Patrick Keenan, the Irish educator who reviewed the colony's educational system in 1869, found that Guppy was "master of his own arrangements" and that not only was he lax in performing his duties but his occasional post as secretary to the board of education meant that he was, in effect, reporting to himself. Yseult Guppy Bridges's portrait of her father's scholarly life in *Child of the Tropics* shows us how he found the time to pursue his scientific studies and in effect explains why the civil service post that paid him five hundred pounds a year was not a priority. Her account also sheds further light on the "advantages" that made writing "easy" for someone like Guppy.[26]

Lechmere Guppy, the son of the English-born mayor of San Fernando and a Creole mother, married a member of the Rostant family. Yseult's evocative memories of her childhood include the Black *marchands* whose street cries marked the rhythms of their labor and her household and whose speech she imitated as she pretended to sell fish to her father. Her mother's intricate greetings—the angle of a handshake, the disapproving "peck" or the "affectionate salutation on both cheeks" (31)—signified the social status of, or displeasure directed toward, the recipient. She presided over the verandah, family members, and "more frivolous acquaintances" (32) and exercised a "despotic" rule over her servants (26). Yseult and her father's friends were allowed to penetrate the study, with its microscope and telescope, where Lechmere worked most of the day after fashioning bookshelves, scientific display cabinets, and dollhouses in the adjoining carpenter's workshop.

The family received periodicals from London, as well as the "yellow-backed French novels and the lighter English fiction" over which her mother laughed and cried. Yseult describes herself as "entirely self-taught," like her father, devouring the books in the house: "the older novelists, works on science, philosophy, history, religion and the classics, beside poetry, drama, and the popular fiction of the day, a selection of which arrived from time to time in a great box from Mudie's. The volumes on the shelves in the study alone were diverse enough to provide a liberal education" (24).

The daughter here delineates two spheres of reading: her father's passionate and "serious" relationship to books and her mother's "light" reading in the drawing room, which punctuated her careful regulation of the social order. The father's seriousness, scholarship, and solitude corresponded with a more expansive attitude toward his social inferiors: his wife drew the lines, so he did not have to. "How did it come about," Yseult asks, "that two such people, seemingly so utterly different as my mother and father, should have fallen in love and married? He, as uncompromisingly English and intellectual as she was profoundly French and instinctive; he scholarly, shunning society, while to her the social round was the breath of life?" Yseult reads their differences according to prevailing clichés about the essential differences between the English and the French. Yet there is also a gendered division of labor here, and Yseult aligns her intellectual interests with her father's. Her description of herself as "self-taught" differs markedly from Thomas's "self-made" status since she was able to get a "liberal education" at home, including the all-important classics, made possible by the financial circumstances that enabled her father to order the boxes from Mudie's, the famous London bookseller.

The Guppys had the tastes and financial abilities of well-off London residents. Yseult's knowledge, unlike Thomas's, was acquired at home and was thus "natural" and "unlabored." Her memoir does include a vigorous discussion of her time at school, but I am arguing that the schoolroom did not *define* her relation to "knowledge" and "culture," as it was perceived as doing for Thomas. One's relationship to knowledge and culture acquired *at leisure* in the home, in a context where one is not really *studying* (unlike Thomas's burning of the midnight oil), mystifies the process of acquiring such knowledge. Those bookshelves fashioned by her father for his study represent the labor of the distinguished scientist who constructs them because he is thrifty, because he needs the recreation, or both. His manual labor, as opposed to that of those who work for him in his home or on his estate, does not define his social status.

Besides complaining about Thomas's failure to be considered for the post of inspector of schools, letters to the editor commented on Thomas's mid-1871 appointment as clerk of the peace at Cedros. Letters and editorials commented that this appointment would "prove fatal" to the survival of the *Trinidad Monthly Magazine,* of which he was the editor.[27] Thomas said that he was going to take the position out of a "sense of duty" since Cedros would mean "isolation and probably suffering." He was "a son of the soil, sprung from the people, and resolved to stand or fall with them." A year later it was suggested that he had been "cajoled" into accepting this position with the promise of a higher salary that apparently never materialized.[28]

Thomas's appointment as acting stipendiary justice of the peace in Cedros in late 1874 earned him accolades since this was a position usually reserved for Whites. The *San Fernando Gazette* noted the appointment in its 9 October issue in terms that are by now familiar to us—the details of Thomas's physical appearance, the fact that he deserves the appointment (he had not "bribed" his way into the position), and of course his moral character:

> For readers beyond the colony, we may state that Mr. Thomas is a gentleman of pure African descent and *looks it,* a self-made man of strong and indomitable character and of an ability, *acquired and natural,* that lifts him a full head

and shoulders above his fellows. Mr. Thomas is the author of the learned and very amusing "Creole Grammar" published in 1869; on a visit to England in the course of last summer, he became an object of marked and unremitting attention by the learned of the Philological and other Societies, and the members of their families. Mr. Thomas deserves all the honors granted him by a government which can discern exceptional merit. He has acted in the same quarter as Clerk of the Peace, and the routine and rationale of duty is therefore familiar to him, for he discharged it with care and conscience. We have known Mr. Thomas some years and feel he deserves these remarks at our hands. The case may be thought a rare one, but it points a moral invaluable everywhere and specially here—to strive and persevere in self-improvement, and avoiding the lower temptations, preserve one's self-respect and that of the world.

The reference to the "learned and very amusing" *Grammar* here suggests that while his scholarship was taken seriously, this did not necessarily alter the perception of the language itself as lacking in prestige.

The next day, 10 October, a letter to the editor of the same paper noted "with satisfaction" the lecture given before the Trinidad Athenaeum (started by Thomas and others in the early 1870s) by Louis Tronchin on the topic "Mathematics vs. Philology." Referring to Thomas's promotion, the letter writer hoped that "the time is not very far when Mr. Tronchin too will be raised a step higher. He has been long in one place and done so well that it is time he should be advanced. Onward ye sons of Trinidad; better days are in store for you. Work and keep together; no-one shall dare to rob you of your rights." Commentators hoped, then, that Thomas would not be an exception.

Shortly thereafter the *San Fernando Gazette* published an address to "Mr. J. J. Thomas. Esq" over the signatures of Michel Maxwell Philip, the Colored solicitor general, twenty-one other listed names, "and 92 other signatures."[29] Referring to his appointment to "the important district of Cedros," the address states that Thomas's conduct had "ever been an avowal of your implicit confidence in the zealous friendship we have professed and will always entertain for you. We lay open our hearts before you regardless of what those, who feel not with us, may say or think." This last seems to imply that some people did not think Thomas deserved the appointment. The letter stated that its signatories desired to emulate Thomas's boldness and honesty, noting that one did not gaze on a fortress and think of weakness. Under great difficulties, they noted, Thomas had acquired knowledge and brought it to light. "Those in the New and Old World whose approbation you have received, are themselves eminent and celebrated," the letter continues. They were proud that he had been admitted to the ranks of such celebrated people and that the governor and the government had entrusted him with various positions. This was a testament to his "intrinsic merit," and "his penetration and justice. . . . We fondly hope you will find no check to your continued official advancement, and that under the Providential eye, your career may increase in those advantages of fortune and honor to which none can be insensible. Wishing you health and happiness we are, dear sir, entirely and most truly your friends."

Prominent members of his society were honoring Thomas publicly, in part because they realized that their own positions were not to be taken for granted. Even M. M. Philip, after all, perhaps the highest-ranked person of color in the government, smarted at being denied positions that were reserved only for Whites.

The same edition of the *San Fernando Gazette* published Thomas's reply. Thanking them for their kindness and goodwill in terms that will recall the Wenkstern-Donovan comparison, he states that he cannot doubt the sincerity of motives "which prompted men of your intelligence and social standing to unite in paying so distinguished a compliment to me whose claims to your notice cannot be otherwise than exclusively personal, unfavoured as I have been by the accidents of birth and fortune that invest men with prescriptive respectability." Their congratulations proved that they disregarded "the opinions of those who differ from you with regard to my movement," and he hoped that "this emancipation from the paralysing dread of people's sneers and censures" would be "perpetual." He thanked them for praising the role of the governor since it would have been "indecent" for him to do so.

The same issue carried an address to Thomas by the president and secretary of the San Fernando Young Men's Mutual Improvement Association, congratulating him as a member of the association "and secondly as a Creole of the Island" and declaring him "a fit example for the emulation of every member of our Association." In his reply Thomas thanked them for making him a member and stated that he had always felt "the warmest sympathy with men who, like yourselves, are labouring with such disinterested earnestness to popularize intellectual pursuits in my native country." Though he would not be able to attend meetings regularly, he declared: "You do me no more than justice when you attribute to me the earnestness of national and official feeling which ought to characterize a true Creole and Public Officer."

Thomas had proved himself as an excellent teacher in the primary ward school system, a scholar of philology recognized on both sides of the Atlantic, one of the leading figures of Trinidad's intellectual life, and a conscientious civil servant. As one of the system's stellar teachers who had been passed over for the premier post in education, what would his appointment as headmaster of the newly overhauled secondary institution in San Fernando allow him to demonstrate? He was appointed headmaster of the San Fernando Borough School in late 1883, replacing Samuel Proctor, who had been headmaster for twenty-seven years. Proctor's farewell speech, published in the 22 December *San Fernando Gazette,* clearly indicates the stakes for those whose access to social mobility depend on state-funded education. As he saw old students occupying important posts, he knew that his work had not been not in vain. Learning was now "within everyone's reach, and scholarship allows many poor boys to get a profession. But it was not so in my day." With the revamped curriculum, "the rising race will get a classical education at a moderate rate."

It was Thomas who was charged with overseeing this new dispensation. In January 1884 Thomas delivered a lecture at the city's Baptist Tabernacle. Admission to the proceedings, which were chaired by Michel Maxwell Philip and attended by Mayor Robert Guppy, was priced at one shilling. It was reported that it was Thomas's idea to address "the people among whom he must for the future dwell," and whose children he would teach, on the topic "Teaching as it is, and teaching as it ought to be." It was the best attended of any event in that city, the paper reported, since people were interested in the chance to give their children the "advantages of metropolitan schools" without the "inconveniences which hitherto ran counter to their intentions."[30]

When the school opened, on 22 January 1884, Thomas addressed students and parents on his ideas about discipline.[31] By February Thomas had responded to Father Violette's sermon about the "so-called High School" and the "charge" of a "freemason conspiracy" by noting that students "of the most heterogeneous training and qualifications could not be expected to have mastered the classics in the first fifteen days of the school." The classics, then, were being used to assess the worth of the institution. "I, who am born of the people, and who belong to them," Thomas declared, "have better opportunities of knowing their feelings and their needs than any outsider, however sincere he may be in striving for their welfare."

It was the "resumption of a defunct power" to tell parents what kind of instruction their children ought to have. The "familiar mouthing of creeds and formularies in schools" in order to make children "religious or even well-behaved" was no longer considered progressive. Since his own early training had been "sectarian," he was entitled to warn his "countrymen" that they needed a "greater fund of knowledge to equip them for the struggles of the world, than [for] unreasoning acquiescence in the decisions of infallibility."[32]

Thomas's letter received a response from Emilie Maresse-Paul, published in the 16 February 1884 issue of the *San Fernando Gazette*. Written in French and addressed to "Mon cher ami," Maresse-Paul congratulated him on his courage in confronting the priest. Courage was a rare virtue in those days, she noted, and many people preferred to forget their personal dignity rather than risk offending a power as arbitrary as the church. Priests considered it a sacrilege to have an opinion that they had not sanctioned or to support a school that they had not established.

Father Violette had tried to put the pulpit beyond the reach of anyone refuting his absurd arguments and unjust accusations. Maresse-Paul believed that Thomas was strong enough to fight this battle, but she warned him to be careful. Ridiculing the church's curses and excommunications ("ses anathèmes") would earn him hatred: "Et laissez-moi vous le dire c'est une terrible chose que la haine d'un prêtre!!" She advised him to summon all the energy of his character to help him to confront this foe and to remember the friend who took pride in thinking like him. A member of one of the distinguished Colored families was supporting Thomas publicly and showing, once again, the cleavages in francophone Catholic identity that were revealed during this period along racial lines.

But Father Violette would not be Thomas's only challenge. He had been headmaster for a year when Joseph Chilberry, one of the school's most "promising pupils," accidentally shot himself at his home in Claxton Bay. Thomas was attending a funeral in San Fernando when he received the news, and neither he nor his assistant was able to attend Chilberry's funeral. He seems to have tried to teach the next day, but he retired to his quarters at recess. "I feel too unwell to attend school any more today," he said in a note to the assistant master, requesting him to close the school for the day and to grant the boys their wish to observe a week of mourning by wearing crêpe armbands on their left sleeves.[33]

Later that month the report of the school's examinations and awarding of prizes, an event open to parents and borough officials, suggested a disappointment of another kind. The examinations had been postponed from December, when Thomas stopped the proceedings, explaining that he had not been consulted about the program and that there had not been enough time to showcase each boy's progress.[34] When the event took place again in March, the first-prize student, Edgar Carter, seemed to apologize for the students' shortcomings. Their headmaster had done his best to teach them English grammar, French, and Latin, Carter noted, but their "deplorable" English had forced him to "subordinate some studies and lay aside others altogether for the purpose of grounding us more fully in that knowledge of our language, without which every other requirement would be a mere delusion and pretence."[35]

If Thomas worried that the public performance of his students might lead some to question his capabilities as a teacher, the controversy over the expatriate head of the Girls School was an occasion for further questioning his judgment, as well as his intellectual priorities. In September 1884 the direction of the Girls School was transferred from Thomas to Josephine McKay, who came from Scotland to take up the position. Though he would insist that his objection to her was founded on her failings as a teacher, perhaps he also resented this change from the custom of giving the headmaster responsibility for both institutions. On the one hand, a woman was being put on an equal plane with him, and he may have resented this. But on the other hand, he may have wondered whether the Borough Council was sending the message that an expatriate White person should not have to report to a Black Creole.

In his letter to the *San Fernando Gazette* on 25 October Thomas referred to McKay's cruelties even to young students and noted that his own children attended the school. No matter how proficient a teacher was in her area of study, he said, she should demonstrate "love and kindness" in her treatment of students, "particularly of the future wives and mothers of a community." Though he refrained from detailing her abuse "because I am dealing with a matter concerning a member of the weaker sex," everyone knew about it, and he hoped that the newspaper would look into it.

Thomas's opposition to McKay was supported by reports of McKay's cruelty, including an incident in which she had knocked a tooth out of a student's mouth and then offered her a brass coin as "hush money."[36] A letter to the editor detailing this incident noted that it was not the first and reminded readers that working-class mothers had been imprisoned without fine for cruelty to their children.

By the middle of the following year Thomas had resigned from his position. "Mr. Thomas has made for himself a position in the world of letters superior to that of any living West Indian *littérateur* and consequently it is to be regretted that he will no longer be able to impart to the rising generation that culture which he possesses in such an eminent degree."[37] His letter of resignation, sent from Grenada, mentioned his failing eyesight, but clearly the borough officials' refusal to dismiss McKay must have had something to do with it. By mid-1886 Thomas had published two pamphlets, *Rowdy Dowdy* and *Rowdiana,* satirizing Miss McKay in verse:

> Deformed, crooked, old, and sere,
> Ill-faced, worse-bodied, shapeless everywhere,
> Vicious, ungentle, foolish, blunt, unkind;
> Stigmatical in making, worse in mind.[38]

Rostant, the editor of *Public Opinion,* used the occasion of the publications to criticize Thomas for wasting his talents. Calling the pamphlets "a magnificent piece of invective in the style of *Napoleon Le Petit,*" Rostant said that even if McKay were unfit for her post both in temper and education, this would not justify Thomas's cruel satire. The reading public had to allow "for a man whose nerves were unstrung by ill-health, or who could ill-brook the petty annoyances and hindrances which he had to endure from a person so inferior to himself in mental calibre." Rostant noted that the members of the Borough Council should have allowed "for the shaken nerves of a man chafing under what he conceived to be wilful and malignant injustice." In addition, Thomas had a heightened sensitivity to "dermaphobia," though one of the officials was the "same hue as he."

As to the "literary merits" of Thomas's pamphlets, it was regrettable that Thomas was wasting his "valuable life" "without an attempt to enrich his native land with some work that would redound to his own credit and the honor of Trinidad. His mastery of the English language, his extensive readings, his long experience, make him, in our opinion, especially qualified to write a historical novel that would combine, in an attractive garb, the main features and most salient facts of the moral and political life of Trinidad during some of the most interesting phases of her short history." Though the pamphlets had been "hurriedly written," they showed "the vigorous and powerful touch of a man, whose flexible pen can do full justice to any subject he may choose to approach. Mr. Thomas is yet comparatively young and we sincerely hope he will set seriously to work on subjects more congenial to his undoubted literary merits, than the sayings or doings of a McKay."[39]

Clearly, then, for Rostant at least, the *Creole Grammar* had not been sufficient. Thomas was simultaneously being praised for his literary talent and being chastised for wasting it on pursuits other than nationalist texts, which in this case were being identified as historical novels. He was being cast as someone who was both mentally unstable and obsessed with complexion in an era when such problems had supposedly been erased.

Replying to the letter in the same issue, Thomas credited Rostant with at least admitting that McKay was "unfit" yet berated him for ignoring the fact that in spite of her "utter unfitness, she was maintained for *one year and nine months* in that post" (his emphasis) at a salary of forty pounds a month. A week later he continued his response to Rostant in a letter in the 7 June *New Era* under the heading "The Reviewer Reviewed." He clarified that the main object of the criticism in his pamphlets was not Miss McKay but the municipal authorities who permitted her to continue in her position even though it was generally agreed that she was incompetent and cruel to the students. His "cruel epithets" were not "splenetic outburst[s] of irritation, but a well-weighed deduction from her conduct." His characterization of her behavior in the pamphlets as "ruffianism" was correct for someone who, "because a child cannot do a sum, deliberately takes its little hand, places it on a desk, and proceeds to crush it with a stick." Echoing the letter of "A Parent," he chastised Rostant for ignoring the fact that McKay had gotten off with only "hard words" instead of the imprisonment with hard labor, for an exemplary term, "which a beneficent legislation imposes even on mothers who permit their temper to rise into delirium in the correcting of their own children."

Turning to McKay, whom he refers to in the letter as "Miss" or "the woman McKay," Thomas noted, underscoring the references in his pamphlets to her physical appearance: "The exterior and bearing of a female who is to be a pattern to girls, are matters of the first importance, outweighing, in that respect, mere scholastic proficiency. It is therefore natural, when any female is presented to us as a trainer for our daughters, that our first impressions of her fitness for such duty should be derived from observing her looks, dress, and deportment." Women had a duty to look attractive, Thomas indicated, a duty that complemented their intellectual capabilities, and McKay had clearly abnegated such duties. It is difficult to know here whether Thomas thought McKay's gender made her incompetence particularly reprehensible or whether her identity as a British expatriate from Great Britain—in a context where Creoles in such positions were few and far between—caused him such fury that he resigned his position. Yet his description of her is so vicious, and physically so—"deformed," "ill-faced, "worse-bodied," "shapeless"—that one wonders whether an incompetent expatriate male teacher would have elicited a similar reaction from him.

On the matter of "dermaphobia," Thomas responded to Rostant's implication that since one of the Borough Council members was of "the same hue" as Thomas, color prejudice was not an issue. Thomas said he attributed "dermaphobia . . . the fear, on the part of a dark-complexioned person, of those who have a fairer complexion than he," to Wharton, a non-White member of the council. "Your arguing, therefore, that Mr. Wharton is of the *same hue* with me (a statement for which he will not thank you!) is not a refutation, but a strengthening of my contention. If Mr. Wharton were white and the McKay coloured, or if I were equally white with that individual, his conduct would have been far otherwise." There was "overwhelming evidence" of McKay's "incompetency, vulgarity and violence," Thomas continued, and the council's attempts to keep her in her position: "When I see Mr. Wharton conspiring to deprive a fellow-creole—talented, a good teacher, a lady—of bread, in order to please 'Miss' McKay, whom all now admit had nothing save her skin to recommend her, I am forced to accept the evidence that facts present." There is the suggestion here, then, that a female "fellow-creole" had lost her position at the school because of the expatriate headmistress. Perhaps this is part of the reason for his anger and his decision to resign his position: the town councillors were willing to jettison Creole "ladies" for outsiders, and Thomas was showing his solidarity.

Thomas then addressed Rostant's comments about his intellectual pursuits: "You speak, Sir, of talents 'wasted' by me, in exposing public imposture, fraud, civic corruption, cruelty to the young, and the degradation of our educational standards. You pity me for being so misguided in the selection of my subject as not to have known that a historical romance was worthier of my skill. Permit me, Sir to differ entirely from you." Thomas noted that vindicating right and rebuking wrong could never be a waste of talent, and his pamphlets vindicated "local instruction and my own claims as an individual and a Teacher." He was not attacking "a woman not worth the while" but exposing the men who kept her in her position. Addressing Rostant's well-known feuds with other journalists, Thomas concluded: "Finally, Sir, let me ask: does it lie with you, the Editor of *Public Opinion,* to rebuke any one for wasting their time and talents? Is it not you, Sir, who, endowed with great gifts for political writing in the interests of the community, spend your time in writing retaliatory diatribes against a purely personal adversary?"

Here were two prestigious men rebuking each other publicly for wasting their intellectual production on unworthy endeavors. In according "vindication of Right and the rebuke of Wrong" as much if not more importance than the "historical romance," Thomas anticipated his own response to Froude three years later. His letter of resignation from the high school was written from Grenada in mid-1885, and he seems to have spent most of the next three years there. In 1887 he gave a series of lectures on education and language, for which it was anticipated that he would have a large audience and would "stimulate the peasantry to a love of learning."[40] A description of one of his lectures noted his concern for the relevance of education to West Indian conditions.[41] He would happily strike Algebra and Greek from the curriculum, it was reported, so that students, the majority of whom would be connected to the land, could learn the technical aspects of agriculture. Thomas proposed that teaching certificates should include proof of a mastery of "practical tropical agriculture."

Similarly, since the eastern Caribbean was in constant communication with South and Central America, as well as Martinique and Guadeloupe, students should gain mastery of French and Spanish rather than "[prattling] about sines and co-sines." Instead of "mouthing the intricate abstractions of Euclid" without knowing their practical application, students should learn "elementary practical geometry." Finally, critiquing "high-class education" for teaching the "mythical characters" of Rome and Greece without the history of those places, Thomas denounced the lack of teaching of West Indian history. Noting that West Indians would be "less servile" if they knew their own history, Donovan's *Grenada People* hoped that Thomas was not proposing that the teaching of English history should be sacrificed, since West Indians needed to "rise to the level of the true Englishman" and share in the "Imperial partnership."

Thomas also tutored students while in Grenada, and in 1888, when he was about to leave for England to pursue publication of *Froudacity,* he was presented with a gift of money at the home of the headmaster of the St. George's Roman Catholic School. E. F. Julien and Hallam Massiah addressed him in Spanish, thanking him for the "kind and careful manner" with which he had taught tutored them while living "for some months" in St. George's. Thomas sent two letters in reply from Barbados, while en route to England, though he directed Massiah, the second recipient, to the longer, first letter, as he was "suffering much from illness." He wrote that he was proud of their Spanish grammar and that he had been glad to aid in their "enlightenment" and "general elevation." The money would "smooth away many obstacles which penury opposes, to aspirations such as those now occupying my thoughts and shaping my movements." He hoped to be reunited "in renewed health" with friends who "lightened the weight of disease and exile from a heart of one who pants to be useful in his generation."[42]

Clearly, then, in addition to being very ill, Thomas felt himself to be in "exile" from Trinidad. Notwithstanding this, it was Rostant who came to his rescue in 1888 when word arrived from London that T. Fisher Unwin, the publisher whom Thomas had found for *Froudacity,* felt that since the book was a defense of people of African descent, this constituency should raise the money for its publication. Rostant launched a fund-raising drive through the Trinidad Literary Association, attracting four hundred subscribers.[43] The incident underscores Thomas's vulnerability in the metropole, which, as we shall see, promised both prestige and danger for the Black intellectual. On the one hand, his trip to London gave him the opportunity to publish as a book the series of articles that he had published in the Grenadian newspapers and to do research in the British Library for a revised edition of the *Creole Grammar.*

At the same time, one wonders what the prospects would have been for publishing *Froudacity* in Trinidad, considering that in 1888, as we have seen, the Legislative Council there voted funds for the publication of Lionel Fraser's proposed *History.* Thomas's quarrel with the San Fernando Borough Council and his resignation from the high school may have convinced him that he had burned his bridges as far as Trinidad was concerned. In the late 1880s perhaps he could no longer count on the sort of connections that he had had in 1869, when Wenkstern, a friend of Governor Gordon, published the *Creole Grammar.* At the same time, he now had the opportunity to publish his work in London, which promised a certain kind of prestige. Ironically, the experience killed him. Very ill when he left Grenada in July 1888, he died of tuberculosis in September 1889, within weeks of the publication of *Froudacity.*

While chapter 4 deals with *Froudacity* itself, it is useful here to note that in the final year of his life Thomas's prestige and his ability to write "easily" continued to be the subject of public discussion. Thomas was himself accused of committing a "froudacity" in attributing the term to an Australian writer. In a letter from London to Trinidad in 1889 Thomas declared the term *froudacity,* like *boycott,* to be "a new addition (in this case an Australian one) to the language, and . . . already accepted as meaning the circulation of statements known to be untrue. In fact, the magazines and other publications of the Antipodes commonly speak of 'froudacious statements.'"[44] The criticism of Thomas appeared in the *Argosy,* the Demarara newspaper that published Darnell Davis's review of Froude's book.[45] It was "absurd" for an "ardent West Indian" to take away "from his own land, to give to Australia, the credit of having added the word to the language." In failing, as a "West Indian," to have read "at least all the more prominent reviews of Mr. Froude's 'Bow of Ulysses'" Thomas had "not added to our high opinion of him."

The *New Era,* which reprinted the *Argosy's* letter, came to Thomas's defense, calling the critic "sharp" and "trivial" and noting that anyone who knew Thomas would realize that he would never deprive "a brother West Indian" of the credit due to him. Furthermore, if the editor of the *New Era* had never heard of either Davis or *Timehri* until this criticism, then Thomas, "who for some time past, has relinquished that particular field of literature," could not have been expected to know about it either. *Timehri* was "like the modest violet, destined to blush and die unseen," and it was its poor circulation, rather than Thomas's failure, that had accounted for the oversight.[46] In a letter to the *New Era* from London dated 7 August Thomas thanked the paper for its "masterly defence," which had absolved him from having to respond directly. The "malicious ineptitude" of someone charged with enlightening the Demarara public had proved this "intruder into the sacred precincts of literature" to be unworthy "of serious literary powder and shot."[47]

After *Froudacity's* publication, reviewers compared Thomas and Froude, the *Port of Spain Gazette* noting that Froude was historically inaccurate but that the "sparkle and flowing elements of his style" more than made up for it. Thomas, on the other hand, suffered from "inflated diction" and "cumbrous and involved" sentences, and he went overboard in his point-by-point refutation and excess of "local" and "personal" details.[48] The *Christian Leader,* an English periodical, thought that Thomas was "at times a little too rhetorical" but proved himself "a scholar possessed of extraordinary erudition." The review noted Thomas's "noble" recounting of the "glorious" work of Wilberforce, Sharpe, and Clarkson and wished that Carlyle were still alive to read Thomas's comments on religion. "In this controversy with the 'nigger' whom he despises," the review continued, "Mr. James Anthony Froude gets decidedly the worst of it. Mr. Thomas demonstrates to the fullest how unsuited Mr. Froude's capacity is for appreciating the political and social issues he has so confidently undertaken to determine."

For the *Star,* another London paper, Thomas, "himself a negro," was a "notable critic" whose "grasp of politics" and "command of English" made him "no unworthy foeman." The London *Echo* thought that Thomas, "who by the way is a 'coloured' West Indian," was "one of the most uncompromising and able of [Froude's] critics" in the colonies he had visited.

Though Thomas had "not disposed of Mr. Froude," *Froudacity* was "very well worth reading."[49]

If the company one kept on the obituary pages was any indication of one's prestige, then Thomas received posthumous notice that suggested he was on par with illustrious names. Noting his "valuable contributions" to linguistic studies and his "unselfish" efforts to improve his "fellow negroes," the English periodical *Academy* announced Thomas's death in a substantial column on the same page as the equally lengthy obituary of the novelist Wilkie Collins and the short notice of the death of the poet Eliza Cook. In Trinidad, readers heard of Thomas's death at the same time that they learned of the death of Frederick Warner, the prominent White Anglo-Creole solicitor and member of the Legislative Council. Thomas's career "differed widely" from Warner's, as the 25 October 1889 *New Era* pointed out, since Warner came from an "ancient and aristocratic West Indian family." A good Anglican and a patron of the dramatic arts, Warner stood "above the middle height," was "of splendid physique," and was "the beau ideal of Anglo-Saxon manhood." Just before his visit to Europe, where he died, he had been appointed a commander of the Order of St. Michael and St. George for his services as a legislator.

Thomas's "poor but respectable" parents could not afford to give him the "educational advantages which might have enabled him to achieve even greater renown than is attached to his name in the Republic of Letters," the *New Era* reported, but natural ability and a "plain education" had established his claim to be considered "one of the first, if not the first scholar of his race and country." Arthur Hamilton Gordon had heard of Thomas's abilities and offered him a civil service position, reflecting Gordon's liberalism. This had given Thomas the "comfort" and "leisure" to produce the *Creole Grammar* and ushered in the "happiest period of his life," when he was admired by all classes of his compatriots, was able to indulge his love of literature, and was introduced to Canon Kingsley, "whom he subsequently visited when on a trip to the Mother Country." Retiring on a pension because of ill health, he had thereafter "adorned" many subjects with his contributions to the press, and his satire ranked with the most brilliant passages in *English Bards and Scotch Reviewers* and Pope's *Dunciad*.

Because Thomas had died in "far from affluent circumstances," the *New Era* continued, his friends had had to make contributions for a "suitable funeral." His mourners included "fellow West Indians," "men of his colour from both hemispheres, and literary men of all shades of complexion." For this paper, Thomas's death provided the opportunity to show the stature that he had achieved as a Trinidadian, a race vindicator, and a man of letters. Noteworthy here is Thomas's association with prominent White men, Gordon and Kingsley, as well as what many would have regarded as the distinction of sharing the spotlight with Warner. Both men had been "eminent Trinidadians," and their names were "household words with all classes of the community."

The *Grenada People,* Donovan's newspaper, referred to Thomas's life-long "love of literature and of his race," his "indomitable courage" and "self-will," his "omnivorous" reading, and his "prodigious memory." This in spite of being "weak and shattered" by illness. Rejecting the *New Era*'s narrative of White liberalism, the editorial noted that Thomas's progress in the civil service had been hampered by his refusal to "cringe and fawn," the only way that men of his "race and complexion" could rise. Though he had surpassed everyone else in the civil service examinations, he had been given the "comparatively insignificant office" of secretary to the board of education, whereas a less successful candidate had been given the "lucrative and honourable" post of clerk to the Legislative Council. Thomas had finally retired from the service because of this injustice, the paper noted. Thomas had been "too educated" to be "ashamed of his complexion," loving his race "with a burning, absorbing, consuming love" and devoting his "last energies to their defence." The charity of his friends had saved him from a pauper's funeral, while many of those for whom he had given his life were wealthy enough to have contributed to his publication of *Froudacity.* Doing something for his widow would "wipe away the stain of ingratitude."[50]

The *Sierra Leone Weekly News* informed its readers that Thomas had "succumbed to the rigors of the climate after seeing two editions of his book through the press," referring here to a second edition of *Froudacity* published in the United States. *Froudacity,* written by "a pure Negro of Trinidad," ought to "be in the hands of every intelligent African." Though the title clearly suggested Froude's "audacity," a reviewer in the London *Saturday Review,* who "could not help being respectful," tried to prove that it could refer to Froude's "capacity" or "sagacity." Quoting segments of Thomas's text, the paper noted that it had been written to defend Negroes in the West Indies but "is a defence of the whole Negro race against the indiscriminate charges which are brought against them by thoughtless or prejudiced foreigners." Rev. P. H. Douglin, whom Thomas quoted in *Froudacity* (191–92), was "well remembered by us for his effective labors in this settlement."

Dominicans appeared to feel as strongly as Sierra Leoneans did that Thomas had vindicated them. In early 1890 the *San Fernando Gazette* noted that the Dominican public had begun a Thomas Memorial Fund in order to erect a "full-size bronze statue in an attitude of triumph, with the right foot clutching a serpent and the uplifted right hand a book labeled "Froudacity." "Such is West Indian appreciation of the late John Jacob Thomas in Dominica," the article noted. "We are glad to say that this is not the first occasion that we have been pleased to observe the patriotism of Dominicans in matters of this sort in which West Indians are concerned. Matters in Trinidad, as regards this subject, seem to be in abeyance, we regret to say."[51] Just as Thomas had vindicated Donovan and others, as well as himself, those he survived took up the cause of vindicating him.

2 "Her Majesty's Ethiopic Subjects"
London, Englishness, Pan-Africanism

If the writer of the work referred to below did not, in a letter to the Secretary of the Philological Society, speak of himself as "born of African parents," no one probably—not even a member of the Anthropological Society—would discover from an examination of it the colour of the pigment within his *rite mucosum,* or be able to measure from it the greater proximity of the writer over the reader to the anthropoid apes. If we are not mistaken indeed, it is the first grammatical work composed by a person of pure negro descent, and has a certain historical value from this point of view. Otherwise, except so far as its subject-matter is concerned, it has nothing particularly remarkable about it.

—*Spectator* (London), September 1869

[Thomas] has been invited to assemblies public and private, is to be enrolled a Member of the Philological Society, has been pleasantly noticed in the Metropolitan Press, and has had to do the amiable at exhibitions and at the table to the fair dames and daughters of scientific husbands and papas. It is not every day that they catch a real African lion in London, and of course they make much of him when they do.

—*Trinidad Chronicle,* November 1873

WHEN ONE European paper noted of Thomas that he had died "fighting the battle of his people" and that had he "remained in his own warm climate his valuable life would have been prolonged for a good many more years," it was both a recognition of Thomas's dedication to "his people" and an interesting metropolitan commentary on which locations suited him best.[1] For while it is certainly reasonable to assume that an English winter was deadly to Thomas's frail health, the reference to "his own warm climate" also has an anthropological resonance. It is to this combination of metropolitan (un)suitability and pan-Africanist vindication that I now wish to turn. I locate Thomas in a metropolitan arena in order to examine his identity as one of, in his words, "her Majesty's Ethiopic subjects" (*Froudacity,* 56), considering the British Isles, and sometimes London more specifically, both as a site of a certain kind of prestige for a British colonial subject and as one of the contact zones of a global pan-African community. In making London the nodal point of pan-Africanism and colonial subjectivity here I risk suggesting that one is only possible through the other, and only in London. But that Thomas died there is incidental: he visited twice and happened to die there on the second visit. As we have seen, Trinidadians did not have to be located in England in order to regard it as the mother country. London usefully brings together the prestige and perils of England, as well as its location, physically and imaginatively, as a contact zone.

When John Jacob Thomas stood up to read his paper "On Some Peculiarities of the Creole Language" during the 7 November 1873 meeting of the Philological Society in London, it was in many ways the triumphant culmination of the acclaim he had received for his published study of Trinidad's Creole language four years earlier and proof of the accomplishments of those "of undiluted African descent" almost four decades after the abolition of slavery in the anglophone Caribbean.[2] The two quotations above, however, indicate the tenuous nature of any claims that Thomas could hope to make on the categories "gentleman," "scholar," "respectable," and "human." The first, from an 1869 review of Thomas's *Grammar* in a London paper, bestowed on a British colonial subject the honor of being noticed by the metropolitan press, and yet it also starkly set the boundaries of his humanity in that forum. Anthropoid apes, after all, were hardly part of the community of *Homo sapiens*, let alone gentlemen or scholars. Since the reviewer refers to "the *greater proximity* of the writer over the reader to the anthropoid apes" (emphasis added), there is at least the concession here that Thomas was not actually an ape, though he is certainly posited as being nearer to one than the White, well-bred, literate males who were the assumed readers of the review. The quick descent from admission of African parentage to the designation "anthropoid apes" suggests the perilous situation for Black persons of letters on the mid-century metropolitan intellectual scene.

Scientific "facts" of the day "placed" Thomas firmly for this reviewer and the readers of the *Spectator.* Even theories that were unpopular with "respectable" scientists could find currency with scientific figures willing to be cast as disreputable and with a general public that drew its ideas from sources ranging from sensational reports about explorers' discoveries in the central African interior, to reports of rebellions in the Americas and in Asia, to minstrel shows. Ideas alive in the culture regarding non-Europeans coalesced around particular figures or events at various points, producing, variously, feelings of sentimentality associated with abolitionist portrayals of Black people, theatrical productions of Harriet Beecher Stowe's *Uncle Tom's Cabin* (which were enormously popular in the British Isles), or accounts of widow burning in India; and feelings of outrage and betrayal at the "savagery" of the subject races associated with the "Maori Wars" and the "Indian Mutiny" in the 1850s and the Governor Eyre controversy in the mid-1860s. While it is useful to trace some of these ideas to particular moments and persons, as I do here, it should be understood that these ideas did not circulate in a straightforward fashion, pinpointed by recalling a particular year or a particular thinker. Rather, they moved back and forth and against each other, often contradictorily, gaining credence in some aspects, losing it in others, in response to concerns about working-class unrest in England, Irish intractability, national or class feelings of piety, anxieties about "foreign" competition for jobs on the docks, or the classed and gendered struggles of various constituencies for authority. That is to say, events and currents in the global context played off those in the British Isles, providing a rich context for reading those who read persons like Thomas.

In late 1869, when the London *Spectator* review was published, James Hunt, a scientist known for drawing connections between Black people and apes, had just died. He and other polygenesists had contested monogenesist theories of human origin associated with the Ethnological Society, a "liberal" body that believed, in Darwinian fashion, that human beings and civilizations could change over time. Even if it were allowed that there were vast differences in development, this school held that all groups of humans were essentially from the same species. Hunt believed that physical types were permanent rather than mutable and that humankind had evolved from distinct racial groups. The differences between these two groups, however, did not mean that adherents of both groups did not believe, stridently or quietly, in racial superiority, with one or another group of Europeans at the top.

Race, as used by prominent scientists and nonscientists, ranged vigorously and imprecisely in meaning over "blood," biological descent, intellect and culture, national and geographical origin, and destiny. Those who believed that Anglo-Saxons were the dominant of the Germanic races, which in turn dominated all others—European and non-European—were not necessarily the same as those who saw important anatomical distinctions between, say, Celts and Saxons. Believers in Anglo-Saxon superiority might work tirelessly to oppose imperialism, believing that some groups were uncivilizable and that British resources were better spent otherwise or simply that it was wrong to rule over others. It was sometimes clear, and sometimes not, that race as biology extended to intellectual capability, or again, that environmental or political circumstances affected racial differences rather than that conflicts between races were inevitable, a consequence of human nature (Lorimer, "Race, Science").

Led by Hunt, a disciple of Robert Knox, scientists associated with polygenetic theories broke away from the Ethnological Society to form the Anthropological Society in 1863. As they saw it, they were engaging in a revitalized anthropology that would not hesitate to relate theories of the relationship between humankind and animals to political, nonscientific issues of the day (Rainger; Stepan, ch. 2; Stocking; Haller). The new organization managed to draw to it well-known scientists even though Hunt and some of his colleagues were regarded by many as crude believers in the essential inferiority of certain racial groups. Hunt, like Knox before him, was discredited in some circles, but this had no necessary bearing on the popularity of his ideas, and extreme positions often had the effect of moving "moderate" views further to the right.

Determined to address politics, Hunt publicly supported the actions of Edward Eyre, the governor of Jamaica, who in 1865 was accused by "liberal" opinion and then the courts of using unnecessary force to quell Black freeholders demonstrating against unfair anti-squatter legislation in the town of Morant Bay in St. Thomas-in-the-East, Jamaica. Hundreds of Black people were hanged or flogged, their houses burnt to the ground. Rumors that White men, women, and children had been massacred by "Negro savages" dominated early reports in the British press, as well as newspapers in the United States, where the end of the Civil War brought an intense interest in the future of Black freed people in the Caribbean. The events in Morant Bay galvanized Victorian public figures from late 1865, when news of the event began to reach the British press, until 1869, as the matter continued to drag on through the courts.

Hunt commissioned papers titled "The Maroons of Jamaica" and "The Negro as a Slave and as a Freeman" and otherwise showed his support for Eyre. Thomas Carlyle, Charles Dickens, Alfred Lord Tennyson, and others also glorified Eyre as a savior of besieged Anglo-Saxons in Jamaica. These defenders of "traditional values" found themselves publicly pitted against John Stuart Mill, Charles Darwin, Herbert Spencer, and others, an urban-identified grouping committed to "rationality and scientific inquiry" (C. Hall, *White, Male, and Middle Class,* 278). In this sense the struggle over the ethics of Eyre's actions in Jamaica was one between liberal champions of a free market economy who believed that White women and non-White people were civilizable, on the one hand, and defenders of conservative values associated with church, landowning, and military interests who believed in the moral right of the English to maintain order and confirm their superiority, on the other.

It is therefore possible to read Thomas's 1869 reviewer as sneering at Hunt and his Anthropological Society. By this reading, the passage stating that "not even a member of the Anthropological Society . . . would . . . be able to measure . . . the greater proximity of the writer . . . to the anthropoid apes" would be suggestive of fanatical, absurd, Hunt-like views about Black inferiority not shared by liberal and enlightened members of the reading public. Just a few years previously, in 1863, William Craft, a fugitive from slavery in the United States, had been present at a meeting of the Anthropological Society, where Hunt presented evidence, confirmed by "other distinguished anatomists and physiologists," that the Negro race "seemed to be an intermediate form between the highest and lowest existing races of man."[3]

Hunt said that the proof was to be found in bone density, brain size and capacity, the voice (which "resembles sometimes the alto of an eunuch"), and even the feet, noting "the resemblance of the foot and the position of the toes of the Negro to that of the ape; and many observers have noticed that the Negroes have frequently used the great toe as a thumb." All of these factors underlined their incapacity for civilization, their lack of history, and their inability—at least the inability of "the pure Negro"—to "advance further in intellect than an intelligent European boy of fourteen years of age." Those who appeared to disprove these facts were "not pure Negroes; but, in nearly every case where they had become men of mark, they had European blood in their veins."

Stating that "though he was not of pure African descent he was black enough" to respond, Craft declared that if God had not given the Negro "thick skulls their brains would probably have become very much like those of many scientific gentlemen of the present day." Appealing to climate as a more reasonable explanation of racial differences and to lack of opportunity rather than "natural" inferiority as the obstacle to Negro progress, Craft also insisted on his African ties. His grandparents were "of pure Negro blood," and he had recently visited the King of Dahomey, where he had found "considerable diversities even among the Africans themselves." His claim to firsthand knowledge thus challenged the "facts" being debated by the Anthropological Society, as his reference to "the treachery of some white men" who had shipped his grandfather to America questioned the anthropological assignment of superiority, moral and otherwise, to his possession of "European blood." Craft ended by expressing disappointment "that scientific and learned men should waste their time in discussing a subject that could prove of no benefit to mankind."[4]

Notwithstanding the shakiness of James Hunt's status in some of London's scientific circles when this meeting took place, in 1863, he would still have been understood to be "obviously" intellectually superior to an escaped slave from the United States, who was at that very moment learning to read. To be sure, liberal, or at least less crude, members of elite society, including Lady Byron and Harriet Martineau, who were two of the Crafts' patrons, would have been aghast at Hunt's remarks and might well have congratulated Craft on the eloquence of his rebuttal (Lorimer, *Colour, Class*, 47–48). Still, Black public speakers could not count on escaping the ideas circulating about race and nature; hence the duty of vindication with regard to this subject. Even if we could interpret Thomas's *Spectator* reviewer, then, as ironizing and thus further discrediting the views of Hunt's society, the words echoed and reinforced prevalent ideas about the connection between apes and Black people. John Jacob Thomas, then, perhaps could not hope, six years later, to avoid this fate even if, unlike the Americans William and Ellen Craft, he was neither escaping slavery nor physically present in London at the time of the review of his book. Judgment of his work was inevitably and securely tied to his perceived subhuman (even if near-human) place on the evolutionary scale.

And yet it was Thomas himself who invited the simian analogy, the *Spectator* reviewer suggests. He was the one who introduced himself as "born of African parents," sealing his doom by undercutting any claim to "objective," "neutral" assessments of his intellectual production. Would it not have been better to keep silent and earn, fair and square, the commendation "nothing particularly remarkable about it"? Like Craft, Thomas insisted on specifying his and his parents' origins despite what he must have known would be the price of claiming Africa as an important and valid part of the way he identified himself. The very viciousness of the racist claims about Black people that made the work of vindication imperative conspired to undermine him by reminding everyone of what many would perceive as his barely human status. In bearing witness to his "African parents" he risked the ignominy not only of being tied filially to apes but also of losing intellectual credibility. Properly intellectual work, after all, was objective and value-free; the "real" scholar, surely, did not make these kinds of autobiographical gestures.

Thomas's assertion of the significance of his origins and thus of the capabilities of persons such as himself, as well as the value inhering in his *Creole Grammar,* managed to earn from the *Spectator* reviewer the dubious distinction for the grammar that it was the "first grammatical work composed by a person of pure negro descent." While this fact assigned it "historical value," it was otherwise unremarkable: Creole speech was unremarkable, as was what Thomas had to say about it.

But does Thomas really fare any better with the second quotation, four years later? On the face of it, it is certainly more promising. Written by a Trinidadian editor in 1873, days after Thomas's lecture to the Philological Society in London, it seems to promise entry into the fraternity of not simply humanity but its most worthy echelons. Here is Thomas the respectable gentleman observing the courtesies to the "fair dames and daughters" with his gentleman counterparts. There is Thomas the scholar receiving intellectual recognition as naturally as everyone else. Listened to in halls of learning, fêted on the social circuit—here was the London in which noted West African figures such as Bishop Samuel Ajayi Crowther and the Caribbean-born Edward Blyden of Liberia moved so freely among Victorian elites. The Black public figure among a community of equals. Thomas is indeed more "pleasantly noticed" this time around.

At the same time, an asterisk beside his name in the 7 November 1873 minutes of the Philological Society directs the reader's attention to the margins and a penciled announcement: "A pure Negro."[5] True enough, the phrase "real African lion" signals Thomas's celebrity, denoting him as the literary sensation without whom London parties were doomed, and it signals as well that the lion, connoting bravery and eminence, its image prominently displayed on the heraldry of the British aristocracy, was arguably less objectionable than the ape.[6] Yet the image of the virile lion among all those fair dames and daughters seems to pull in a much different direction from that of society lions and aristocratic heraldry. Hear him speak. See him use the right spoon. See them "catching him." *In London.* As opposed to his presumed "natural" habitat—the Port of Spain Public Library or the central African interior?

Ranked on a scale, were African lions more or less exotic, more or less civilized, than Bengali ones such as Keshabchandra Sen, who visited England in 1870, giving lectures and meeting with the queen and the prime minister? One of many newspapers reporting his visit, *Punch* proclaimed on 16 March 1870:

Let's beard this "lion" in his den
This BABOO KESHUB CHUNDER SEN.
So come to tea and muffins, then,
With BABOO KESHUB CHUNDER SEN.

(qtd. in Chatterjee 38)

How did Keshabchandra Sen and Thomas rank with maharajas such as Dalip Singh, who lived in England from the 1850s (see Gell), or Hawaiian queens? When the queen of the Sandwich Islands visited Charles and Fanny Kingsley in their home in 1865, Fanny Kingsley noted: "The feeling of having a Queen civilised and yet of savage, even cannibal ancestry sleeping under one's roof in Charlie's and my room—eating at one's table—talking of Tennyson and *Tom Brown's School Days* (!) of the delight with which she and the late King, her dear Husband, had read *The Water Babies* to their little Prince; strange—it was passing strange, and made me feel that we had been living for twenty-eight hours in a dream!"[7]

Civilized and yet savage. The ability to read and discuss the well-known writers and texts of the day was no guarantee that your hosts would not think of you in terms that suggested reversion. Perhaps "*real* African lion" was meant to juxtapose Thomas with those who *claimed* to be African but really were not, such as the "frauds" who in the 1850s attempted to fool an unsuspecting and sympathetic reading public into believing that they were fugitive slaves (Lorimer, *Colour, Class,* 46). Or there may be a veiled reference here to "real *African* lions" as opposed to North American ones, including those, like the Crafts, who paraded as the real thing but whose "mixed" blood compromised their supposed authenticity, given the assumption that "European blood" placed one higher on the human scale at the same time that it compromised one's "authenticity." Thomas's claim that he had been "born of African parents" takes on particular significance here, suggesting his identity as the real thing, close to a particular experience and history.

At the same time, under what conditions would Thomas have been an *African* lion, coming as he did from the Caribbean, which had a long history of distinguishing between "seasoned" Creoles and "saltwater" or "Guinea" new arrivals? Since Thomas had been born in the Caribbean, could he really claim to be African? Since the reviewer applying this term to Thomas was *Trinidadian,* was he perhaps reminding Thomas of his exceptionality, as a dark-skinned Black man, in the middle-class Trinidadian context?

If lions and apes were the only analogies available, to say nothing of the mention of animals—any animal—and exhibitions in the same paragraph, then the prospects for this colonial visitor seemed grim. The latter recalled the spectacle of Sarah Baartman (later Bartmann), the South African woman who was exhibited as "the Hottentot Venus" to great acclaim from 1810 to 1814 in England, where she appeared at 225 Picadilly and in the Chancery Court, among other London venues. In Paris, where she appeared until her death in 1815 or 1816, patrons paid three francs to see her exhibited nude except for a brief skirt or apron from 11:00 A.M. to 10:00 P.M. at rue St. Honoré. Since her guardian specialized in exhibiting wild animals, the admission fee included the viewing of a rhinoceros.[8]

One could, of course, argue that this punning on the Trinidadian editor's reference to "exhibitions" ties Thomas unnecessarily to the spectacle of Bartmann, as well as to other bodies on public display on the antislavery platform at Exeter Hall or at various colonial exhibitions throughout the century, since his circumstances were altogether different. Making much of the "catch" of a "real African lion," however, suggests an editor who is either sneering at Thomas (*London* might fête you, but we at home will remind you who you really are) or wryly but sympathetically noting the inclination of the British public to consume someone like Thomas as an exotic (we are proud of you, but we have no illusions about your hosts). It is not so clear, then, that the designation "African lion" guaranteed Thomas a more egalitarian reception in London than did the speculation in the *Spectator* review on the significance of the color of his nostrils.

"A REAL AFRICAN lion in London" can be linked to notions of authenticity circulating around Thomas and others like him in Britain. As we have seen, one of these concerned the extent to which he could assume that his status as a human being and intellectual was disconnected from prevailing ideas about Black people's proximity to apes and cannibals. Another resonance of "real African" was derived from the thriving institution of blackface minstrelsy in Britain. The intense interest in caricatured African American speech and bodily gestures on the part of British visitors to the United States such as Charles Dickens and William Thackeray was matched by the British audiences who flocked to see White men from the United States as well as Britain dressing up as Black men and women on stage. Indeed, one writer claims that "although of American origin the minstrel business was brought to its highest state of perfection in [England]" (qtd. in Brody, 74). Performing solo or in troupes, White men, their faces blackened with cork, entertained British audiences from the early 1820s. The most popular American minstrels performed in England, but minstrelsy was also increasingly institutionalized on the British side of the Atlantic, where by the 1860s there were fifteen permanent companies, who performed in London and other cities and for Queen Victoria (Lorimer, *Colour, Class,* 191).

Minstrelsy was given a new lease on life by the publication of Harriet Beecher Stowe's *Uncle Tom's Cabin* in 1852: "Indeed, 'without minstrelsy, *Uncle Tom's Cabin* would not have existed,' and without *Uncle Tom's Cabin,* minstrelsy in Britain would not have flourished" (Brody, 81). Stowe's novel and its theatrical offshoots added to the ongoing representation of, and thus reflection on, Black people, slave or free, in the British isles and throughout the British empire. Mrs. Stowe's characters, as well as blackface minstrelsy in general, offered "Black people" who were knowable, representable, familiar as the advertisements for soap that could wash "picaninnies" white and the Mulatto and Juba dolls marketed to children.

Spectators judged the authenticity of these performances on the presumption that they were competent to judge authentic Black behavior. When Samuel Hague formed the Georgia Minstrel Troupe from one of the many itinerant bands of freed slaves earning a livelihood by putting on shows after the Civil War, he took them to Liverpool, where they performed at the Theatre Royal in July 1866. When audiences seemed less than enthusiastic, Hague hired White men to supplement the troupe (Reynolds, 162–63; Lorimer, *Colour, Class,* 88, 238 n. 74). Thus Black performers were competing—unsuccessfully—with White counterparts in blackface. When the Jubilee Singers from Fisk University performed before Queen Victoria and the prime minister to great acclaim, they were competing with other African American entertainers, as well as with fugitives from slavery, students, and evangelists, for the attention of the British public. Their success depended on their ability to convince audiences that their causes—abolition, temperance, evangelism—were genuine and deserving of the public's moral and financial support.

Henry "Box" Brown, who had escaped from his American owners in a box, found himself having to defend his reputation when a Wolverhampton newspaper accused him of exaggeration and buffoonery in his dramatic presentations on his escape, which featured portrayals of slaves being whipped and burnt alive (Lorimer, *Colour, Class,* 53–54). The newspaper called him a "bejewelled darkie" who exhibited the "foppery, conceit, vanity, and egotistical stupidity of the Box Brown school." Brown sued, claiming that the articles caused a decline in his audiences and thus in his potential income. He was awarded damages after witnesses testified that though bejeweled, he was quiet and well-spoken. He thus found himself judged by a knowing British public, assessing, sympathetically or not, what was genuine and what was excessive. He was caught between two constituencies: those who thought that he overperformed and those who did not think that his performance detracted from a fundamental possession of the appropriate comportment and speech. Both on the antislavery platform and in court his spectators ultimately decided his fate.

Black performers were closely scrutinized by their British audiences, then. Their creative and intellectual production could have a particular kind of prestige in Britain, not least because of its association with freedom (Britain had abolished the slave trade in 1807 and the institution in 1834), and the prestige of its intellectual life—particularly, but not only, for persons from English-speaking territories. But recognition could not be divorced from spectacle. Black visitors were caught between promise and danger, between a well-developed abolitionist industry offering an oasis of freedom, for instance, and a significant constituency of those who were derisive of excessive or inadequate "performances" by Black people themselves, as well as of excessive sentiment by others on their behalf.

On the latter point, one newspaper editor would put it this way in the 1860s, during the Morant Bay–Governor Eyre controversy:

> What have the English people done that the irrepressible negro should make an interruption into their daily press, disport himself at their dessert, chill their turtle, spoil their wine, and sour their pine-apple and their temper? Are we henceforth to be separated, as a nation, into negrophilites and anti-negroites? Is every dinner-party and every tea-party, every society of geographers and every society of social twaddlers, to be worried and wearied by prosy controversialists in the brutal inferiority or the angelic superiority of the sons of Ham?[9]

"English people" and the "nation" are clearly marked off here from the offending "sons of Ham," who interrupt the normal business of a daily life that otherwise has nothing to do with them. As if the very sweetness of their dessert and the acquired taste for it were unrelated to a historical and ongoing relationship with these sons and daughters of Ham.

Black visitors to the British Isles represented a range of experiences. Prominent visitors from the African continent expected to move among Victorian elites and contrasted their reception by the British upper class with the discriminatory treatment they received at the hands of British officers in the territories from which they had come or to which they returned to work. Set apart from Black people who were competing for working-class jobs, they gained degrees or qualified in the medical or legal professions in England and Scotland. Bishop Ajayi Crowther, born in Yorubaland and educated partly in Sierra Leone, studied in England, gaining fame as a translator with the 1841 Niger expedition. From the 1850s to the 1880s he gave lectures at Cambridge, had an audience with the queen, and received an honorary degree from Oxford for translating the Scriptures into African languages (Lorimer, *Colour, Class,* 60–61; Crowther and Taylor). Dr. James Africanus Horton, of Sierra Leone and the Gold Coast, trained as a surgeon. Edward Blyden, born in St. Thomas, in the Danish Caribbean, migrated to Liberia after studying in the United States. Prominent on the London scene whenever he visited, he was an honorary member of the Athenaeum, contributed to *Fraser's Magazine,* and represented Liberia at the Court of St. James's.

For Black writers and public speakers traveling from the Caribbean and North America in the decades before Thomas's visit in the 1870s, Britain offered intellectual prestige (though often not without irony), a respite from slavery for some. Francis Williams, who attended Cambridge in the 1750s, impressed David Hume as a "parrot who speaks a few words plainly" (123n. See also Sandiford; Drayton; and Lindo). In 1773, some twelve years after being sold into slavery at age eight, Phillis Wheatley traveled to London with the son of her Boston owners for the publication of her first book of poetry, on which a reviewer commented: "These poems display no astonishing power of genius" except "when we consider them as the production of a young untutored African." Here Wheatley's "untutored" and "African" characteristics guarantee her public notice, redeeming her lack of "genius" (Richmond, 33).

Whereas Wheatley returned to slavery in Boston after her short visit, and Williams returned to Jamaica, where he opened a school in Spanish Town, teaching Latin and mathematics, Mary Prince's journey to England with her owners in 1828 held no such guarantee of return, as we have seen (Prince; Ferguson; Pouchet Pacquet, "Heartbeat"). The fugitives Harriet Jacobs, Frederick Douglass, and William Wells Brown all spoke favorably of their reception in England, as did the evangelist Amanda Smith.[10]

After his negative experiences with White denominations in America, Alexander Crummell took a degree at Cambridge in 1853 before leaving for Liberia, allowing him, as his biographer notes, to acquire "at the source [the] civilization of a British gentleman and so become a far superior representative of modern European Civilization than the white Americans who sought to ostracize him. What sweet revenge!" (Moses, 51). Similarly, the orator and former fugitive Samuel Ringgold Ward traveled to England in April 1853 to lecture under the auspices of the Anti-Slavery

Society in Canada; he recalled when he was prevented from leaving his cabin by American Whites traveling on his ship, he was visited by William Thackeray, who "still honours me with his friendly acquaintance" (235).

In the 1850s, when Mary Seacole published her *Wonderful Adventures of Mrs. Seacole in Many Lands,* about her travels as a hotel proprietor and medical practitioner throughout the Caribbean and Central America and in Sebastopol during the Crimean War, she was telling the British public that her dusky skin notwithstanding, she had mothered their sons at the battlefield and trying to persuade them that she now deserved their patronage and support (Seacole; Pouchet Pacquet, "Enigma of Arrival"; Gikandi). Unlike Williams and Prince, she desired to remain in England, asserting her right to British patronage as a British subject.

Michel Maxwell Philip's *Emmanuel Appadocca, or Blighted Life: A Tale of the Boucaneers,* published in 1854, while he toured Europe after finishing his legal studies and prior to returning to Trinidad, is a novel about a pirate's quest to avenge his White planter's abandonment of him and his Black mother. The preface announces that the author's feelings are "roused up to a high pitch of indignant excitement, by a statement of the cruel manner in which the slave holders of America deal with their slave-children," thus indicating its affinities to the slave narratives of Jacobs and Douglass, as well as to William Wells Brown's novel *Clotel* (see also Cain, xv; Cudjoe, preface, ix; and McDaniel). Both Seacole and Philips were born free during slavery to White fathers and Black or Colored mothers. Seacole's apprenticeship in herbal medicine and hoteliering, occupations dominated by Black and Colored women in Kingston, and Philip's ties to a propertied family well known for its political activism on behalf of political rights for free Coloreds in Grenada and then Trinidad give their respective texts the complex double edge of negative, stereotypical renderings of dark-skinned Black persons and affinities with enslaved Black constituencies. Both texts present protagonists who cross several borders and are confident about their ability to make demands upon powerful White Americans and Europeans.

The significance of Britain for all of these visitors was connected to their experience in their place of origin. For most, their visits seemed to promise a different relationship to the space to which they were either returning or moving. In many cases, the authentication of their hosts was important, recalling the prefatory letters by prestigious Whites in slave narratives. Thus, one can only guess at their silences: did Ward's conversations with Thackeray on board ship include a discussion of the caricatures of Mr. Sambo and Miss Swartz in *Vanity Fair?*

While both of the quotations that head this chapter tie Thomas to London, the first as his work was reviewed in a London periodical but before he actually visited, the second during his first trip in 1873, London is but one of the contexts for understanding him. That I have considered his relationship to England at some length may seem odd, then, since he certainly spent much less time in London than did many of his wealthy Colored and White Trinidadian compatriots or, indeed, the thousands of British Caribbean residents who would begin to flock to England in the early twentieth century. In addition, many of Trinidad's cultural elite considered *Paris* as much a symbolic center as London, if not more so. Trinidad's newspapers are replete with obituaries and other accounts of successful Black persons in France during the 1860s and 1870s, and thus my concentration here on an anglophone orientation risks obliterating such complexities. Finally, the repeated reference to African American figures instead of, say, to Latin American or, for that matter African or Asian ones risks giving undue privilege to a North American context that is already well documented, not to mention canonically dominant, in relation to the Caribbean and to a racial context that risks discounting both White and Colored Trinidadians who read and discussed his work.

Yet, it is worth noting that Frederick Douglass and other African Americans were known to Trinidad's reading public since news items from the United States were reprinted in the local papers, including references to its growing ability to acquire wealth. From the early part of the century African Americans debated schemes for emigration to Trinidad and other Caribbean territories.[11] In addition, "Americans," or "Merikins," who fought on the British side in the American Revolutionary War were given land in Trinidad. They resided in company villages in the south, where their Baptist services were reviled by some observers as noisy and savage (Brereton, *Race Relations,* 158–59). "African American" histories, then, are not inseparable from "Trinidadian" histories per se, though exploring these connections is not my major concern here.

I have situated Thomas in relation to England because it is one of the necessary contexts for "reading" him as a colonial subject of the empire of which it was the administrative center—the seat of empire and home of the queen, Parliament, and the military complex that kept order "at home" and "abroad"—as well as the symbolic intellectual and cultural center, housing the British Library, Oxford and Cambridge Universities, and those Victorian men and women of letters who authored the volumes over which Thomas and his peers labored, and whose journal and newspaper reviews set the standards of taste by which aspiring intellectuals were judged. England—sometimes London more specifically—interpellated figures such as Thomas from all over the British Empire, as well as beyond, figures who, whether or not they traveled there physically, regarded it as the center of a literal and symbolic universe.

Thomas's race, quite apart from either his intellectual achievements or his Caribbean origins, determined both the ways in which Londoners regarded him and the ways in which he wanted to be regarded, though not exclusively so. While focusing on Thomas's relationship, as a "pure negro," to his Trinidadian and wider Caribbean milieux, it is important to contextualize him as well both as someone whom elite Londoners read in particular kinds of ways and as someone who consciously identified himself as part of a transnational community of Black intellectuals.

Black persons with varying degrees of relationships to colonial states or republics combined transnationally, without the concrete political and geographical entity of a state, though some did talk concretely about acquiring this. Martin Delaney, for instance, had plans for a railway system that would traverse the African continent, a "GREAT THOROUGHFARE for all the trade with the East Indies and Eastern Coast of Africa, and the continent of America."[12] In *Froudacity* (1889) Thomas refers to the responsibility of this transnational citizenry, this "transnation," to a besieged African continent.[13] The "naturally opulent cradle" of the African continent, "too long a prey to violence and unholy greed," craved the assistance of its diasporic subjects. Since the "intra-African Negro" was "powerless to struggle successfully against personal enslavement, annexation, or volunteer forcible 'protection' of his territory," it was up to those "extra-African millions" to come to the continent's rescue (179). The logic of history had determined that "Egypt, Assyria, Babylon, Greece, Rome, and others had successively held the palm of supremacy," and after the present "pre-eminence" of the Anglo-Saxons, eventually it would be the turn of "the African race" (180).

Thus, the readiness of those "extra-Africans" was imperative: "apt apprentices in every conceivable department of civilised culture" (179), surgeons, solicitors, teachers, journalists, "here in the West Indies, and on the West Coast of Africa, . . . men who not only teach those immediately around them, but also teach the world," including "a full-blooded Negro [who] took the highest degree Oxford has to give a young man."[14] Thomas turns his attention to "the Blacks of the United States," who "despite the lingering obstructions of caste prejudice, have positively achieved wonders":

Leaving aside the writings of men of such high caliber as F. Douglass, Dr. Hyland Garnet, Prof Crummell, Prof E. Blyden, Dr Tanner, and others, it is gratifying to be able to chronicle the Ethiopic women of North America as moving shoulder to shoulder with the men in the highest spheres of literary activity. Among a brilliant band of these our sisters, conspicuous no less in poetry than in prose, we single out but a solitary name for the double purpose of preserving brevity and of giving in one embodiment the ideal Afro-American woman of letters. The allusion here can scarcely fail to point to Mrs. S. Harper. This lady's philosophical subtlety of reasoning on grave questions finds effective expression in a prose of singular precision and vigor. But it is as a poet that posterity will hail her in the coming ages of our Race. For pathos, depth of spiritual insight, and magical exercise of a rare power of self-utterance, it will hardly be questioned that she has surpassed every competitor among females—white or black—save and except Elizabeth Barrett Browning, with whom the gifted African stands on much the same plane of poetic excellence. (191–92)

Thomas sees himself as part of an international cadre, a "vast body of African descendants now dispersed in various countries of the Western Hemisphere," charged with carrying out, with "unity of purpose . . . the obvious duties which are sure to devolve upon us, especially with reference to the cradle of our Race" (191–92).

"Full-blooded Negro," which resonates with "born of African parents," indicates one layer of the complicated meanings around what these connections meant to him. While, as we have seen, any connection to Africa tainted one as inferior and thereby represented a challenge to disprove the assumption, the intellectual achievements of the "full-blooded" were particularly pleasing since they were presumed to be the truly inferior, the lowest-ranked on the scale of ability. The meanings attached to race, then, pulled in different directions. Race mattered, and "the Negro Race" (comprising anyone of African descent) constituted an important context of Thomas's self-identification. At the same time, "mere colour" or "the miserable skin and race doctrine" (190, 193) by which persons such as Thomas in the Caribbean and around the world were kept from realizing their destinies was wrong. Special significance attached to "full-bloodedness," and at the same time all members of the race, "full-blooded" or not, shared in its slights and triumphs.

The passage also indicates that men and women of letters in particular were charged with carrying out the "duties" of the race, or "the vast engine essential for executing the true purposes of the civilised African Race" (193). The ability to read those texts that nourished the intellect, as well as those that viciously attacked the capabilities of the race, and the discipline entailed in mastering the canon and acquiring a command of the proper rhetorical styles, particularly given the many hurdles placed in the aspirants' way, were laudable and necessary but also useful since the printed word promised dissemination that transcended the boundaries of space and time.

The reference to Mrs. Harper, despite Thomas's giving the middle initial as "S.," is probably to Frances Ellen Watkins Harper, well known throughout the mid- to late nineteenth century as a prominent African American poet, essayist, abolitionist, and public speaker. Harper's fiction, including her 1892 novel, *Iola Leroy,* was published in installments in the *Anglo-African* (see Foster). That Thomas may have met or corresponded with her or with any of the other figures he mentions here is a tantalizing thought. Thomas was obviously very proud of Harper's achievements and particularly impressed by the way she and others of "our sisters" demonstrated that "Ethiopic women of North America" shared the public sphere, the operation of that "vast engine," with their male counterparts. That Harper and others move "shoulder to shoulder with the men" in Thomas's passage suggests an equality that pleases rather than threatens him.

Yet "shoulder to shoulder" seems also to rub against the grain of the assessment that "she has surpassed every competitor among females." The earlier image of equality with Ethiopic men now passes into a sphere in which only women compete, perhaps suggesting an interesting doubling of realms for Black women such as Harper. They are grouped on the one hand with Black men and on the other with "females—white or black." Elizabeth Barrett Browning is the standard in the latter arena. White, English (her Jamaican family ties notwithstanding), and a prominent writer of poetry protesting slavery, she provides both the standard against which Harper, "the gifted African," is judged and found more or less equal, standing as she does "on much the same plane," *and* the limits of Harper's abilities: Harper "has surpassed every competitor . . . save and except."

The double move here in the assessment of Harper can be more fully understood if we add the consideration that Ethiopic men in North America, the Caribbean, and West Africa not only operated the vast racial engine jointly with their sisters but also found themselves in competition with elite White Victorian men in an intellectual field that was highly gendered and self-conscious about performing a robust manliness. For Thomas and his fellow Black male intellectuals, all elite Victorians, male and female, set standards of civility and taste against which they measured themselves.

They even measured elite Victorians themselves against this standard and found them wanting, as Craft's admonition to Hunt or Thomas's response to Froude suggests. This was by no means the only yardstick that Thomas and others used, but it was an important one, and when it was applied it placed them on a ladder of civilization whose lower rungs were occupied chiefly by lower classes of all kinds in the United Kingdom, the Caribbean, and throughout the world, who did not sufficiently aspire to its standards.

While all elite Victorian Whites set this standard, the women of this group were not necessarily regarded as "moving shoulder to shoulder" with men. Elizabeth Barrett Browning, to go back to the quotation above, is still being compared to "females—white or black." The editor in Trinidad who noted that Thomas socialized with "the fair dames and daughters of scientific husbands and papas" was distinguishing between males who engaged in intellectual inquiry and females who adorned social events with their beauty and grace. Whether or not Thomas may have shared this image of "manly" men and the fairer sex, it was part of a standard against which he and others were assessed.

We have seen that James Hunt informed his 1863 audience that the Negro possessed the "alto of a eunuch." This image of castrated masculinity would have been understood to represent a questionable sexuality, no less damning than his assessment that the intellectual limit of "pure Negros" was "intelligent European boy[s] of fourteen years of age." The standard of intelligence being applied was clearly White and male, though it is not as clear whether male *and female* Negroes were being held up to scrutiny. For Black men, both of Hunt's comments present a masculinity that is negative both in relation to normative notions of rugged heterosexuality and in a thwarted, deformed sense: the best that can be expected from this group is the sexual and intellectual maturity of an adolescent boy.

If females are being considered in the analogies with eunuchs and fourteen-year-old boys, then they are included in the slight to mental adequacy, and with regard to sexuality they are masculinized. According to prevailing standards of femininity this would count as a loss, though it also ironically places them on the same plane as their male counterparts. "Shoulder to shoulder," as it were. Victorian male travelers noted this equality between the sexes among the Black working classes they observed in the Caribbean. They regarded it as an aberration and spoke of it with derision, though they also reserved a grudging admiration for the women. Consciously or not, Black men and women who set store by elite standards had to contend with these often contradictory attitudes, and their discourses indicate their attempts to challenge or measure up to the intricacies of these classed, sexed, and gendered identities.

Thomas, Harper, and other Black public figures were part of Benedict Anderson's conception of an "imagined community," a term that usefully draws subjects together into a comprehensible constituency while also having elusive and liberatory resonances (Anderson, 6–7). The term seems to reserve a space for desire, so that Thomas is as much bringing this community into being by invoking it rhetorically as he is noting its existence. He stresses what brings its members together instead of the many differences in gender, ideological orientation, geographical origin, and life experience that separate them from one another. As books and pamphlets changed hands, and as newspapers of various sorts made their way across the world—stitched into sailor suits, hidden under legal cargo, borrowed from libraries, sold at antislavery meetings, read aloud at Sunday School meetings and Emancipation Day anniversaries, reviewed in noted periodicals, debated in literary societies—the words written by and about this community were consumed hungrily by its members.

When these members met face to face, it was another way of confirming the community's existence. The British Isles, and London in particular, was one such place where many constituents of this community met one another as subjects of this or that colonial state, as fugitives from this or that territory. At the same time, in Britain the community as defined above by Thomas came into contact with communities from Asia, Latin America, and elsewhere, as well as with constituencies from North America, West Africa, the Caribbean, with whom they might not have come into contact "at home."

In this sense, if London is one of Mary Pratt's examples of a "contact zone"—"the space of colonial encounters, . . . in which peoples geographically and historically separated come into contact with each other and establish ongoing relations" (6)—there were, of course, other such places. Liverpool, Edinburgh, Paris, and Amsterdam also served as contact zones, as did the whole western coast of Africa and the Caribbean. The contact zone of Trinidad brought together constituencies from all over the world. London, then, was one of such zones where people met to bring news about, and to strategize about getting to, other contact zones. So Craft, as he said, visited the king of Dahomey because many from around the world were interested in trading possibilities there. Fugitive slaves–turned–Presbyterian ministers J. W. C. Pennington and Henry Highland Garnett toured England in the 1850s exploring the possibilities of African American emigration to the Caribbean (Blackett, "Hamic

Connection"). And that other "lion," Keshab, after criticizing the English for the spiritual and economic poverty he found there, returned to India —speaking English only once a year—and dedicated himself to introducing "ideas of neatness, order, punctuality and domestic devotions, which form such striking features in a well-regulated middle-class English home" (Chatterjee, 39). Venezuelan-born Andres Bello spent the years 1810 to 1829 developing his nationalist projects in London as a diplomat and with his periodical *Repertorio Americano* before going to live and work in Chile.

Douglas Lorimer argues that after the 1860s elite Black visitors experienced a hardening of attitudes on the part of their hosts. Respectability and gentility could no longer compete with race as attitudes of xenophobia and ethnocentrism increased because British Whites were becoming disillusioned with the possibility of developing middle-class constituencies in the Caribbean and West Africa. Since this process seemed to be taking so long, perhaps Black people *were* innately inferior. In addition, incidents like the "Indian Mutiny" and the Morant Bay rebellion underscored the presumed ingratitude and innate savagery of non-White subjects. While it may be true that in terms of a general trend Black elites found whiteness to be a precondition for gentility toward the end of the century, it seems more accurate to note the simultaneous promise and danger for Black people in the British Isles at all times. Their acceptance had never been guaranteed nor consistent.

In laying all negative reactions at the door of American racism, African American visitors may have granted their Victorian hosts too much, ignoring the class dynamics dictating that their hosts' magnanimity extend to neither White English nor any other working-class groups. As a native of a British colony, engaged with other Trinidadians in the demand for increased political representation, Thomas seemed as enthralled as his African American counterparts by English liberalism. *Froudacity*'s critique of imperialist discourse is that it is untrue to the best ideals of English thought.

Whatever we choose to make of these visitors' positive conception of England, it is at least clear that England was central to their formation as intellectuals and "citizens." It figured prominently in their identities as "Trinidadian," "American," "extra-African," as they, together with White Creole elites in their respective "national" spaces in Trinidad, the United States, and elsewhere, accrued an intellectual capital in which mastery of English texts and culture figured prominently. England also figured in their construction of transnational, diasporic identities, in which the appropriation of English language and culture was for them a prerequisite for the rehabilitation of the African continent. Denied political power in the lands of their birth, they were searching for alternative nations, or at least for viable ways to write national narratives without political power.

London and the British Isles, then, constituted a zone of contradictions related to the history of the presence of Black people in Britain and across the Atlantic. The holdings of its libraries and museums and the leather chairs of its reading rooms were seductive and suggestive of its independence of the labor of others because of an innate superiority. The sources of this civilization, or at least the nature of Britain's interaction with these sources, were therefore masked. White Ladies' Road and Black Boy Inn in downtown Bristol may have been explicit about such sources, but the representation of the jewels in the royal crown as gifts from this or that maharajah benignly reconfigured these connections. "The West" produced two simultaneous histories of itself in the eighteenth and nineteenth centuries, as Homi Bhabha has noted: At the same time that

> certain master narratives of the state, the citizen, cultural value, art, science, *the novel,* when these major cultural discourse and identities came to define the "Enlightenment" of Western society and the critical rationality of Western personhood, [the West] was producing another history of itself through its colonial possessions and relations. That ideological tension, visible in the history of the West as a despotic power, at the very moment of the birth of democracy and modernity, has not been adequately written in a contradictory and contrapuntal discourse of tradition. (218)

Thomas and others lived through London's contradictions by embracing its promises and confronting its perils but also, since London was neither the beginning nor the end of their existence, by using their reception there to help to negotiate their projects elsewhere.

That Thomas died in London in the process of getting *Froudacity* published and preparing a second edition of the *Creole Grammar* marks him, in one sense, as another colonial subject so enthralled by the promises of Englishness as to be overwhelmed by it: an anglophone predecessor and parallel to the Haitian intellectual Edmond Laforest, who tied a Larousse dictionary around his neck and drowned himself in 1915 (Gates, 13; Dash, *Other America,* 55). While London helps to contextualize Thomas and others, however, it cannot provide the whole picture, and in any case it is Englishness—not at all reducible to London, England, or Britain—that is more crucial here. One need not have visited London to have faith in its cultural and intellectual institutions, and one might live there all one's life and not have such faith. That Thomas placed a high value on Englishness should be considered in the context of his commitment both to the rehabilitation of the "Negro Race," as we have seen, and to Creole projects in the Caribbean. The following events suggest how diasporic arenas sharpen rather than displace local or national situations, while local contexts shed important light on diasporic situations.

William Herbert's letter published in the 13 January 1870 issue of the *Star of the West* expressed concern about the international reception of a local issue. When a White expatriate, a Dr. Bakewell, sent an offensive letter to a Colored Creole, a Dr. Espinet, that was later published in the newspapers, a storm of controversy was set off. Bakewell apologized publicly, noting that his earliest childhood memory was of contributing money to the Anti-Slavery Society and that he was presently risking his life with the "mostly coloured" population of Mayaro, in southeast Trinidad, during the cholera epidemic. This was not enough to prevent Bakewell from being tarred and feathered by hired ruffians in the streets.

Herbert chided Dr. Bakewell for his "imprudent and improper" slurs and Dr. Espinet for publishing a private letter, but he was preoccupied by the attack in the streets. His letter expresses regret for the "stigma" that the incident had brought to "the coloured people," thus indicating that Dr. Bakewell's attackers were known to be "coloured." It expresses the hope that "all men of colour, not connected with the abominable affair, who are true to their race, and have the future of that race at heart" would condemn the incident, "which not only disgraces the whole colony, but suggests serious reflections as to the state of civilization of the race to which it has hitherto been my proudest boast to belong."

Wherever the news travels, Herbert's letter laments, "it will be said everywhere that the coloured races are brutal and degraded, that their barbarous passions can never be subdued, and that they are incapable of experiencing the humanizing effects of civilization." The incident will "deprive us of friends" and "enable our enemies to state that brutality is our normal condition," particularly because "the melancholy affair of Jamaica, distorted and misrepresented as it undoubtedly was, created an intense prejudice against the coloured people in England." Five years after the events in Morant Bay, then, the reputation of the "coloured races" everywhere was vulnerable, and English reactions were critical.

In September 1872 the *New Era* published a letter written by the editor of the *Negro* in Freetown, Sierra Leone.[15] The author of the letter is not specified, but Thomas's reply, written after some time, indicates that it was Edward Blyden. Addressed to the Hon. William Grant, of the Legislative

Council of Sierra Leone, the letter refers to Grant's proposal for an educational institution to be staffed by Negroes. Blyden endorses the idea, noting that it would be a good thing for Sierra Leone and the western coast of Africa in general, since parents felt that sending their children abroad was not addressing the "specific wants of the country."

Outside of Sierra Leone were "influences" that confused "the instincts of race" and diminished "the proper manhood of the Negro," so that he had to "shape his feelings" to the "prevailing tastes around him." Thus, "wherever you find him educated in the schools abroad, you are apt to find him a man of distorted tastes, confused perceptions and defective and restless energy." The exceptional man "in whom the race feeling is not destroyed" was "a target for the assaults of his own people and of the unsympathising strangers among whom he dwells; and he must consider himself fortunate if he does not go down to a premature grave, hastened thither by sheer grief and disappointment." Sending children abroad to be educated would thwart their "natural bent" and "native instinct" and make them "useless to the race." Blyden continued, "As a people not far removed from ancestral barbarism," we need the counsel of Europeans, "not to Europeanize us, which must always be the labor of Sisyphus, but to help us to understand our own needs, to speak our own thoughts, to express our own feelings, and act ourselves out. Every state and nation and race must fight its own internal battles." It was the "strong race feeling" that had given Jews their "unquenchable vitality."

In practical terms, Europeans could not withstand the climate, and Sierra Leone's graveyards were proof of this. "Earnest and well-cultivated Negro instructors" would "perform continuous and uninterrupted labor in the schools" and "exert a wholesome influence upon the masses and guide public opinion aright, or, rather, develop and organize a public opinion, which, perhaps, does not yet exist."

Two weeks later, the *New Era* published a letter from Thomas entitled "Negroes and their Nationality," in which he showed his keen attentiveness to African affairs and their relation to his local community and endorsed the qualities he admired in a writer.[16] Leaving aside for the moment "the late disclosures of Livingstone; the significant intimation of England's views relative to the ineffable atrocities which have changed into a vast Golgotha that paradise, planted by the Creator's hand, and extending from the heart of Africa to its eastern shores [and] the gigantic progress in the task of self-elevating already achieved by the Negroes of the United States," Thomas wanted to address the "noteworthy efforts of the Blacks in Sierra Leone." Apart from the letter's "high literary merits," Thomas admired the "unprescriptiveness and thorough freedom of intellectual movement," its "serene candour," and its lack of both "truculent envy of the more fortunate race" and "parrot-shrieking of truths trite to everybody." There was no "purblind beating about the bush, while the point to come at stands saliently and clearly before the intellectual eye," nothing to violate "the proprieties," and no "vagueness and circumlocution—the coward's refuge, the dunce's vice."

"On my own behalf and that of all Negroes," Thomas thanked Blyden for his admission that Black people could not afford "to decline foreign assistance." It was "fatal" to "rebel against this law of international borrowing," and history had demonstrated that "Greece borrowed letters and science from Phoenicia and Egypt; Rome, intellectual culture from Greece; and all the nations of civilized Europe are debtors to Rome on similar grounds." Equating "national" and "racial" categories, Thomas noted that the letter revealed the "movement now in progress for infusing a national sentiment or, as the writer terms it, a race-feeling, into the minds of the juvenile Negroes of Sierra Leone." "In truth," he stated, "there is no more serious question in connexion with our ultimate position among the nations than this question of the higher education of our offspring." This "miscegenetic training" induced "moral flunkeyism" and was responsible for "the guilty reticence with which, year after year, we sneak through the twenty-four significant hours of the first of August, which should have been the great commemoration day, the Passover, for us, the Israelites of the Antilles."

Though it was true that "in Trinidad, as compared with many other countries in which Negroes exist, the conditions are somewhat unfavourable to the existence of the race-feeling," it was better to ignore such feeling entirely than to be apologetic about it. Various conditions accounted for development of race-feeling: "consistent oppression" such as the "Brethren of the United States" faced; "autonomic advantages," as in Liberia and Haiti; and "the beneficent action of official appreciation and support," as in Sierra Leone. If "the Negroes of the West Indies" could appreciate the "significance of the relative position of their race in respect of contemporary nations," it would be a "triumph for the cause of human progress."

Until Trinidadians "attained, like our friends in Sierra Leone, the means of influencing our children, as they are now striving to do theirs," they must patiently work toward that end and congratulate them. For Thomas, Trinidad's lack of overwhelming percentages of people of African descent, as in West Africa and Haiti, or of conditions of extreme oppression, as in the United States, were not reasons to dispense with a "race-feeling."

This flew in the face of appeals to Trinidadian exceptionalism, as when, as we shall see in chapter 4, requests for an official celebration of the jubilee celebration of Emancipation were turned down in 1888 because Trinidad's non-immigrant population of African descent was not substantial enough.

Interestingly, Thomas's reference to "international borrowing" resonates with his desire that Trinidad's students not learn the classics without a thorough grounding in Greek and Roman history. This historical context rendered normal Black people's attempts to "catch up" since all the great empires had borrowed from others. Similarly, Blyden's reference here to the labors of Sisyphus echoes his letter to Gladstone some years earlier. Here, that Black people in West Africa could not be Europeanized is not presented as a deficiency. Europe supplements rather than displaces their efforts.

In April 1885 Philip Rostant reviewed a concert held in Port of Spain on 22 March to raise funds for the African Methodist Episcopal (AME) Church, whose bishops were shortly to visit from Canada.[17] Noting that open-air meetings held in that city a few months earlier had been under the auspices of the *British* Methodist Episcopal Church, Rostant implied that the change from *British* to *African* had been a shrewd way to attract a larger audience since 150 persons had paid one shilling apiece to attend. Rostant did not know whether this was the average attendance for this group "or if people came to see a female lecturer, which is why we went." He condemned the event as "openly and avowedly a class meeting, intended to revive among us feelings and prejudices which exist less in this country than in any of the other colonies where slavery formerly prevailed, and which as a consequence of the rapid progress of education, must sooner or later die out if not kept alive by such *lectures* as the one pronounced by Mrs. Riep at the meeting."

Rostant chastised the chairman of the evening's proceedings for failing to "keep the lady within moderate bounds" and scoffed at the lecture's references to the two opposing purities of race, in which she used coffee and milk as examples, and to the "vain ambition caused by ignoring the maternal relationship (Africa) for the paternal (Europe)."

"We do not wish to be hard on a lady lecturer," Rostant asserted, and he was sure that the organizer of what was a "quasi-religious meeting," opened with prayer, could not have known "to what length this impulsive lady was prepared to go" in using "language which may be adapted to the readers of Zola, but was certainly too realistic for an audience composed in a great measure of young girls," and "openly pooh-pooh[ing] the idea that St. Paul, the great apostle of the Gentiles, was competent to give an opinion on the demeanour that is befitting to women in Church matters." But if the AME Church wanted "to sow disunion of discord, it will have no success among the well thinking portion of our people."

A letter from "Impartiality" in the *San Fernando Gazette* two weeks later accused Rostant of misrepresenting the AME Church to the public.[18] Noting that an announcement in the *New Era* the previous year had set out clearly the relationship between the BME and AME branches of the organization, the letter "allowed" that "a national feeling was evinced and observed by the meeting for the moral, social and political elevation of the African race." But "Impartiality" denied that those gathered had been reviving prejudices, since this implied that none currently existed in Trinidad and that everyone was content. He allowed that the lecturer was "terse, blunt, appropriate, forceful and truthful" and that this had thus been "unpleasant to the *would-be* European taste." No young girls had found it "indelicate," and, knowing Zola, the writer expressed surprise that "a professed gentleman" would insult a lady thus, since there had been nothing "indecent" about her language. The participants owed Rostant a debt for "the notoriety and prominence he has given us and our cause, eliciting sympathies latent in the bosom of the coloured people of this Island."

Edgar Maresse-Smith admonished Rostant in that issue. In an earlier letter, predating Rostant's notice, he had reviewed the event's "literary treats," finding the lecture to be particularly good.[19] He had noted then that his perspective was not religious. Rather, "my standpoint is that of a person who, having African blood flowing in his veins, and not being, like many others, ashamed of the land of his mother, looks with pride and satisfaction upon any success achieved by those who, in common with him, are descendants of Africans." In his letter of 25 April he noted that Rostant's review referred to a Mr. Smith who took part in the proceedings, even though none did, to make it appear that Maresse-Smith's earlier favorable review had been written from the biased perspective of a participant. Mrs. Riep, Maresse-Smith declared, was "a lady whose intelligence and talents place her on a pedestal of respect, there being so few ladies in the whole Island, who can boast of equal abilities." Anyone familiar with "the crude style" of Zola's *Nana* or *Pot-Bouille* "would readily understand all the injury which such a comparison carries with it."

Commenting on Rostant's reference to the "quasi-religious" nature of the evening, which had supposedly been violated, Maresse-Smith noted that "priestly influence" was "so much on the wane" that the Church had to make "large concessions to the increasing intelligence of the age." Although the Roman Catholic Church condemned the stage and theatergoers, that church was now "compelled to eat her own words" since "purely religious meetings [were] unproductive."

Turning to Rostant personally, Maresse-Smith noted that he had attended the event and heard things "that did not please his aristocratic ears for he is above everything an aristocrat." Rostant was sensitive in matters of race because "in defiance of his crisped hair and the copper color of his skin," he had "elected to be a white man": "harmless folly if Mr. Rostant would persuade himself of his béquéism and allow others to think as they please. But he finds that he dupes no one and therefore falls into convulsions as soon as the word 'African' is pronounced within his hearing, for fear that a hyphen will be gleaned between himself and the detestable African race. Hence Mr. Rostant's overflow of fury at poor Miss Riep."

A performance sponsored by the North American–based AME, then, provided an occasion to "out" Rostant as a mere would-be *béqué* (White) and for Maresse-Smith to assert himself, a Mulatto, as a proud Afro-Trinidadian who had joined with others to assert the validity of "class feelings" in Trinidad. In the process, the conservatism of the Catholic Church was publicly noted, and the role of "immodest" women in the public sphere was both condemned and lauded.

Finally, the following exhortations from a Jamaican editor in 1895 stress the interplay of diasporic and "local" contexts, in this case the education of women:

> The race rises as its women rise. They are the true standard of its elevation. We are trying to produce cultured men without asking ourselves where they are to find cultured wives. We forget that cultured families constitute a cultured race and that a cultured race is an equal race. The elevation of women to equality with [their] white counterparts is the Condition *Sine Qua Non* of the elevation of the Negro race.
>
> Every pound spent to educate the black boy tends to elevate a class only, but every pound spent to educate a black girl, tends to elevate the whole race. Fathers and mothers, bear these facts in mind, and send as many of your black daughters to England as you can. Some tell you that your girls can be just as well educated here. Ask them, why then do they send theirs to England.[20]

Here, women are crucial to the project of enabling the race to stand "shoulder to shoulder" with other cultured races, just as Mrs. Riep did in Trinidad and Mrs. Harper did in North America. This is why, for instance, Thomas was so alarmed at their absence from Grenadian lecture halls. Their intellectual capital was to be invested in the domestic sphere, their "culture" and respectability confirming that of their husbands, families, and all people of African descent.

To properly "read" the quotation it would be necessary to know what specific conversations were going on in Jamaica in the 1890s, just as Trinidad had its own local contexts and other territories had theirs. When the *Grenada People,* W. G. Donovan's newspaper, noted with pleasure on 13 July 1887 that Mr. J. J. Pierre of Snug Corner was doing the "unthinkable" for Black Grenadians by sending his eldest daughter to school in England, the paper noted that Black children in that territory felt themselves to be inferior to the children of Whites and of "yellow negroes" and that it was not unusual for Trinidadians to send their Black daughters abroad to be educated. This use of Trinidad as a standard reminds us that compared with the European visits of families of propertied Coloreds, Whites, and Blacks, Thomas's visits to Europe were unusual only in their brevity. Indeed, Yseult Guppy Bridges noted that it was only during their essential finishing year in England that White Trinidadian girls would "have a chance to eradicate the insidious singsong Creole accent and [acquire] poise and complexion" (157).

Sending one's daughters to England, then, had several layers of meaning and positioned such travelers in a range of relationships to the British Isles and to their "local" contexts. For Robert Love, the editor of the *Jamaica Advocate,* no doubt, education in England would enable this girl to be a better Black daughter, a better Caribbean daughter, when she returned. Sending these daughters to England was proposed, not with the intention of enriching English institutions, but with the hope of improving the prospects of the global Black transnation, as well as of the specific territory.

3 Can Anything Good Come out of Cedros?

Creole Grammar, Theory and Practice

At Cedros, thudding the dead sand
in spasms, the tarpon
gaped with a gold eye, drowned
thickly, thrashing with brute pain
this sea I breathe.
　　　　—Derek Walcott, "Tarpon"

ON THE OCCASION of the reissue of his *Creole Grammar* in the late 1880s Thomas explained how he, "then only an obscure young teacher in a remote district of this out-of-the-way dependency of Great Britain," had come to write the *Creole Grammar:*

> The thing, like most notable facts in human affairs, was the outcome of a very simple incident. In fact, it sprang out of my having paid a visit to a sick friend—the Rev. J. W. Mathews—who, together with his entire household, consisting of five persons, was writhing in the purgatorial agonies of the redoubtable "Cedros Fever." A native of Barbados, proficient in classics, and other branches of the then so-called "liberal" education, Mr. Mathews was, as often happened with scholars with reference to modern languages at that period, utterly helpless as regarded the French, which, as a matter of fact, he had never heard spoken nor even looked at in books. What, then, must have been his plight with regard to unliterary Creole, after only a few weeks' sojourn amongst people who spoke that alone! On the occasion of my calling, as above stated, to see the poor fever-stricken family I found the reverend patient utterly distracted at his inability to make his own wants and those of the other sufferers in the house understood by the only servant they had—a Cedros girl who knew not one syllable of English! Mr. Mathews, in course of a conversation between us on the subject, expressed his astonishment that not a grammatical text-book, nor even a vocabulary, existed for helping strangers in the matter of understanding and of making themselves understood by, the mass of the population

who spoke the patois exclusively. Nor was my own wonder less than his on witnessing, as I then did, not only the inconvenience but the positive danger of that state of things. As the matter was one which fell within the scope of my regular private studies, I resolved then and there to attempt supplying this glaring need.[1]

Here are the "labors" of being posted in Cedros. The diligent schoolmaster and the learned Barbadian clergyman are like minds in the unlettered "purgatory" of a posting on the southwestern coast, many times removed from a civilized center.[2] A "remote district" in an "out-of-the-way dependency" (recalling Borde's reference to his own double disadvantage, "unskilled and inexperienced to write a history, be it that of the smallest and most remote corner of the earth"), Cedros offers fever, isolation, and Creole speech. This is what it means to be posted there. Classically trained though he may be, Rev. Mathews (Black? Colored? White?) is lost in Cedros. His "liberal" education, which Thomas may be gently mocking here as inadequate to the needs of the region, has left him without a mastery of French. Though French would not solve all of his problems in a place where only "unliterary Creole" is spoken, he would certainly not feel as completely adrift as he does—an anglophone Barbadian in a francophone world.[3]

In one sense, then, an implied hegemonic power is accorded to Creole since even elites proficient in the classics are helpless without it. No amount of formal education will help them if they do not know the language. On the other hand, Creole speakers are not represented here as powerful or even competent. Their speech is "unliterary," and they speak *only* Creole. The "Cedros girl" is defined in terms of her *lack* of English rather than in terms of her mastery of the language spoken by "the mass of the population." This is not the only time that a "Cedros girl" will give Thomas an occasion to think about the boundaries and rules implied by a grammar. Perhaps linguistic and moral chaos is best embodied in females who are ill-spoken or who speak out of turn. Thomas, as master of both English and Creole, will be the mediator between the foreign clergyman's family and the local woman who serves them. His grammar will make the language comprehensible to churchmen and others, bringing light where there is darkness and order where there is chaos. It will cure the Cedros fever.

As the interaction between Thomas and Mathews indicates, the translation facilitated by a grammar is made necessary by the presence of "outsiders," though these may include persons who are familiar with Creole speech, as we will see. This is a collaboration of elites, one in the know and one not, but both marked by their distance from "unliterary" Creole speakers. Those among whom they labor, bringing religious, moral, and intellectual light, can hardly appreciate their efforts and will have no need of a grammar. Thomas, engaged in "regular private studies" at night in addition to laboring in the schoolroom by day, will write a grammar explaining Creole's tenses and conjugating its verbs even as he is mastering the Greek and Latin in which his Barbadian colleague is proficient, and which Woodbrook has denied him.

Rev. Mathews's predicament is only one of the reasons Thomas gives for deciding to write the text. We shall see how his *Grammar* participates in a rich and noisy grammatical context in which verbs, racial types, and morals are endlessly conjugated. In making sense out of chaos Thomas captures and even honors this noise, but he also helps to regulate and reduce it. Just as the contours of Creole language and identity are demarcated by Thomas and others, places such as Cedros are deemed insignificant. The energy and violence of Cedros's waters, teeming with Walcott's silver tarpon, are modalities that are unfathomable to both scholars, perhaps exemplifying the nonliterate discourses that Wilson Harris contends still need to be unearthed in the process of comprehending the region's history and society.[4] The Cedros of Thomas's and Rev. Mathews's imaginations is a swampy purgatory far from the libraries and debating societies of Port of Spain and San Fernando rather than the continental gateway for mainland Warahoun Amerindians making their yearly pilgrimages to Trinidad's interior.

THOMAS'S PREFATORY remarks in the *Creole Grammar* make clear his concern that members of Trinidad's working class were being rendered voiceless by legal and religious institutions. Creole speakers were at a disadvantage in the churches, where Mass was conducted in French, and even "the best interpreters" in the courtroom, he pointed out, produced imperfect translations because of "the prevalence of the opinion that Creole is *only* mispronounced French" (iv).[5] Working at night for almost three years, he painstakingly recorded the proverbs and songs that he heard all around him.[6] Creole speakers and the French dictionary were his two sources of reference for his research: "As regards French, I had but a few school-grammars and two third-rate dictionaries, at whose mercy I stood for everything not within my previous knowledge. . . . I labored almost unceasingly at my task; sometimes threading my way with confidence, frequently having to condemn or re-write whole pages, which a chance remark of a passer-by or closer inquiry had proved erroneous" (v).

Here was a laborer who was dependent upon the passerby as the primary source for the validity of his conclusions, in one sense indicating the integrity of his methods and in another confirming his vulnerability: does the "chance remark" cover all possible errors, and might it not be a remark typical only of Cedros and not of the rest of Trinidad? But Thomas was also well aware of the hierarchies governing his field of inquiry: some grammars and dictionaries were for *students* rather than for scholars, and some were even worse: "third-rate."

Gertrude Aub-Buscher notes that Thomas's text is truly one of its time, "influenced . . . by methods more applicable to the highly inflected classical languages" and generally tending "to explain Creole forms too much from the point of view of French."[7] Yet Thomas himself indicates the limitation of an undue focus on French. After pointing out that the use of certain French past participles would render a sentence unintelligible to the Creole speaker and also bring scorn on the speaker for being "too Frenchified in his *patois*," Thomas notes: "Whosoever condescends to talk Creole, must, for the while, forget his French, and believe (for it is a fact) that he is using a dialect fully capable of expressing all ordinary thoughts, provided the speaker is master of, and understands how to manage, its resources" (104–5).

The grammar is divided into sections titled "Orthoëpy and Orthography," "Etymology," "Syntax," and "Interpretation—Idioms," yet only the first three sections answer to the project of a grammar, strictly speaking: "The composition of its vocabulary as a whole, the accidents of its individual words, and their arrangement into sentences" (113). Thomas promises not to "abuse" the "indulgence" of the reader if the fourth section exceeds "the limits of our present undertaking, which is a grammar and not a dictionary," an excess made necessary by both "the peculiar nature of the subject, and the fact that there is, as yet, no work devoted to the exposition of the patois—of this Island at least" (113). Thomas compares French and Creole words "in order that some notion may be formed of the divergence of the Creole from the French with regard to the import and use of individual words" (113). In addition, to indicate "the extreme fancifulness" of Creole idiomatic expressions and the consequent difficulty in interpretation, he gives the Creole text, the literal translation in Standard English, and then the corresponding idiomatic expression in Standard English. Clearly, then, he is interested in definitions and etymologies, as well as in how these words operate in the culture at large.

The idioms are followed by proverbs, rendered in Creole and then in English, and the list includes "some which are not current here," which presumably means that Thomas took them from the wider francophone region. The learned commentaries following each group of proverbs are pointedly moralistic, befitting the genre of the grammar, though in its race vindication Thomas's text exceeds precise generic and functional boundaries. "Ravette pas jamain tnî raison douvant poule" is translated as "Cockroach never is in the right where the fowl is concerned" and is followed by this commentary: "The reign of injustice, during which the insect symbolised the Negro, and the bird, his oppressor, is slowly passing away. There is now some chance for the roach, and day by day he is vindicating his claim to a little more" (127).[8] Some definitions also seem personal. "Faut paouôles môr poû mounes pé vive" is marked with an asterisk, indicating that it is not "current" in Trinidad, and is translated as "Words must die that men may live" (126). Thomas's commentary here—"Very short will be the earthly existence of a person who does not allow slander to die a natural death, but fumes and frets at every thing said against him"—would seem to be the perfect weapon for an enemy to direct against him. Rostant and others would have agreed that he "fumed and fretted" at every slight. Was Thomas conceding that the inevitable price was a short life?

Not a quaint, coffee-table text, then, Thomas's grammar vindicates the roach, who is increasingly coming into "his" own. The "truthful and ingenious" proverbs indicate that "everything in Nature symbolises to the Negro something in man or man's affairs . . . worth volumes of comments and labored definitions," though "the unlaboured proverb is, generally, the truest and most significant" (120). Thomas deems proverbs an important "insight into the mental habits and capabilities of the people who invent them." They are "the ornament of African discourse," "instruct[ing] and delight[ing] the Negro race in all ages and stages of its existence. . . . We prize them as beautiful no less than intelligent deductions from the teachings of Nature, that free, infallible, and sublime volume, which Providence has displayed to all men, but more distinctly to those who have no other revelation and guidance" (120). The Creole speakers whom he shows to be founts of philosophy and wisdom "have no other revelation and guidance." Here, Negroes are more receptive than others to the divine revelations of Nature, but they are thereby lacking in more secular sources of wisdom. In this sense Thomas is the roach's defender in the face of the fowl, as his own definitions labor the proverbs into significance.

The *Creole Grammar* concludes with translations of various kinds of canonical texts into Creole. Thomas "paraphrases, more or less free[ly]," the fables of Perrin, Aesop, and La Fontaine, "a sample of Haytian, by

M. l'Hérisson, surnamed the Béranger of Hayti" (128), and Jesus's encounter at the well with a woman of questionable morals and ethnicity in the Gospel of St. John. As Thomas explains, the Creole version is translated closely from the Latin, and he also consulted the Greek text. Each passage appears in the *Creole Grammar* in three renderings, Creole, French, and English. Thomas points out the accommodations he makes both for Creole limitations—"answered and said" are rendered as "made for answer" or "answered," as in "Jésis fair li poû la réponse" or "Jésis répône li"—and for English and French limitations: "In the 12th verse, we begin the woman's question with *die moén*, 'tell me,' for which there is no equivalent in the English nor French translation; but we think it answers to the interrogatory particle in the original, which is represented in the Latin version by *num*" (128). Thomas thus demonstrates the ability of the Creole language to handle biblical, Greek and French "classics."[9]

"We should have invited the reader's attention," Thomas begins the section on proverbs, "to the beautiful sayings which form the ornament of African discourse; but neither our space nor our present limited knowledge will allow our writing a formal dissertation on the subject. We trust, however, to be able to do so at some future period" (120). It is not clear whether Thomas is referring here to his own future plans for studying proverbs in African languages, but he notes the importance of this particular parent in the project of establishing the character and sources of the Creole language, as well as his own linguistic inadequacy at that point in time. In this sense the *Grammar* is provisional. It also clearly plays a role in "fixing the birthplace" of Creole texts, as well as national and racial ones:

> Even among the few [Creole Proverbs] we shall cite, there may . . . be some which are mere translations of French, English, or Spanish originals. . . . We have been much hampered in our choice by the ever-present consciousness of the extreme difficulty of fixing the birth-place of a saying, especially when we find its parallel in so many different languages. Nevertheless, after deducting from our proverbs those of whose foreign extraction the acute reader is certain, enough will yet remain to prove that the Africans are not after all, the dolts and intellectual sucklings that some would have the world believe them. (120–21)

Underlining Thomas's contention that Creole is not merely mispronounced French, the pure substance that remains after the "foreign extraction" has been weeded out will demonstrate the intellectual capacity of the race. "Mere translations" of "originals" from elsewhere cannot suffice. By this reckoning, "French," "Spanish," "English," and "African" are distinct, albeit parallel and overlapping; they are translatable into one another, for example. With the *Grammar*, Thomas "fixes" Creole as powerfully marked by an African provenance and significant and valuable because of this. He also proffers an idea of languages as being singular, knowable, and representing distinct sources even if one has to work hard to demonstrate this. "Fixing a birthplace" secures the place of "African" "originals," repudiating those who would claim that only French, Spanish, and English qualify as original and worthy sources. "Fixing a birthplace" would also seem to leave little or no place for those words, proverbs, and concepts that are neither French, Spanish, English, nor African (Amerindian and East Indian, for instance) or are not clearly traceable to one recognizable source.

But what of the African source that Thomas promises to be able to say more about in the future? Besides taking Thomas to task for giving the incorrect sources of some Creole lexical items, as well as for missing the scatological meanings of some words, the *Spectator* reviewer of the *Creole Grammar* referred to at the beginning of chapter 2 noted his failure to account for African etymologies: "What is still more to be regretted is that he seems to have taken no trouble whatever to separate the pure African element, or to trace one single word to a specific African source."[10] Here, a metropolitan reviewer was chiding "one of her Majesty's Ethiopic subjects" for leaving out the "African source" even while confirming Thomas's assumptions about purity and specificity.

By Thomas's own account two decades later in *Froudacity*, he had been "familiar since childhood with members from every tribe in Africa" (142), yet such familiarity did not guarantee him the means to trace African etymologies in the way in which he indicates he traced French ones, that is, with "a few school-grammars and two third-rate dictionaries." Third-rate or not, grammars and dictionaries were "legitimate" sources of philological inquiry, whereas oral interviews with African-born Trinidadians were not, though it is entirely possible that lack of time and resources, rather than disparagement of such oral sources, prevented Thomas from pursuing this line of research. In any case, the distinction between "Creole" and "African" cultural spheres within the Caribbean may have led to a general discounting of the specific impact of the various African languages on Creole speech. That is, the languages of African-born persons entering Trinidad after a certain period would have been deemed completely separate from a Creole language whose features were considered to have been stabilized under specific conditions by the late eighteenth century.

Even if we assume that tracing Yoruba, Arada, or other etymologies *in the Caribbean* (as opposed to within the African continent) would have been considered to be "intellectual" or contributing to the store of what counted as legitimate "knowledge," it is not clear what Thomas's chances of tracing the African influences on Creole speech (those predating the arrival of African immigrants in the mid-nineteenth century) would have been. During slavery, the manner of controlling Africans was not uniform across the Caribbean (Cuba encouraged ethnic African solidarity in order to stave off racial solidarity, for instance), but in many territories there were penalties for using African names, languages, and musical instruments. While African languages *qua* African languages existed in the Caribbean, therefore, particularly where there were recent immigrants (or, in the case of Cuba, new arrivals of slaves), African words and phrases existed in religious ceremonies and folk songs or as a subterranean presence under the syllables and syntaxes of other languages spoken in the region, occurring in their interstices, to be read "between the lines," their impact registered as a resounding absence in the colonial dictionary: "origin unknown."[11]

Perhaps no less surprising than the difficulty or inability of a Caribbean linguist of African descent to trace the specific and multiple African "birthplaces" of Trinidadian Creole in a manner that would have satisfied the *Spectator* reviewer was the familiarity of European philologists and missionaries with these languages. A glance at the proceedings of the Philological Society meetings for the year in which Thomas presented his paper in London indicates interesting proof of this metropolitan familiarity. For April 1873, there is a record of the receipt of a letter from W. H. I. Bleek, author of a comparative grammar of South African Bantu languages: "For more than two years we have been hard at work studying the Bushman language from the mouths of two natives, who are, for a time, staying in my house. . . . A dictionary has been commenced; and the grammar becomes gradually more and more clear to us." (Bleek, 186–87 n. 1).

Though the methods here recall Thomas's (laboring to overhear the speakers of Cedros), Thomas is perhaps more native informant than colleague of Bleek and company. His invitation to address the Philological Society represented his recognition by the metropole, his reward for attempting to use the strategies of classification and containment on which they were the experts. In this sense his *Creole Grammar* assisted them to collect more efficiently. An announcement in the *Trinidad Review* of 22 November 1883, entitled "Creole and Creoloid Dialects" requested "written specimens" for a publication "dealing with Creole and Creoloid idioms" by Professor Hugo Schuchardt, of the Imperial Academy in Gräz,

Austria, and noted that "Mr. J. J. Thomas, whose services have been enlisted for that interesting work," would act as a liaison for anyone wishing to send material to him. Both this announcement and the letter quoted at the beginning of this chapter noted that Schuchardt had become acquainted with the "Creole French" of Trinidad and other Caribbean territories through Thomas's *Grammar*. According to Derek Bickerton, "Although the languages he worked on range around the globe, Schuchardt never left Europe—all his information on pidgins and creoles was derived either from the work of others or from a voluminous correspondence he kept up with denizens of the tropics" (viii; see also Schuchardt, 90).

Thomas was a "denizen of the tropics," one of Schuchardt's native informants, doing the groundwork that would then be theorized by scholars such as Schuchardt or the members of the Philological Society. On one level, then, the *Creole Grammar* was inseparable from the project of civilizing "native sounds" into intelligible discourses for the consumption of European scholars. Not unlike the genre that he challenged in *Froudacity*, grammars and travelogues alike functioned as guidebooks for travelers or for those who, like Schuchardt, stayed at home. Such guides sought to bring oral discourses into "harmonious compatibility" with written European languages, promising "the uncanny return to familiar surroundings" after the fear of the unknown represented by African and Creole languages (Woodward).

In another sense, Thomas's research enabled Schuchardt and others to extend their linguistic investigations, and he was recognized as an authority on the region. The librarian of Yale College, in New Haven, Connecticut, noted that one of the sources for his research on Creole grammar was Thomas's *Grammar,* "the most extended and valuable work on the grammar of the [Trinidadian] language."[12] Prestigious philologists with access to institutions and resources mined Thomas's work for examples for their own large-scale, comparative projects at the same time that he was receiving "pleasant notice" internationally.

By November 1870, a little over a year after the publication of the *Creole Grammar,* evidence of Thomas's further research appeared in the form of an essay that he sent to *Trübner's American and Oriental Literary Record:* "We have been favoured by Mr. J. J. Thomas with the following extracts from a very curious Essay."[13] Noting that Creole is spoken "not only by the Negroes and the coloured people, but also by most of the white natives of Hayti, St. Bartholomew, Guadeloupe, Deseada, Dominica, Martinique, St. Lucia, St. Vincent, the Grenadines, Grenada, Tobago (in one district only), and Trinidad," Thomas posits that while "the general

structure and grammar" are "identical . . . in almost every island it presents certain peculiarities of detail, arising chiefly from local influences,
whereby the nationality of any one speaking it may at once be determined."
Here is a wider regional context for Creole, then, which nevertheless continues to allow for "fixing birthplaces" according to "nationality."

Thomas then addresses the issue that he had regretted saying so little
about the preceding year: "With regard to the Creole spoken in Hayti, it
appears to contain more of the African element than that of any other
island: a circumstance not to be wondered at, considering the history of
Hayti. . . . An important and very curious question, which remains as yet
undetermined, is the extent and nature of the modifying influence which
the idioms of Africa had on the formation and characteristics of the
Creole." Noting that there could be "no reasonable doubt" about "the
operation of such influence," because of the "origination of the Creole by
Africans," he proposed the further factor of "the striking analogy of form
and grammatical construction presented by the Negro-English or *Bouriki,*
as compared with the Negro-French [French Creole]. The Verb being the
vital element in all languages, we shall give a few illustrations from that
source, leaving the inference to the judgment of the reader."

One of Thomas's examples of this relationship between Bouriki and
Creole French is the use of the prefix *ca* (Creole) or *da* (Bouriki) with the
(French or English) infinitive to form the present tense. He concludes:

> Putting together these and a hundred other coincidences of a similar nature
> observable in dialects derived from languages so different in grammatical
> structure, we can see no other way of accounting for these peculiarities, save
> by supposing them to have sprung from a common source, foreign to and inde-
> pendent of the direct original of either dialect. There seems to be wanting but
> little evidence more to prove the existence of a dominant African language,
> bearing to the dialects whose peculiarities characterize the Creole, a relation
> similar to that borne by Sanskrit to the Indo-European languages, or less
> remotely, the relation which the Latin bears to the Romance dialects. We may
> suppose the existence in this stock-language of some verbal particle analogous
> to *ca* and *da,* and also of some verb of identical force with the past participle of
> the substantive verb.

Notwithstanding his critics—Van Name, the Connecticut librarian,
found it "improbable" that items playing such a crucial role in Creole
vocabulary should be traced to an African root, offering the French
quand or *comme* as more plausible sources for *ca* (144–45)—Thomas
pursues here a conception of Caribbean Creoles that ties them to each

other as closely as, or even more so than, what ties each Creole to English and French. This conception is in tension with another of his assertions about Creole languages: that they are derivations of an originary European language. Both ideas come together in the passage above: certain features of Creole languages suggest that they have "a common source, foreign to and independent of the direct original of either dialect." The "original," that is, French or English, is thwarted by and attempts to tame the "foreign and independent."[14]

Thomas offers a notion of Creole that stresses its Negro character; he states that "a dominant African language" accounts for many of its most significant features. This "African element" varies from territory to territory, as do various other features of Creole. Caribbean Creoles have crucial similarities but are also distinguishable from one another by the European languages that provide their respective vocabularies. All territories where "Negro-French" is spoken share basic grammatical features yet differ discernibly in "certain peculiarities of detail." In addition, Creole is spoken by "Negroes," "coloured people," and "most of the white natives" of each of these territories. Here, the Creole language is a trope for identities that coalesce, dissolve along, or cut across lines of nationality, region, race, or "origin" ("French," "English," "African").

In the 1870 *Trübner* piece we can see how the 1869 *Creole Grammar* is the Trinidadian component of a wide-ranging, regional project of Thomas's that considers the relation of Trinidadian Creole not only to the Creole spoken in other territories with a history of francophone settlement but to that of anglophone territories as well. Thomas's inclusion in this periodical suggests the transatlantic character of metropolitan philological and intellectual discourses, which encompass "American and Oriental" (evidenced in the full title of the periodical, *Trübner's American and Oriental Literary Record*). Both the reference to his "curious essay" and the poem by Bret Harte entitled "The Heathen Chinee: A Specimen of Californian Humour," appearing on the same page as Thomas's excerpt, remind us of the dual promise and danger of an international readership.

Thomas's excerpted essay concludes with a list of works published in Creole in francophone territories, including two on Mauritius Creole.[15] He notes that there are "many amusing productions written on passing events, and for local circulation in the different West Indian Islands. A judicious collection of these, with proper editing, would not be labour thrown away." They include religious catechism,[16] along with what he terms the "the classic works of the Creole dialect": M. M. Marbot's "travestie of La Fontaine's Fables," *Les bambous* (Martinique, 1846),

M. L'Hérisson's (Haitian) *Poémes creoles,* and F. Chrestien's *Les essais d'un bobre africain* (Mauritius, 1831). Several of his examples come from Trinidad, including two religious texts by H. L. Jobity (a farewell to Archbishop Spaccapietra in the 1850s and Creole proverbs compiled for the pope), an anonymous satire of Governor Eliot in 1853, and *"Maman moén vlé mâüer (Mother, I wish to marry),* a very diverting song; in fact, a comic master-piece, by Syl. Devenish, who in this department of literary work, stands unapproachable among our native Trinidadians (MS, 1867)."

Here are Thomas's predecessors and contemporaries. Many are Europeans or White Creoles, and their texts are an indication of the occasions for publishing in Creole: a religious catechism, adaptations of La Fontaine, addresses to Catholic officials, and satires of British officials. Significantly, Thomas refers to the Haitian (and probably Black) writer François Romain L'Hérisson, as well as to François Chrestien, the Mauritian writer of *Les essais d'un bobre africain,* written in the manner of La Fontaine. The *bobre* provided the mournful string accompaniment in traditional Mauritian *sega* music. Either these two writers and texts were recognized in the francophone world as "classics" or Thomas was establishing them as such. The list not only gives us an idea of the texts to which Thomas had access when he was writing his *Creole Grammar* but also indicates an audience for his text comprising persons who were familiar with Creole texts and whose authority to judge him he must have felt very keenly. Indeed, the *Spectator* reviewer of Thomas's *Grammar* notes Thomas's ignorance of Marbot's *Les bambous,* published anonymously in Martinique, "but known to be from the pen of a very able French official born in the island."[17] Furthermore, this reviewer continues, not only does Thomas's limited knowledge of Spanish account for his erroneous derivation of *blankite* (a term of scorn for a light-skinned person) from *blanket* instead of from the Spanish *blanquita,* "little white," but even his French is faulty, as when he conjugates *aller* with *avoir* instead of with *être.*

A reviewer in the *Anti-Slavery Reporter* noted that the *Grammar* was "remarkable as a literary effort" because its author's race showed the "natural capacity of the negro for purely intellectual pursuits" and because a "self-educated man, deprived of book-help," could not know what had been "already written upon the science of languages."[18] Creole was no patois, as Thomas claimed, since "any so-called patois traced to its origin, is the fountain-head of the language of which it is alleged to be a variation of a corruption." Rather, Trinidadian Creole was "an obvious corruption of two or more foreign tongues." Furthermore, Thomas failed to account for the fact that the "modern French" sanctioned by the French Academy was different from the "provincialisms" existing all over France. Thus, the examples of "'patois,' or Creole tongue," were "nothing more when analyzed than corruptions of French or of Spanish" that Thomas was "elevating" to "a real language."

Reviewers also indicated prevailing conceptions of the connections between Creole speech and female sexuality. The *Spectator* reviewer recalled "darkened rooms behind unglazed lattices" and "dames plump of form, and luxuriating in that easiest of dresses, the cinctureless *gaule* or long white dressing-gown," noting that the surest way to the "good graces" of an "old French West Indian lady" was to "talk Creole with her." This echoed the entry for *Creole* in the Larousse dictionary, published the same year as the *Grammar:* "A corrupted French in which several Spanish and Gallicized words are mixed, [Creole], often unintelligible when spoken by an old African, is extremely sweet when spoken by white Creole women."[19] Whitened and feminized, Creole speech provides the singsong backdrop to the leisure hours of White males in the Caribbean. Creole was not linked only to White women's bodies, of course; we have seen that Yseult Guppy Bridges recalled Black *marchands* on her verandah. Furthermore, although Thomas does not make these sorts of connections in the *Grammar,* as we shall see in chapter 4, "fascinating daughters of the sun" who helped to relieve governors and other officials of the "tension and wear of official duty" are brought into play in *Froudacity* (188). For these male commentators, women's bodies were constructed as a powerful site of Creole authenticity.

For the *Spectator* reviewer, Thomas's attempt to politicize the Creole language is commendable since his Black Creole informants are "a shrewd and observant race, not without depth of insight." But if the proverb "Words must die that men may live" recalls the silence forced upon slaves, it also anticipates the fate of Creole: "With the advance of education it is losing itself again in French, it is retreating before English. Within the next century, probably, Mr. Thomas's work will only be a literary gravestone, commemorating its existence." Thomas clearly disagreed with this conception.

In his preface to the *Creole Grammar* Thomas notes that he had "no other materials than a collection which I had made of *bellairs, calendas, joubas,* idioms, odd sayings, in fact, everything that I could get in Creole" (v). The dances known as *bellairs* (or *Bel Airs* or *bèlès*), *calendas* (or *kalindas*), and *joubas* (or *jhoubas, jubas,* or *gioubas*) were dance and musical events that were central features of Black working-class life. Varying in details of choreography, occasion, dress, and instrumentation from period to period, as well as from territory to territory across a francophone zone stretching to New Orleans, these songs and dances were alternately condemned as reprehensible and defended as quaint by elite observers.[20] Thomas indicated that this "noise" was a rich source of the words and meanings he mined for his research. Quite possibly he attended these events in Cedros and in Port of Spain: Donald Wood notes that in the process of trying to get them transcribed Thomas lost a valuable collection of Creole folk songs that he had gathered in Cedros ("John Jacob Thomas," 16). Here, then, is another source for his research on Creole speech, which Thomas posits as being equally as valid as the written Creole texts of his White compatriots.

The *Spectator* reviewer faults Thomas for missing the scatological references of the idioms and proverbs he interprets; this is because Thomas is at pains to show that the "Negro" character of the Creole language he presents is *respectable*. There may be a pedantic, "labored" heaviness to the proverbs Thomas glosses in the *Grammar*: "*Qui méler zéfs nans calenda ouôches?* What business have eggs in the dance of stones? This is to meddlers in matters they know nothing about; to men eager after, and moving in, society which they cannot enjoy without injury or self-abasement; in short, to all who, through their own folly are, and suffer for being, where they ought not to have intruded" (126). But there is surely nothing respectable about the following obeah-related terms: "*Yon nômme simpe.* A simple man. A man ignorant of witchcraft; having no obeah charms"; and "*Mârer yon moune.* To tie a person. To cast an obeah spell over him" (118–19). While Thomas would most certainly have deplored obeah, the explanations are offered here by someone familiar with the discourses of his compatriots, no matter how transgressive.

A Trinidadian reviewer of the *Creole Grammar* in early 1870, noting that Thomas had been asked by "a gentleman well-known in the literary circles of Paris and who is connected with the publication of various Philological works, to send him something else in Creole," advised Thomas to utilize his collection of fables and "droll tales" to produce a "work of a more popular character than a grammar could well be."[21] After all, "if a mere Grammar could abound in oddities and drolleries, what amusement might we not look for in a book of tales, anecdotes, fables and other such light matter!" By definition pedantic, the genre of the grammar was not designed to entertain the public in the way that a coffee-table collection of "droll tales" might. Yet the remark may also have been a veiled response to his text's privileging of Black Trinidadians. The social equality of the cockroach is deliberately (mis)read as "oddities and drolleries." This public advice to Thomas about his intellectual pursuits raises the question why his was the only grammar of Creole in Trinidad, when there were many elites who could have produced such a text. Thomas shared with such persons a desire to defend francophone culture. But perhaps his zeal, occasioned by having merely intellectual rather than other kinds of capital, which made the production of such texts urgent, the advocacy of Black working-class interests, and the desire to indicate the African contribution to the national cultural equation accounted for Thomas's text.

THE *Creole Grammar* can be read against the backdrop of Trinidad's intense interest in language and speech in the 1870s and the assignment of cultural and racial attributes. It appeared in the same year as Patrick Keenan's report on Trinidad's educational system. Keenan, the chief of inspection for Ireland's Board of Education, visited Trinidad in response to Governor Gordon's appeal to the Colonial Office for an assessment of the territory's schools. Keenan's report covers such wide-ranging matters as the hazards of traveling through Trinidad's forested interior on horseback and on foot, the problems caused by the proximity of schoolrooms to teachers' living quarters, and the lax record keeping of teachers. He suggests that "considerations of the weightiest moral importance" favor the importation of European female teachers to supplement the teachers of the government primary schools, "all persons of colour."

Keenan's report notes that the public education system ignores Indian children, his tour of the few Presbyterian institutions devoted to their education suggesting to him that male Indians were intellectually superior to "Creoles of African blood," having better memories and a good grasp of numbers. On the other hand, Indian females were "immeasurably inferior" to their male counterparts, and all Indians had "serious moral defects," including untruthfulness. His report finds instruction in Trinidad's public education system to be irrelevant to the needs of students, who were often taught by teachers unfamiliar with their first languages (Spanish and what he termed "French"). Although the Irish National Board publications in use in Trinidad's schools were very good, they were not relevant to the geography and culture of the country: "As the Irish element preponderates in the Irish books, so the Trinidad element ought to preponderate in the Trinidad books." Though the aim of "every lover of the colony" was for everyone to speak English, as in some schools in Ireland, Wales, and Scotland, children should be taught to read in their first language and then taught English through that language. "The padlock at present on the lips of the children of the French and Spanish-speaking districts would thus be opened."

Though Thomas and Keenan were committed to the anglicization of the classroom and lamented the poor performances of students in Trinidad's schools, both also advocated the use of Creole—Keenan would have said "French"—to teach English more effectively. In this sense Creole was a stepping-stone to the hegemonic language of a British colony, though both men would have differed on whether it was a language in its own right.

In "Creole Literature," a lecture given by Thomas in San Fernando some six years after the publication of the *Creole Grammar,* Thomas compared Trinidad's Creole with others in the region. While "the Negro corruptions of the English, Dutch and Spanish languages are spoken exclusively by the unlettered of African descent [in Caribbean territories dominated by English, Spanish, or Dutch settlers], with the Creole [in Trinidad and other French-dominated territories] the case is far different. Like its parent the French—when the latter was as yet a *patois* of the popular Latin, and just gathering coherence and power in the hands of the Troubadours,—it has worked and won its way upward from the cabin of the vulgar into the mansion of the educated gentry." Thomas continued: "Lips to which the language of Voltaire and Macaulay is familiar, disdain not, in the sweet intercourse of home-life, to fashion themselves to the utterance of the Creole with its quaint phrases and grammatical artlessness."[22]

Here, French is the "parent" of Creole and also the patois of an older "parent." Thomas suggests that unlike other Caribbean territories, in which the educated elite hold Creole languages in contempt—the word *Creole* here is used exclusively in connection with the francophone territories— Trinidad is blessed with an elite constituency that respects the language. His nationalistic ranking of Caribbean Creole languages is very interesting, indicating that the superiority of Trinidad's Creole had much to do with the elite's endorsement of it. They had invested it with the social magic that was lacking in other Caribbean territories, which were marked by "Negro corruptions" uttered by the "unlettered of African descent."

The reference to Voltaire and Macaulay signifies an educated elite's consumption of both francophone and anglophone canonical authors, a reminder that, the cultural friction between French Creole and Protestant factions of Trinidad's elite notwithstanding, their separation from non-elites, secured by the possession of economic and/or educational capital, was ultimately a more significant social distinction. Creole's quaintness and "grammatical artlessness" are indications of its unpolished nature in relation to the language of Voltaire, perhaps, but this suggests a guileless authenticity, not unlike the distinction between William Donovan and Otto Wenkstern.

It was silly to despise Creole, a language known to everyone on the most intimate terms:

> Is it not, I ask, the very climax of illiterate absurdity, to feel or, what is worse, to affect contempt for a language which is on our lips or sounds in our ears every day and at every turn—at home, and in the bustling scenes of business; a language the ignorance of which in this Island (to go no further) is a sorely felt inconvenience in every department of life; and which, moreover, has vitality and acceptance enough to hold its own successfully for more than a half century. In the first instance, against the encroachments of the French, and subsequently, against the influence of the French and English together?

Contrary to the *Spectator* reviewer's prediction, Creole definitely was not dying a slow death, and it was precisely its *popular* nature that should make "us" embrace it. It was on everyone's lips, in every sphere of life, public and private (including, we might assume, Thomas's own home), and without it one was hard pressed to survive in Trinidad. Moreover, Creole "holds its own" against both French and English, so that it was distinct from both, and notwithstanding the "parental" relationship of French, it was beaten back by Creole.

It is this ability to "hold its own," its "exclusive prevalence" in "most Primary School districts," that makes instruction in English so difficult. This instruction is not misguided by any means, though its methods are: "Still is this Creole the popular speech of this Island, though obvious policy has dictated, and intelligent zeal and energy have been employed for its eradication. The established system of Primary Instruction, which might have been as thoroughly effective of its purpose as it is, without doubt creditable to our social economy, gives evidence, both in the quality and amount of its results, of a deplorable waste of intelligent power." There was obvious value, Thomas declared, in using Creole to give instruction in English. Otherwise, Creole's "potency" meant that English could only be "half acquired" in the classroom. We have seen that his experience at the Boys Model School years later suggested that this was easier said than done. In any case, Thomas's defense of Creole in the 1875 lecture was not by any means a plea for its displacement of English acquisition, and as one of the territory's most well known teachers of English, he did not mean for it to usurp what he clearly saw as Creole's important place in Trinidadian society.

Newspapers of the day recorded the "noise" of working-class Creole speech, including the elaborate rituals of wordplay associated with the daily "cussing" and "'buseing" of policemen and other figures of authority. Newspapers also contained numerous advertisements for language instruction, indicating that those who aspired to "civilization" needed the social magic of language mastery. "Popular Instruction," began one 1869 notice. "New courses of the French, Spanish, English and Italian languages. Pupil learns to read, write and speak the language without the necessity of laboriously and tediously studying the genders, declension, conjugations, grammar, nor any book. He has only to be provided with a few sheets of paper to write his exercises. J. R. Bowen. Author of the system."[23] We can only imagine Thomas's reaction to this promise of mastery without the necessity of labor.

Languages offered for instruction in the territories' schools or by private tutors did not have equal status, so that Spanish, for instance, was ranked lower than German. Carl Campbell suggests that this was because of Prussia's prestige, whereas despite (or because of?) "many hundreds of Spanish speakers in the colony, and millions next door in Spanish America . . . Spain was not one of the great nations" (*Young Colonials*, 25). Not just within Europe, however, but also within Trinidad Spanish lacked prestige. Most of those who had it as a first language were perceived to be rural, isolated agriculturalists (in places such as Cedros) who were immigrants or descendants of immigrants from the South American mainland. "Peons," or "payols" (from *espagnols*), as they were called, had no prestige, so neither did the language. Sylvia Moodie points out that the community of elite Venezuelan expatriates could have "rejuvenated" the language but that Spanish was ultimately trumped by French (Moodie; see also Moodie-Kubalsingh). At St. Mary's College, where many students were from homes in which Spanish was spoken, Spanish was optional, while French was compulsory. Carl Campbell notes that teachers in the Canadian Presbyterian mission schools for Indians were encouraged to teach in Hindi as well as in English in order to attract students (and thus potential converts). He suggests that the colonial authorities permitted this because Indians were not yet seen as more than a transient constituency (*Young Colonials*, 231).

The ability to move easily and elegantly from one language to another was certainly a sign of one's social status. Sylvester Devenish was said to have "picked up a working knowledge of modern Greek, became fluent in Spanish and acquired a smattering of Italian, Polish and Hebrew. Later also a little Ibo" (A. de Verteuil, *Sylvester Devenish*, 105). Not all of these languages would have conferred obvious distinction, but given his social and economic status, Devenish did not require marks of obvious distinction. The languages he knew and the fact that they indicated a "smattering" rather than mastery as such would have conferred a rugged, practical cosmopolitanism (as in "a working knowledge of Modern Greek").

Some six decades later, C. L. R. James would recall Michel Maxwell Philip's mastery of Latin, Greek, French, Spanish, and Italian, noting that he had "read a few lines of the classics every morning of his life and so kept his knowledge fresh. His facility in French was perhaps not so extraordinary at a time when educated persons in Trinidad commonly spoke both languages; his powers in Spanish have already been indicated and there is the testimony of a Spanish priest who said that unlike so many people in Trinidad who spoke Spanish, Mr. Philip's Spanish was that of a Spaniard. When he started to practise at the bar, seeing that Hindustani would be useful to him, he soon mastered it" ("Michel Maxwell Philip," 254–55). "Hindostanee" was also one of the languages of which Thomas was known to have a working knowledge, in addition to Greek, Latin, French, Spanish, Italian, and German.[24]

Creole was the first, if not only, language of most of Trinidad's lower classes, though percentages shifted with the influx of immigrants from non-francophone territories throughout the late nineteenth century. Familiarity and intimacy with Creole was also the province of elites, who spoke it with their servants and sang folk songs in Creole at social events. However, as the above references show, whereas speaking *only* Creole marked one as lacking in distinction, speaking Creole as someone who had mastered French, English, and other languages marked one in a different way—as a well-heeled member of the society. Language mastery was an outward sign of one's inherent distinction: some constituencies could never take for granted that such mastery would earn them respect. If one was not deemed to be naturally distinguished, speaking English marked one as laboring absurdly, like Trollope's monkeys.

Consider this excerpt from the *Trinidad Chronicle*: "'The March of Intellect.' The following was related to us by a gentleman who overheard the remark, a few days ago, in passing: two ordinary-looking black men, without jackets, were leaning idly on the western gate of Trinity Church, engaged in conversation. To the surprise of our informant on nearing them, as he passed up the street, he heard one of the two say to his companion: 'Well now, I can tell you how it was—you see Sir William Draper was a friend of the Marquis of Granby, and so when Junius attacked the Marquis—' Our informant heard no more, having in his walk passed beyond hearing."[25] Unlike the "jacket-men" who shed the jackets that are the outward sign of their essentially elite selves when they visit working-class arenas such as the calypso tents, these men do not wear jackets at all. Even if they had jackets, however, they would be considered to be absurd mimics, just as they are when they discuss the marquis.

"Junius" was the pseudonymous writer of letters in the London *Public Advertiser* attacking George III, Lord Granby, and other aristocrats in the late eighteenth century. Sir William Draper wrote a letter in defense of Granby (Drabble, 523). That these men are discussing an antigovernment, Whig figure, therefore, might well cast an ironic light on the discussion of the incident in a British colony. There are also strong parallels to be drawn between the contentious and highly charged exchange of letters in mid-nineteenth century Trinidad and a similar exchange in eighteenth-century England. In the context of the anecdote, however, these jacketless men are held up to ridicule and carefully distinguished from the "gentle-man" narrator, who would be taken seriously for uttering the very same words. Possessing *only* linguistic competence, without other forms of capital, was not enough to secure unquestioned prestige.

Visitors and residents alike sought to pinpoint the linguistic and racial characteristics that constituted Trinidad's national grammar. W. H. Gamble, a missionary, noted that "Africans" were superior to "Coolies" in learning languages, though the latter trumped the former in their reli-ability as laborers. "Yarrabas" seemed to "value the benefits of civiliza-tion and Christianity," while "Congoes" had "little or no strength of character." While "Madras coolies" made good house servants, "Tamil-speaking Coolies" were eager to speak English, and "Bengalis" were not. In such a rich linguistic situation—"quite a Babel," as Keenan put it in his report—most store clerks were able to conduct business in English, French, and Spanish, and some "managed to learn to speak a few words of Coolie as they term it, meaning, of course, Bengali" (31–40).

Arthur Hamilton Gordon, governor of Trinidad (later Baron Stanmore), was attuned to linguistic facility while he traveled through the Caribbean. He described a fellow traveler, Trinidad's chief justice, W. Knox, as a "good Italian scholar" who had taught himself Hindi "since Coolie cases became numerous and important." At the other end of the spectrum were the Black men and women who boarded the ship when it stopped in Grenada to coal: "Mostly unfeminine looking women of the most repul-sive appearance. They all yelled and shouted at the utmost pitch of their voices and at night when the scene was lighted by torches and by fires which had been kindled on the wharf, the scene was weirdly picturesque and highly demoniacal."[26] Their Creole-speaking voices intensified the sense of unnatural gender and unnatural freedom: their proper place was the sugar plantation.

Charles Kingsley, the novelist and canon, accompanied by his daughter Rose, visited Governor Gordon in the Christmas season of 1869. For Kingsley, the women are particularly reprehensible. His biographer, Susan Chitty, notes that his "happy experience with male West Indians," particularly "industrious" ones, helped to wipe out memories of less happy ones with females (*At Last,* 1:265). When his daughter calls out to one woman to call another one, the woman pretends not to hear and then says to her companion: "You coloured lady! You hear did white woman a wanting of you?" (1:265). In this arena, clearly, elites are out of their depth.

That Black working-class reprehensibility was closely tied to the independence that jobs such as coaling represent is made clear by Kingsley's remarks on the "evils" of coaling, which was "demoralizing in itself, as it enables negroes of the lowest class to earn enough in one day to keep them in idleness, even in luxury, for a week or more, till the arrival of the next steamer" (1:32). Wage-earning Black people had agency, which was threatening to a sugar economy in need of their labor. Labor in any other context was therefore "idle," particularly because it left open the possibility that one might not perform the same job in the same way every day, the sign of the moral human being.[27] Later, as he visited the provision grounds of Black Trinidadians, he would again insist on their idleness in the midst of noting their labor (1:221). Like coaling, the cultivation of their own crops on their own land (or as squatters on crown lands) signified their control over their earning power.

On land, Kingsley notes the "weary din of the tom-toms which came from all sides of the Savanna save our own" (1:264). Observing a "dance" in a "Negro garden" below the governor's home, featuring "a few couples, mostly of women, pusetting to each other with violent and ungainly stampings, to the music of tom-tom and chac-chac, if music it can be called," he asks one of the servants if he and his party can go for a closer look. However, the Black man is reluctant: "Ah massa: when cockroach give a ball, him no ask da fowls." Hearing or even seeing does not guarantee access. That these "cockroaches" do not encourage "fowls" to invade their space is an indication of their awareness of the threat of consumption if fowls were to have complete access. Thomas, we will remember, viewed the roach as "day by day vindicating his claim to a little more." "More" here might symbolize the right to one's own physical and cultural space, unobserved by intruders. Even in the face of elites' disapproval or the laws of the courts, "ungainly" dancers, "vulgar" coalers, and "idle" smallholders asserted their right to hold balls without consulting fowls.

If Black people offend Kingsley's sensibilities, Indians please him. Attending the races in Port of Spain, he literally engages in "race-tracking" as he compares the women of the two groups: "The Negresses, I am sorry to say, forgot themselves, kicked up their legs, shouted to the bystanders, and were altogether incondite. The Hindoo women, though showing much more of their limbs than the Negresses, kept them so gracefully together, drew their veils round their heads, and sat coyly, half frightened, half amused, to the delight of their 'papas,' or husbands, who had in some cases to urge them to get up and ride, while they stood by, as on guard, with the long hardwood quarter-staff in hand" (2:262).

Vulgar Negresses provide an unpleasant contrast to docile women who are graceful in their submissiveness to their "papas": "No wonder that the two races do not, and it is feared never will, amalgamate; that the Coolie, shocked by the unfortunate awkwardness of gesture, and vulgarity of manners of the average Negro, and still more of the Negress, looks on them as savages; while the Negro, in his turn, hates the Coolie as a hardworking interloper, and despises him as a heathen" (*At Last,* 1:194). At the orphanage for Indians in Tacarigua, Kingsley reflects on gender equality: "The girls, I was told, are curiously inferior to the boys in intellect and force of character; an inferiority which is certainly not to be found in Negros, among whom the two sexes are more on a par, not only intellectually, but physically also, than among any race which I have seen" (2:253). The "evils" of early, arranged marriages among Indians and the high rate of wife murders do not detract from the ability of Indian men to be excellent house servants, as in the case of the "pretty, gentle, graceful" young man who is serving a prison sentence for murdering his wife (2:49).

Kingsley's hostess, Lady Gordon, the wife of Trinidad's governor, ranks the races of her servants: "Welsh, Scotch, and Portuguese, white, black, coloured and Coolie; they each hate and despise the others." While Matthew, "the coolie boy" is "dark but gentlemanlike and very good-looking," Negroes give her no such pleasure: "The more I see of the black servants, the more I hate them." She enjoys the reactions of her friends when she wears Indian jewelry: They "say I have turned Coolie, for I have got bangles on both arms, and only want a ring to be complete. No one else here has ever thought of wearing these things and they look surprised when I pull up my habit sleeves and display a row of bangles."[28]

The bangles, turbans, and veils of Indians, then, are enthusiastically documented as evidence of their exotic dignity. In Kingsley's text, yet another group of "Indians" functions as a pleasant antidote to the presence of Black Caribbean people when he reflects that the history of Trinidad might have been different "if at that early period, while the Indians were still powerful, a little colony of English had joined them and intermarried with them" (*At Last,* 1:108). Here, English and Amerindian men share power, with Indian women cementing the relationship. "Indians" are restored to Trinidad, happily coexisting with the English rather than suffering a terrible fate at the hands of the murderous Catholic Spaniards. Since Black Trinidadians had been introduced to replace a decimated Amerindian population, in Kingsley's fantasy of contemporary Trinidad they are not needed.[29]

In "The Legend of La Brea," a poem published in *Macmillan's Magazine* and reprinted in the *Trinidad Chronicle* Kingsley pitted Amerindian nobility against Black brutishness. An "ancient Spanish Indian" lectures a carefree, thieving "negro hunter" on the environmental and moral evils of hunting for birds near the Pitch Lake. Kingsley's Negro hunter gnaws on his sugarcane, rolls his eyes, and dozes, his idle existence paid for by the British people:

Never jollier British subject
Rollicked underneath the sky?

. . . .

He had all we have, and more.

Superstitious and cowardly, and fearing only his "sturdy mate's" physical abuse, he is advised by the "stately, courteous" Indian to "take care" lest the Pitch Lake boil over as punishment for his theft. The hunter's response, that "dere's twenty tousand birdskins, / Ardered jes' now fram New Yark," suggests that wicked American capitalists encourage the impressionable and foolish hunter in his mischief.[30] Similarly, in *At Last* Kingsley and his daughter listen as the coalers sing about America: "You go to America? You as well go to heaven" (1:31–32). "New York" lures idle Black bodies with easy money, leading to idleness and the further jeopardy of the plantation economy.

These disturbing scenarios are offset in *At Last* by fantasies such as the White men who are husbands of Indian women in Kingsley's reading of Trinidad's history and correspond with a Scotsman he meets in Trinidad, who has a "handsome Creole wife, and lovely brownish children" (1:201). This couple prompts a meditation on the civilizing possibilities of an even better union. A young English couple who are refined but "unable to keep a brougham and go to London balls" could "retreat" to the West Indies, "leaving behind them false civilization, and vain desires, and useless show; and there live in simplicity and content 'The Gentle Life.'" Such a couple "would be a little centre of civilization for the Negro, the Coolie" (1:202–3). The Caribbean provides a solution to excess populations that strain English resources, or more specifically here, gentry with insufficient income to maintain an estate with servants in England. Their failure to do so becomes a virtue since broughams and balls are "false civilization" and "useless show," and in the Caribbean they will be units of civilization for Black and Indian servants forever destined to be laborers.

It is clear throughout the text, however, which group of laborers is superior. Unlike "Negroes," who, if they once had the "skill" and "thoughtfulness," had "lost them under slavery," "Hindoos" were "trained by long ages" in the scientific agriculture that would secure a viable future for the region (2:279–80). The "race of Hindoo peasant proprietors" would "teach the negro thrift and industry, not only by their example, but by competing against him in the till lately understocked labour market." He continues: "[Hindoos] have acquired—let Hindoo scholars tell how and where—a civilization which shows in them all day long; which draws the European to them and them to the European, whenever the latter is worthy of the name of civilized man, instinctively, and by the mere interchange of glances; a civilization which must make it easy for the Englishman, if he will but do his duty, not only to make use of these people, but to purify and ennoble them" (1:190, 193).

At the very moment when Kingsley's brother-in-law, Friedrich Max Müller, was demonstrating the Sanskrit origins of the English language to the Philological Society in London, Kingsley indicated the "prize" for possessing a culture that "drew Europeans to them": Indians could and should be "made use of" in the Caribbean. The future of the plantation economy required the last hope, "Hindoos," to deliver what Black people had failed to deliver. The latter's "laziness" guaranteed Indians' "civilization" and, most importantly, industry. The darker races in the Caribbean were exotic or savage in the context of their availability to the sugar industry.

Though most of Kingsley's text is given over to detailed descriptions of Trinidad's flora and fauna, supplemented by his own illustrations, his comments on Trinidad's people earned him criticism. A costume in the 1870 Carnival depicted him brandishing a copy of *Good Words* (the periodical in which early versions of *At Last* appeared) and supporting Governor Gordon, "the noble Arthur, evidently the lord of misrule," who wore a Russian imperial crown and carried a wizard's wand.[31] Kingsley's participation in public debates about state funding of public education, detailed in a chapter titled "The 'Education Question' in Trinidad," elicited criticism even before he left Trinidad.[32] "We will not abandon our Catholicism to please a 'guest of the Governor,' as certain good people thought it pious and edifying to do, at last week's meeting at the Town Hall!" one journalist proclaimed angrily. "A *Catholic* mayor, a *Catholic* Solicitor General" used language tantamount to a renunciation of the Christian faith, "even as professed by the Anglican Church!"[33]

True Catholics, the editorial continued, would not "renounce the creeds for the amusement of Mr. Kingsley, agreeable and charming novelist and magazine writer that he undoubtedly is, though he failed to make himself particularly pleasant to Dr. Newman, when he told him—it was only Dr. Newman!—that he must either be a fool or a knave—to profess so great an absurdity as the Catholic religion!" Referring here to the schism in the Church of England in the 1840s led by John Henry Newman, a Roman Catholic convert whom Kingsley famously attacked, this local journalist scoffed at Kingsley's insubstantial faith and berated his compatriots for abandoning theirs.[34] M. M. Philip, in fact, was the traitorous solicitor general referred to here, and his obituary notes that it was he who invited Kingsley to the meeting.[35]

A letter to the editor from "Colibri" in the *Star of the West* on 27 July 1870 questioned Kingsley's presentation of the thieving "negro hunter" in his poem of that year: "[The poem] should have been headed—'A Satire on the Negroes of Trinidad.'" The correspondent expressed surprise at such a presentation, considering "that the only Negro whom Mr. Kingsley met here in close contact, and from whom he might have drawn inferences concerning the capabilities of the Negro, was Mr. Thomas of wide-world literary fame—a negro from whom, according to one of the London papers, that gentleman procured promotion for his abilities." I have found no commentary by Thomas himself on Kingsley's poem or on his travelogue. If he chose not to respond, one wonders why this would have been so, considering his famous response to Froude eighteen years later. Thomas's *Grammar* appeared earlier in the year that Kingsley visited Trinidad, and the letter just cited indicates the prevailing belief that the attention that Thomas received—including promotions to positions as clerk of the peace in Cedros and Caroni, secretary to the board of education, and secretary to the board of Queen's Royal College—were at Kingsley's recommendation.

It is possible, then, that Thomas's perceived indebtedness to both the governor and Kingsley prevented him from public commentary. When he responded to Froude in 1888 he was in Grenada, which is not to say that he was disconnected from the patronage of governors—we have seen his approving comments on Governor Sendall's attendance at Donovan's lecture in 1887. However, he may not have felt as beholden as in 1871, and in any case Froude was so generally condemned in the Caribbean and in England that criticizing him may not have been as controversial as responding to Kingsley would have been. On the other hand, Thomas may have felt that William Herbert's condemnation of Kingsley was sufficient.

In August 1871 Herbert published a two-column review of Kingsley's book.[36] As Thomas would in the case of Froude's travelogue eighteen years later, Herbert chose to see Kingsley's scenes of flora, fauna, and physiognomy as hostile and racist rather than innocently picturesque. He condemned the partisan nature of Kingsley's text, sneering at the extent to which it was influenced by his host, Governor Gordon: "The fact is, that Mr. Kingsley saw Trinidad only through the spectacles which were supplied by another. . . . He was the unconscious agent of a more powerful will. Without knowing it, he was the tool of a man, with a policy more subtle than the mazes of the Cretan labyrinth, who wielded him as he pleased. Mr. Kingsley was like a kid seethed in its mother's milk." With an eye on the market, Kingsley, the professor of history at Cambridge, the "gentleman" and "scholar," was "a writer of books to sell. . . . He knows what will sell, and prepares the commodity accordingly. Highly-spiced and even sensational books are in demand, and Mr. Kingsley has too much of the tradesman's instinct to leave his clients out in the cold."

Condemning Kingsley's stereotyping of Black and Colored people, Herbert declares:

> [Kingsley] comes in accidental contact with a few African men and women, and forthwith he points to them as types of the whole negro race in the West Indies; when it is well known that the *Creole negroes* who form the overwhelming majority, under the influences of civilization, differ so materially from their progenitors, in habits, in thought, in manner, even physical conformation, as almost to appear to be a distinct race. Yet among these very Negroes are men who might fairly sit as models for so many Apollos, and forms of women which Canova would have been delighted to copy. (Herbert's emphasis)

For Herbert, then, there are Negroes and there are Negroes. Here, he shows himself to be as much invested in ideas about "civilization" as Kingsley; the differences lie in where the lines should be drawn. One wonders how the linking of culture here to physiognomy by Herbert, who was a Mulatto, would have been received by dark-skinned Thomas. The difference between, on the one hand, "Creole negroes" who might serve as models for

Italian sculptors and, on the other, their "progenitors" seems to rest as much in their "physical conformation" as in their capacity for "civilization." "Negroes" they might be, but so different from the lower classes on whom Kingsley chooses to focus that they are practically a "distinct race."

After distinguishing "Creole" from other Negroes, Herbert goes on to critique Kingsley's comments on Indians: "But if all the worst passions in Mr. Kingsley's heart are roused by the negro, the coolies act as a sedative. The milk of human kindness with which Mr. Kingsley's bosom is always full, overflows at the sight of the coolies. They are all ladies and gentlemen." In critiquing British misrepresentation Herbert refers to the "Mutiny" of 1857 as "proof" of Indian savagery. So "perfect" are these Indians that "Englishmen have not forgotten the *perfections* of the East Indian race in the *gentle* scenes of Lucknow and Cawnpore" (Herbert's emphasis). Notably, Herbert appeals to another travelogue as further "proof" of the noncivilized nature of Indians. Kingsley's claims of Indian civility are, he says, "contradicted by every writer on East Indian matters, of whom we have any knowledge," and he cites Robert Minturn's *From New York to Delhi* on the "facts" of Indians' inability to speak the truth. *Some* travelogues, it seems, are tolerable.

If Herbert vindicates Black respectability, then, it is at the expense of nonelite Black people and of all Indians, none of whom seem able to make it into the kingdom of culture. In speaking for the sophistication and respectability of Trinidad's "Creole negroes," their capacity to participate fully in the fruits of modernity, Herbert by no means suggested that all people in Trinidad were respectable. Nor did he question the cultural standards that were at the heart of the genre of the travelogue, even if he had a problem with *Kingsley's* text. As Antoinette Burton has put it, "Herbert was at worst a collaborator in the ideological work of empire, at best an ambivalent and contradictory reader of imperial ideology and its twisted promises" (47).[37] Kingsley, sharing planter anxiety about the labor supply for sugar, juxtaposes Indian docility and dignity with Black laziness and vulgarity, while Herbert smarts at representations of Black people that are not class-specific and at the way in which such representations render Indians superior.

Herbert's review earned him a public tribute over the signatures of "300 gentlemen" that was published in the newspapers a few weeks after his review.[38] Herbert's well-wishers referred to Kingsley's having published a book on West Indian manners in which "our race was singled out and held up to the scorn and obloquy of the world—as being imbued with all the crimes and vices induced by the most degraded state of existence.

That the Rev. author should utterly ignore all trace of intelligence among the people who swelled the congregation that listened to him as a messenger of peace and good-will, certainly betrays a lamentable want of discrimination, and is a grave reflection on his conduct as a pattern of Christianity." The letter continued, "Whatever regret we do feel in being thus maligned does not equal the satisfaction we experience in viewing your courage and intrepidity in exposing and refuting the fallacies and aspersions of Canon Kingsley." Herbert was further commended for the fact "that you should identify yourself with your and our race—which without advantages and with few opportunities has placed itself, nevertheless, on an equality with the favoured class." Concluding, the letter called him a "true sympathiser, friend and defender of our race."

In his reply Herbert recounted the trials of his career and exhorted those who had paid him tribute to work together for the improvement of the race: "Let me hope that when the brain which conceives these ideas, and the hand which traces these lines shall have mouldered into dust, the words which I have written, and to which you have this day listened may have their effect, and be instrumental in however slight a degree in helping to elevate that race—my mother's race—which I love so well."

A letter by Thomas published a week after Herbert's review of Kingsley's text provides a final example of the lively theorizing and practice of Creole linguistics, politics, and morals and returns us to Cedros, where we began. In attempting to shift the conceptual implications of *negro* Thomas relies on the connection between race-tracking and linguistic facility that we have noted in other texts, and insists on the clean separation of Indians and Negroes. [39] Stating that he is writing in response to passages in recent issues of the *Trinidad Chronicle,* he takes as his subject "the action of opinion and language upon each other, and the collective influence of both upon the human character and behaviour." Language was continually being transformed by "time, necessity, ignorance, caprice and innumerable other agencies," so that, historically, where "'Knave,' was once, like *der knabe,* his German relative, simply a boy, what a knave is now nobody need be told." Similarly, "idiot" now referred to a "creature unfurnished with brains, or at all events, with brains capable of sensate thought." But "in Greece, his native land, the *idiotes* was a private citizen, a man of peace, as contradistinguished from the *stratiotes,* or soldier, the historical glory of whose patriotic achievements is allowed to blind us to the violence and lawless capacity which formed his most ordinary character."

These historical examples provided a context for contemporary perversions of language in the Caribbean, says Thomas:

In the West Indies, the word *negro,* a Spanish term meaning "black or dark," is growing more disreputable every day. Not only does it commonly supplant the word "slave" in our vocabulary; but it describes, and that without any possibility of mistake, a man—even though white as driven snow—who displays in his conduct those vices which charitable virtue regards as peculiar to bondsmen. I was not surprised at learning last week a rather novel application of the term under consideration. A Coolie woman who had some business in the Court here on being asked by the Magistrate, through the Interpreter, whether she was free or under indenture, replied: "Siam *naygar* hai," i.e. I am a negro. The critical scholar in Hindustáni will, no doubt, carp at the woman for her grammar, or at me as having corrupted it. I can only say that, striking as her answer was to me, I treasured it up *verbatim* in my mind,—but as the sentiment, and not the grammar, of the reply is the main point at present, I should not mind being thought incorrect in my reproduction of the woman's syntax, provided her peculiar use of the term *negro* is admitted to possess even half the significance I have applied to it.

Thomas also condemned the phrases "insolent negro" and "negro insolence" in the text of a recent contributor to the *Trinidad Chronicle,* who had stated: "In no part of the world can there be found more insolent negroes than . . . the cabmen of Barbados. . . . The most striking difference between the Aden and Barbadian cabby is . . . that the moment you are going to use the whip on him, which is the *sine qua non* in India . . . he shuts up like a book, and at once becomes your slave—as submissive as possible, while if you were to have recourse to the lash at Barbados at present, you would be split like a mackerel." For Thomas, this writer proves that Stowe's Mr. Legree is "at once possible and immortal." By contrast, the governor of Barbados, "a gentleman possessed of the mental capacity and enlightenment which enable men to discern between right principles and wrong methods of asserting them," terms the Negroes "free and independent," a phrase more aptly describing "men who do not become anybody's slave, nor 'as submissive as possible,' under the inducement of a horsewhipping and other degrading treatment."

What did *Negro* mean in the mid-nineteenth century? Which words, concepts, and persons cited in connection with it demeaned or elevated it? For the learned grammarian—were Thomas's readers impressed by his Latin and Greek references or contemptuous toward them?—calling cabbies "insolent negroes" and invoking the whip revived the old days of slavery and indicated that Mr. Legree, Mrs. Stowe's brutal slave driver in *Uncle Tom's Cabin,* was "at once possible and immortal" outside of the realm

of fiction. As Thomas seeks to rescue from slander one immigrant constituency—the Barbadians, who would be particularly reviled in the next
decade as more and more entered Trinidad (Johnson)—he censures the
representative of another constituency for speaking out of turn. Diverging
from a script that he and others have prescribed for her, a script rooted in
the precise placement of races, Thomas interprets the response of the
woman in court as being rooted in a perception that the condition of
bondage and the nomenclature *Negro* were interchangeable.

Interestingly, the writer whom he critiques for his slander of Barbadians
contrasts the latter's "failure" to be submissive—that is the "insolence" of
responding to the threat of the lash by splitting someone like a mackerel
—with the comparative docility of Indian laborers, who were more likely
to "shut up like a book" and become "slaves." As other commentators
have noted, whereas the events of 1857 elicited fears of Indian savagery
within the Indian subcontinent, in the Caribbean Indians' indentured status
enables them to be "made use of" when Black labor was less reliable. They
were thus the docile alternative to Black "insolence." Thomas does not
connect the invocation of Indian submissiveness in the Barbadian example to the woman in the Cedros court. While the implicit interpretation of
Indians' supposed willingness to take the lash when Barbadians will not is
that they perhaps deserve to be "slaves," the Cedros woman's suggestion
that her own indentured status is linked to Negroes is taken by Thomas to
mean that she demeans Negroes by insisting on their enslaved status,
rather than that her status as a laborer is linked to the historical and current status of Black people as laborers.

The interpretation of the woman's response, indeed her very presence
in court, was tied to "knowledge" of the supposedly immutable traits of
Indians. Travelogues, novels, sermons, letters, oral accounts, and sketches
circulated from one part of the globe to the other fixed and tracked her
with the confidence of familiarity, much as Kingsley fixed for his readers
the traits of the banana: "The only spot, as far as I am aware, in which it
seeds regularly and plentifully, is the remote, and till of late barbarous
Andaman Islands in the Bay of Bengal. . . . I owe these curious facts, and
specimens of the seeds, to the courtesy of Dr. King, of the Bengal army.
The seeds are now in the hands of Dr. Hooker, at Kew" (*At Last,* 2:272).
The circulation of seeds and bodies and their elevation from a "barbarous" state were monitored with authority by metropolitan observers in
Trinidad, as at the Bay of Bengal, to confirm, and be confirmed by, the
specimens already examined at Kew or in the halls of the Philological
Society, the Ethnological Society, and other societies.

The testimony of the Cedros woman, then, was framed by the "facts" about people like her. In 1870, the year before Thomas's letter, for instance, Michel Maxwell Philip instructed a jury: "You have sat there over and over as jurors, and you are all aware what value you can attach to the unsupported evidence of coolies. You know with what unscrupulous hardihood they violate the most sacred of the sanctions which they represent as binding them to tell the truth." Philip then offered "proof" of Indians' propensity to lie by reading "from a work bearing on this point of the East Indian character."[40] If we can assume that Philip quoted from a travelogue, then once again it appears that metropolitan authority was acceptable so long as it avoided the slander of "respectable" colonial subjects.

We have seen that Philip, Thomas, and others were praised for their mastery of "Hindustani" and other languages in a society in which an important characteristic of the elite was facility with languages. On some level, then, Thomas's ability to translate the words of this woman may have indicated his and others' ability to serve her and others more efficiently and sympathetically, just as his *Creole Grammar* had the better representation of disadvantaged speakers in the courtroom as one of its aims. But in a context in which a defendant "from a particular class or race" was assumed guilty until proven innocent (Trotman, 87), nonelite speech, as well as nonelite actions more generally, represented something to be eliminated, punished, or reformed.

Thomas is careful to distance himself from what he deems the woman's grammatical shortcomings. Aware that his well-bred readers will understand "Hindustani," he makes his excuses for reproducing her faulty grammar.[41] He insists upon "fixing" her, first, to a standard of Hindi that will admit of no departure from the normative standard that he has learned. In fact, Bhojpuri, the language that many Indians in Trinidad spoke, was often considered to be "bad" Hindi.[42] Further, Thomas fixes her to a rigid social script that "knows" her "authentic" speaking position and will not admit of any identification that veers from this. It is quite possible, of course, that this woman did in fact mean to indicate that her status was demeaned and that this was best described by referring to herself as a "naygar" or "negro" or "nigger," that is to say, that she had learned all too well the negative associations of *naygar* in Trinidadian society. The point is, *could* she claim to be a "naygar" herself, and what did it signify?

For Thomas, this outsider was polluting a Trinidad that was being constructed, if contentiously, by various elements of Trinidad's respectable classes. His letter looked toward a future in which *Negro* and *slave* would be separated in the national grammar. Errant elites such as the commentator on Barbadian cabbies—who should have known better but who persisted in using *Negro* and *slave* synonymously—needed to be alert so that outsiders such as this woman would not take it as a grammatical and conceptual given that the dehumanization and social indignity of slavery was defined by persons of African descent.

What Thomas's translation failed, or refused, to fathom was the power of "Siam naygar hai" to misspeak, misidentify, and unfix across the social and economic boundaries in place in colonial Trinidad. Like Yoruba indentured laborers, also brought in to shore up the sugar industry, she "may have seen little or no difference between [her] status as indentured immigrant and the role played by the slave" (Warner-Lewis, *Guinea's Other Suns*, 7). Might "Siam Naygar hai" not be read as a challenge to those who would use her bangles, her hair, her "docility" to indicate how unlike "naygars" she was (whether this proved she was less "heathen" than they or more so); as her insistence that as an inheritor of a historically specific role in the Caribbean plantation economy and the highly stratified society that buttressed it, she too ought to have been understood as the "not-free," as having a condition defined by servitude, rather than as the privileged possessor of an "exotic" culture and the key to Trinidad's future? Trying to listen to her statement in court might require us both to mishear the more powerful sounds of her inability ever to be a "naygar" and to think about why she and the generations that would follow her seemed to be asked to choose between refuting "naygar" and choosing it as a condition of becoming Creole. In this sense perhaps "Siam naygar hai" marked the limits of her entry into Trinidadian society: remaining at its margins or entering without being allowed to participate in its definition or transformation.

In Part 1 of the *Creole Grammar* Thomas states that "when—as in the case of Africans in the West Indies and America—a barbarous nation adopts a foreign speech, these approximations will be a prominent feature in the dialect thus formed" (1). One example offered is the treatment of "this poor letter," the letter *r*, which for "pure *Patois* speakers is almost non-existent" (4). The absent *r* marks the Creole speaker as ignorant, rude, and even, with reference to an early meaning of *barbarous*, foreign. Accepting prevailing notions about speakers of African languages, Thomas's *Creole Grammar* nonetheless seeks to redeem the "barbarous nation" by showing these speakers to be normal and valuable, rather than pathological, members of the nation. He does so by making clear his own ability to pronounce words masterfully, as he and other gentlemen—scholars, priests, missionaries, travel writers, and journalists—interpret and fix persons according to the grammars of race and nation. Two Cedros women, one "local" and one "foreign," provide Thomas with an opportunity to reiterate the rules of grammar, race, and nation. As he notes their unseemly speech—one misspeaks, and the other speaks only one tongue—he underscores his own mastery as a well-bred and respectable interpreter. In this sense the *Creole Grammar* was part of a conservative project to fix the precise contours of what could count as Creole in the face of the influx of groups from all over the Caribbean and the globe. Anyone entering Trinidad from midcentury on would have to conform to this paradigm.

4 West Indian Fables Explained
Travel and Translation in the 1880s

They chattered like jackdaws about a church tower. Two or three of
the best looking, seeing that I admired them a little, used their eyes
and made some laughing remarks. They spoke in their French *patois*,
clipping off the first and last syllables of the words. I but half understood them, and could not return their bits of wit. I can only say that
if their habits were as loose as white people say they are, I did not see
a single licentious expression either in face or manner. They seemed
to me lighthearted, merry, innocent young women, as free from any
thought of evil as the peasant girls in Brittany.

Froude, *English in the West Indies*

THIS ACKNOWLEDGMENT of a reciprocal gaze by the late
nineteenth century's most infamous travel writer on the Caribbean is not
singular. Froude's comments about women in the market at Roseau,
Dominica, are echoed by Lady Brassey, who, noting Trinidad's array of
races (as well as Mulattoes and the "yellow-faced" of "no particular
race"), concludes that those she encountered were "as much amused with
us as we were with them, which made us feel more easy in using our eyes
and making the best of the opportunity of gazing at all the strange sights
that presented themselves" (14). In a similar vein, William Paton "respect-
fully" and "diffidently" pursues the "Hindu Cooly Belle" pictured in his
book's frontispiece down a Demerara street. But for her "sable" color, he
notes, she could have been a Grecian psyche or a Vassar freshwoman: she
is, like him, a descendant of Japhet, an "Aryan kinswoman" whose skin
is as "brown and dark as rarest mahogany." Perhaps for this reason he is
perturbed that she finds him "grotesque or outlandish" (177).

This acknowledgment of the other's gaze, or even that the other's gaze
permits one's own, suggests the egalitarianism of what Mary Louise Pratt
terms the "contact zone," the space where different languages, bodies,
and histories come together, "the spatial and temporal co-presence of
subjects previously separated by geographical and historical disjunctures,

and whose trajectories now intersect" (6). However, first-class passengers in a steamer have circuits of travel and power that are different from those of people who come on board to coal the steamer, so that the relationship between self and other in travel writing may be characterized as a "calculated nonreciprocity," to use Mario Cesareo's formulation (108).

Indeed, Lady Brassey's complaint that she had to pay duties on the two dogs she attempted to bring into Barbados resulted in the customs officer's receiving a reprimand from the governor. The 21 October 1885 issue of the *Grenada People* printed the petition of thirty women who complained that in conducting trade between Grenada and Trinidad their luggage was checked in the presence of crowds. They requested a more secluded location for the search, as well as a female examiner. When the same paper complained on 29 December 1886 that "poor Quashie" was badly treated by customs officials in the trade between Trinidad and Grenada, while "birds of passage" of the higher classes were not bothered, it was referring to this disparity in travel.[1]

The women who bring produce on foot from all over Dominica to the market at Roseau, where Froude sees them, and those who transport produce between Grenada and Trinidad are plying routes of trade established during slavery, important commercial zones that enabled them to feed themselves and maintain a livelihood independent of the sugar economy. That is, Froude's recognition of their right to discuss him in the Creole language, putting him at a disadvantage, is an expansive gesture that is at odds with his general anxiety about Black people, who do not consistently make their labor available to estate proprietors. Just as Paton rhetorically draws his "sable" Belle into his portion of the human family, Froude finds that the leopardlike gaze of the women in the Roseau market matches the most "graceful forms" of "any drawing room in London" (136). The innocence that he is surprised to discover because it goes against conventional wisdom regarding Black women's sexuality accords with his general theme that they are prelapsarian and thus require guidance. He assumes the authority to distinguish between harmless flirtation and licentiousness, and at this moment in the text the women's assertiveness does not suggest the desire for political self-assertion that he condemns elsewhere.

Indeed, Caribbean reviewers of these travel texts objected to admiring comments about Black and Indian women because of the related depiction of men as lazy, as well as the general failure to note the existence of the "intermediate" classes. Local commentators offered their own readings of working-class bodies and similarly compared and contrasted different constituencies across the region, as well as across the globe. The 1880s narratives of travel that I discuss here are by travelers, by writers of guides for travelers and reviewers of such guides, and by commentators on alien travelers. They demonstrate the concerns of gentlemen at various levels with interpreting and taming the sounds of noisy jackdaws. Like the *Creole Grammar,* they are often concerned with vindication, offering revisionist histories of particular communities, regions, or prestigious men. They condemn expatriate "birds of passage," Europeans residing in the region for relatively short periods of time and therefore having no long-term stake in its future, for preying on resources that rightfully belong to Creoles. They distinguish between authentic cultural traditions and alien incursions or between the excesses of Gladstonian liberalism and strong rule. They invoke women as signs of a constituency's health or decay. Women also represent what a man becomes when he fails to be a real man, since central to such discussions is the reiteration of the difference between a man and a boy, or a little man and a great man. Speaking like a man means knowing when the occasion calls for strident rhetoric, even amid controversy, for deference to one's elders, or for silence. Alternately, a "real" man *acts* heroically on a battlefield, for example, rather than indulging in empty rhetoric.

In the mid-1880s local and visiting elites interpreted aliens abroad as well as in their midst against the backdrop of franchise reform, plans to mark the jubilee anniversary of the abolition of slavery, and the often violent confrontations between the forces of law and order, on the one hand, and the rural and urban lower classes, on the other. Such confrontations occurred during the 1881, 1883, and 1884 Carnival celebrations, and police shot into the procession at the 1884 Hosay festival, killing or wounding more than a hundred participants (Trotman, 263–70; A. de Verteuil, *Years of Revolt;* Singh). In the streets of Port of Spain and San Fernando or on estate roads Creole- and Bhojpuri-speaking people confronted an English-speaking police force: the Black Barbadians who occupied the lower ranks, White Irish officers, and a White English chief. Tassa drumming in the Indian community of St. James so disturbed officers in neighboring barracks that their complaints resulted in an 1883 bill banning drumming or playing of non-European instruments during certain hours and requiring a police permit at other hours. Uproar from elite francophone quarters resulted in the replacement of this bill with Ordinance 11, holding owners of premises where drumming and drum dances occurred liable, that same year. As David Trotman points out, such legislation and the "battles" between police and people indicate underlying, constant fear resulting from previous "mutinies" in other parts of the world but also from memories that drum dances on estates on weekend nights had fostered organizing for rebellion during slavery.

Thomas joined others in commenting on these local events, and by the end of the decade he had contributed the most well known response to Froude's travelogue. But he also offered Trinidad's public an account of his own travels in a lecture on his 1873 trip to Grenada, which he promised to publish separately but which was not published until 1883, in the *Trinidad Review,* presumably when he was editor.[2] In the articles, Thomas gently admonishes Trinidadians for their insularity and shows a keen interest in regional affairs. Compared with the travels of Ulysses, Herodotus, Marco Polo, or those "glorious" modern discoverers, Livingstone and Stanley, his own travels are "non-heroic," Thomas states. He has no encounters with giants or dalliances with nymphs to recount, living as he does in a more "prosaic" age of "disillusion." Nevertheless, Thomas infuses dramatic moments into his account: seasickness on board the sloop, a captain who steers off course, and sympathy for the whales hunted in Grenadian waters. He also includes an apostrophe to the "historic martyrs of freedom," the Amerindians who jumped to their death fleeing their French captors centuries before at the aptly, if grotesquely, named Sauteurs (leapers).

Thomas regrets that Trinidadians have an aversion to travel since so many people from elsewhere regard Trinidad as a chance to start over and since it is dependent on goods from other places. Severe illness and his physician's orders now make it imperative for him to travel, and he recommends Grenada as cheaper and more comfortable than going "down the Islands," referring to the group of islands in the Gulf of Paria where elite Trinidadians vacationed.

Traveling through Grenada on horseback is perilous, Thomas finds, because of the custom of "making roads on the tops of hills, and the verge of precipices." The schools he visits are not as impressive as in Trinidad, and the excellent teachers in the system are badly paid. Young women of the lower middle class lack "acquired accomplishments," if not "native graces," because of the lack of institutions for their training, while laboring women coal steamers, work in lumbering, dig hills, and tout sand, occupations that are reserved for the "rougher sex" in other countries. For Thomas this signifies that the "lower classes" are as hardworking and eager "to turn an honest penny" as they are in Trinidad. The low wages explain why many migrate to Trinidad.

St. George's, the capital, is so deserted, Thomas finds, that "Ichabod is being written on [its] portals," a reference to Washington Irving's "Legend of Sleepy Hollow," and Thomas finds only one newspaper during his visit. Notwithstanding this, and despite his partial paralysis caused by severe rheumatism, he thoroughly enjoys his month's stay, noting the hospitality of estate proprietors and the many visitors who turn his quarters into "a perfect room for Socrates." While the mostly bad orators at the House of the Assembly convince him that more attention should be given to "intellectual weight" than to ownership of property in the selection and number of political representatives, the eloquence of one speaker temporarily banishes Thomas's acute rheumatism. In any case, "well or ill," Grenadians have representative government, which they are right to guard jealously.

While Thomas may have found working-class Grenadians hardworking, other commentators lamented the presence of immigrants from the eastern Caribbean in Trinidad. In 1881, when R. C. G. Hamilton arrived from England to investigate that year's Carnival disturbances, he concluded that in contrast to the old days, masqueraders in recent Carnival celebrations had been "persons of the lowest character, many of them being immigrants from other islands," who seemed to be interested in nothing but creating disturbances. During Carnival, he continued, "it is common" for "the vilest songs, in which the names of ladies of the island are introduced to be sung in the streets, and the vilest talk to be indulged in while filthy and disgusting scenes are enacted by both sexes, which are beyond description and would be almost beyond belief were it not that they were vouched for by witnesses of unimpeachable credibility" (Rohlehr, *Calypso and Society*, 19, 538 n. 58; Hamilton). Such oppositions—"vile" songs and "filthy" acts of men and women in public spaces, on the one hand, and virtuous "ladies" and truthful witnesses, on the other; an older, cleaner Carnival and the disreputable celebrations of the present day; a virtuous Trinidad overrun with disreputable elements from other Caribbean islands—are familiar to us now.

In the same vein, the editor of the *Trinidad Review*, possibly Thomas, opposed the 1883 Music Ordinance by contrasting "old native dances and airs" and "ribald songs and dances," underscoring the point that Trinidad's francophone constituency, elite as well as nonelite, pursued a cultural tradition that was distinctive and worthy of "encouragement" rather than abolition. The ordinance banned the assembly of "Rogues, Vagabonds, and such like" for the purposes of "singing or dancing to the music of drum, chac chac, or any other instrument," and elites resented the colonial authorities' assumption that all local music and dancing equally deserved to be penalized:

If the authorities wish really to put down the ribald songs and dances that outrage the decency of the Colony, they must condescend to learn that there are as well songs and dances that are decent, as songs and dances that are not decent. It can be proved that the indecent songs and dances are not Trinidadian: they being either importations or imitations of the lewd songs and dances of Curaçao, from which island they were first brought over and practised here by one BIMBIM and her equally vile daughters, who, every night, to the peculiar music of their Quelbays went through the most lascivious antics, indicative of the sensuous vocation to which they abandoned themselves. This dance, which cannot be mistaken by the Police, should, with the songs composed for it, be stamped out of the colony like a pestilence; as there is much in it that appeals successfully to the grosser instincts of the uneducated and unwary. On the other hand, every indulgence, if not encouragement should, as in times past, be given to the old native dances and airs, each and all of which possess recommendations that entitle them to exemption from legislative interference.[3]

Here, the ruling anglophone authorities are being scolded for their failure to distinguish between, on the one hand, an idealized "Trinidadian" folk tradition that is so virtuous as to be outside the need of "legislative interference" and, on the other hand, alien entities, this time from the Dutch Caribbean, who threaten to defile the nation's virtue. BimBim and her successors have clearly joined the ranks of local jamettes who populate urban streets, their music and dancing leaving no doubt as to their "sensuous" profession. In the same move this editor is protecting the right of one element of the working class—the "authentic," "Creole," francophone element—to practice its culture, and he is encouraging the authorities to outlaw the cultural practices of working-class immigrants from other Caribbean territories. As Gordon Rohlehr points out, the writer was participating in "the evocation of an idyllic 'Golden Age'" (*Calypso and Society,* 38).

Clearly, this editor watched BimBim and her "vile daughters" closely. He and others were shocked by the confidence with which she and other members of the lower classes asserted themselves in public. Instead of meekly conforming to the standards set by their "betters," in their "appeals . . . to the grosser instincts of the uneducated and unwary" they threatened to undermine society's moral foundations by dragging others down with them. An editorial in the *Port of Spain Gazette* on 2 February 1889 condemned prostitutes in Trinidad's streets: "Courtesans—women coming from the various colonies, French and English, by bands, to swell the ranks of the immoral in Trinidad. They conducted their trade in broad daylight, were generally well-dressed, and often molested decent women in the streets."[4] Again, not only were such women shocking in their lack of subterfuge but they threw into relief the "decent women" whom they attacked and whose moral presence in society was thus made all the more important. Like BimBim, these "courtesans" were an alien infection, though clearly their presence highlighted the existence (since they "swell the ranks") of home-grown versions as well.

The reaction to the Hosay killings of October 1884 also was framed in terms of the violation of both law and order, and of authentic cultural tradition. Though some editorials expressed regret for the excessive force used against the participants, there was general agreement about the need for the close monitoring of nonelites:

> Not only among the Coolies, but also among the lower orders of our Creole population (chiefly composed of the scum of the neighbouring islands with a sprinkling of native incorrigibles) the signs of a growing disregard to law and order have been for some time so evident that even had the late sad events not taken place, a conflict between constituted authority and some section of our lower orders, was, in our opinion, only a matter of time. Let us hope this terrible lesson may have a salutary effect, not only on the Coolies, but on the heterogeneous collections of loafers, prostitutes, roughs, rogues and vagabonds, which infest our two towns.[5]

Strictly speaking, only "Mahomedans," and "but a small portion only of the faithful" at that, were supposed to be involved in the festival: "With the Hindus," the editorial continued, "it has no more to do than with the creoles of this Island. The Hindus follow it because the Mussulmen were their former masters in India, and they take part in the ceremony from habit in much the same way as the creoles were doing here. Their persistence in carrying out the old programme was not justified on any religious or superstitious ground, but was dictated by a pure spirit of opposition to authority."

Not only were "Creoles" essentially foreign to this festival, then, but so were "Hindus." The insistence on a strict reading of "cultural" and "religious" norms in the name of preserving authentic traditions forestalled the possibility of unnatural combinations that would threaten the political stability of the ruling classes as well as the safety of the middle and upper classes. If the lower classes combined across the national, ethnic, racial, and religious boundaries that elites insisted kept them separated, if they regarded their treatment as society's "scum" as the major basis of categorization, they might overturn the economic and social principles to which their social betters held on for dear life. The editorial's interest in preserving the sacred boundaries of ethnicity and religion here, then, disguises a more pressing need to preserve order: if all the participants in that year's Hosay celebration had been "authentic Mussulmen," after all, their activities would have been no less objectionable.

Henry Norman, Jamaica's governor, was brought in to investigate the killings at San Fernando. That he had served at the highest levels of the British colonial regime in India and had also been a soldier during the "Mutiny" in the late 1850s underscores the empire's interconnectedness and efficiency. His report on events in San Fernando drew on his knowledge of Indian matters, as when he noted that the witnesses he had questioned were from Bihar or Oudh and "consequently spoke a language with which I had been familiar during many years." Though he occasionally proffered "a question or two in Hindustani direct from myself, to show the immigrant that I knew what he was saying," he preferred to put the questions through an interpreter, "for although the Hindustani of the immigrants is perfectly intelligible, they often bring in local phrases with the meaning of which I was at first unacquainted."

Making Trinidad's languages intelligible for visitors was the aim of J. H. Collens's *Guide to Trinidad*. Collens, the expatriate English superintendent of the Boys Model School in Port of Spain, instructed his readers in the most efficient ways of extracting service from Trinidad's laboring classes. To get the attention of a "Coolie or East Indian" porter, for instance, savvy visitors were advised to say: "Hi, baboo, load mangé; tum kétna chargum?" which Collens translated as "Hello, poor fellow, do you want to carry load / How much do you charge me?" (49). English, Creole, and Hindi are jostled together here in a hybrid not permitted in Thomas's *Creole Grammar*. Of Thomas's text Collens stated that the attempt to "elevate the Patois to the dignity of a language" was notable since Creole was particularly suitable for humor, wit, and abuse. However, the language lacked "elegance of diction" (49).

Continuing his social mapping, Collens noted that his pupils at the Model School did not believe in the "simplicity of the Saxon tongue" (39–40). They spent hours searching the dictionary for words "which for length might be measured by the yard," and he had to check their "disposition . . . to use long-winded words and high-flown phrases." Of Trinidad's Black population generally he said that they were to be divided among those who would not work, those who did little work, and those who worked regularly.

In its review of the *Guide* the *San Fernando Gazette* of 9 April 1887 said that Collens should have restricted himself to topography and tourists' expenses. Not only were his historical and industrial facts misleading but with the "jaunty style" of an unctuous "porter of some public institution," telling "jumby stories" in order to elicit a tip, Collens reproduced the "calumny of the old school of the slave planter against the black population."[6] This was particularly reprehensible because he was paid by the government to teach his Black and Colored students with impartiality. By dividing the Black population according to its propensity to work on sugar estates and by equating "natives" with "lower classes" (and thus, implicitly, the upper class with those who were "imported") Collens demonstrated the "arrogance of this class when they live amongst us and scrape a few pence together," commanding positions that "native talent" was denied. Those who knew that "the pulpit, the bar, the medical department, the magistracy, and even the press and literature" had "representatives from this portion of the population" would recognize his mischief. "Our people" ought to make sure that such calumnies did not "pass unchallenged" so that the "little ones" would not be bequeathed "vile slanders as historical heirlooms."

Rev. P. H. Douglin, the Black Anglican rector of the St. Clement's Church in Naparima, gave a lecture in San Fernando on 1 August 1887, Emancipation Day.[7] He addressed an enthusiastic gathering of "ladies and gentlemen" on his work with the Rio Pongo Mission in West Africa. Cautioning his audience not to confuse it with "River Congo" or "Rio Pongas," he identified the region as located 120 miles north of Sierra Leone and a major exporter of palm oil to England.

Douglin noted that the mission's establishment by the Anglican Church in the West Indies in 1855 had not been the founding moment of Christian instruction in that region. An early-eighteenth-century expedition had baptized some of the inhabitants but had then left the region "with the rest of Western Africa, in all the gross darkness of heathenism." When Sir John Hawkins had arrived to begin "disastrous labours" there in 1804, he had captured three hundred persons "living in peace and quietness" by "the sword and other means." He had taken them to the Caribbean, where he exchanged them for hides, ginger, sugar, and pearls, and returned to England to get Queen Elizabeth's blessing. She had "strongly objected" but then had been assured that the people of the region had "voluntarily offered themselves as labourers." As various religious missions had floundered, "white men of all nations" had competed for the lucrative slave market and taught the population "tricks and rogueries."

Since the inhabitants of Rio Pongo "up to this day" were "averse to sending, or to allowing their people to go to foreign parts," their love of money and alcohol was exploited by the traders, demonstrating what "the cursed love of money" will do to "an unprincipled Christian man." The Anglican Church in the West Indies, headquartered in Barbados, had resolved to send a mission from a population "mainly derived from Africa, and where not derived from Africa, deeply indebted to Africa by wrongs inflicted, and by benefits obtained." Since "men of African descent" had proved less susceptible to fever than the "Europeans" who had originally been charged with heading the mission, the former now supervised as well as staffed the mission.

Three clergy, three catechists, and three schoolteachers served at five stations, initiating improvements in housing and in communication between Rio Pongo and Sierra Leone and generally bringing light to people "sunk in great ignorance and superstition." Though Africa had been "in the vanguard of civilization" and its people had been the "pioneers of mankind" in the arts and sciences, architecture, navigation, textiles, and other areas, Africans had retreated for safety "far from the light and knowledge of God, which is the centre and source of all improvement and civilization." The "thick forests of ignorance, superstition, vice and ungodliness," where "evil habits" lurked "like wild beasts and venomous serpents," needed to be cleared.

Theological and linguistic translation was an important part of this work. "Rightly directed," Sosoh deities could be shown to be parallel to the Trinity, and the network of "invisible spiritual beings" could be used for good rather than witchcraft. Since the Sosoh language functioned as a means of trade among the "Sosohs, Fallahs, Mandingoes, Bagahs and Tomahs" who visited the region, Douglin and his colleagues had learned the language and reduced it to writing, translating portions of the Bible, the *Book of Common Prayer,* "and educated works." No easy task, it involved "seizing the subtle idioms of speech and dragging forth from these depths where euphony hides them, prefixes and affixes, which are indispensable and which make such a vast difference." But the result was that God was now heard in prayer rather than in oaths, just as slavery had been "mitigated" if not eliminated, and converts were learning to regard their wives as other than "natural conveniences" and to appreciate the value of work. "The whole of West Africa is trembling in the balance," Douglin told his audience. "The Rio Pongo Mission is your Mission." He closed by singing a hymn in Sosoh.

Douglin spoke with authority on African history, the slave trade, and the innate cultural characteristics of "civilized" Bagahs, "heathenish" Black Bagahs, and essentially honest Sosohs now "tarnished" by outsiders. Addressing ladies and gentlemen in the city that was perhaps the center of Trinidad's Black and Colored "respectable classes," the very account of the incident in the *San Fernando Gazette* was framed by the boundaries of "civilized" procedure. The lecturer entered the St. Paul's School Room with his wife and daughter "punctually to loud applause," and the article ended by noting "the very ill-behaviour of a few young men whom we would advise to reserve such buffoonery as they were guilty of at the lecture for equestrian performances." Douglin's San Fernando audience chuckled at the Sosoh belief that kola nuts were the forbidden fruit that Eve had swallowed, thus preventing her from keeping secrets, while they had stuck in Adam's throat, explaining why men are reflective before speaking aloud. Their laughter confirmed their own modernity as believers in the equality of the sexes and as Christians. They endorsed his narrative of a once great continent ravaged by European outsiders and in need of spiritual and cultural conversion.

That his account was similar to contemporary texts on Africa written by European travelers would only have confirmed its rightness: well-meaning English people were like Queen Elizabeth, after all, juxtaposed in Douglin's lecture with evil traders such as Hawkins. Douglin's listeners felt themselves to be tied ancestrally to Africa and judged unfairly by its failings. They had faith in the eventual rehabilitation of Africa in accordance with their and Douglin's definitions of culture and progress, and they took pride in his missionary activities, which demonstrated that Caribbean "extra-Africans" were giving back to their ancestral homeland.

When Douglin told his audience that Rio Pongo was one of the "sunny fountains" about which they sang at their missionary services, he confirmed their stake in the continent as Christians of African descent. Reginald Heber's 1817 hymn "From Greenland's Icy Mountains" was widely used in mission and antislavery circles:

> From Greenland's icy mountains,
> From India's coral strand,
> Where Afric's sunny fountains
> Roll down their golden sand.
> From many an ancient river
> From many a palmy plain
> They call us to deliver
> Their land from error's chain.[8]

That it would also become the official opening hymn of meetings of Marcus Garvey's United Negro Improvement Association in the early twentieth century suggests how Christian missions, British imperialism, and pan-Africanism reinforced and "languaged" each other (see C. Hall, "From Greenland's Icy Mountains"; and Hill, 278).

The *Grenada People* seemed to concur with Douglin's representation of African affairs in its report on King Ja-Ja of Opobo, who was banished from West Africa to the Caribbean in 1888.[9] If Russia, in its dealings with "some Central Asian tribe," had been guilty of similar "land-grabbing propensities," English public opinion would have been deafening. Such "tyranny and injustice" had "kept Africa dark." Was it any wonder that the continent had not been Christianized? King Ja-Ja, a "semi-civilized African potentate," had been tricked into exile because English traders were greedy for more control of the palm oil industry.

As the region's commentators responded to Froude's text in 1888, some linked vindication of Black people in the Caribbean to the rehabilitation of the African continent. More generally, there were objections to his willed ignorance of the "intermediate" classes, which were the same as the *San Fernando Gazette*'s objections to Collens. Whether Creole Black, Creole White, or metropolitan White, commentators agreed that Froude's reading of the region's Black and Colored middle classes was at best insufficient and at worst racist, particularly as this constituency was crucial to the future of the region. This did not mean, however, that their responses were identical. They demonstrate that "Negro vindication" was not just the province of Negroes and also that such vindication might demonstrate the *potential* of Negroes for eventual participation in political life under the constant supervision of Whites or might indicate that they were already fully capable of doing so or that they had a key role to play in the Caribbean, *in addition to* assisting in the rehabilitation of the African continent.

Froude's respondents were in general agreement that his concentration on the views of White "birds of passage," as well as his insistence that there was no future for Whites in the region and that it was therefore destined to go the way of "Hayti," was limiting. None questioned that vodun was a sign of Haiti's "barbarism," though Froude was chided for his hysterical obsession with it and for his use of Haiti as a standard by which other territories should be measured. For these critics, Froude's concentration on Black and Indian nonelites was also problematic. Though some reviewers of his book stressed the potential of working-class Black people to participate in political life eventually, none alluded to a significant place for

Indians in the region's future. Ironically, then, the metropolitan travel-ogue's focus on the region's nonelite masses affirmed their importance, however expediently, while critics of such travelogues tended to see such focus as misguided since it was a deliberate writing out of "intermediate" claims to political agency.

LIKE KINGSLEY before him, Froude regarded the Caribbean as the primal scene of England's naval and political glory. In the seventeenth and eigh-teenth centuries England had proved itself supreme among European nations in Caribbean waters, winning battles and territories from French, Spanish, and Dutch competitors. As well-read products of their country's most prestigious public schools and universities, Kingsley and Froude had read and re-read texts recounting the exploits of the English adventurers and offered their own celebratory readings of the Elizabethans: Froude had won public admiration for his studies of Henry VIII and Elizabeth I, while Kingsley had paid tribute to the defeat of the Armada in his novel *Westward Ho!*

Reading Kingsley's *At Last* prompted Froude's desire to visit the region, and he made a point of visiting the rooms where Kingsley had stayed in Trinidad. Both men prepared themselves for their respective journeys by reading the travel accounts of others: "Looking," writes Kingsley, "upon that upon which my teachers and masters, Humboldt, Spix, Martius, Schomburgk, Waterton, Bates, Wallace, Gosse and the rest, had looked already, with far wiser eyes than mine, and it was not less, but far more wonderful than they had said" (1:157). Froude prepared for his trip by reading naval histories, Jean-Baptiste Labat, and biographies of Lord Rodney. Kingsley's invocation of the "three great names, connected as long as civilized man shall remain, with those waters—Columbus, Raleigh, Humboldt" (1:65) was a reminder that the region had been claimed in print and otherwise and was also, perhaps, an indication of anxiety that these late-nineteenth-century travelers might not measure up to their pre-decessors. Their own texts were in this sense part of a "strategic forma-tion" whereby "groups of texts . . . acquire mass density, and referential power among themselves and thereafter in the culture at large" (Said, *Orientalism*, 20). It was the combined weight of these texts and their readers' acceptance of them as knowledge that gave them and their writers their authority.

Froude was far from feeling like a figure of authority when he entered Caribbean waters early in 1886. At odds with the tone of forthrightness that pervades his text was the fact that he was exhausted from the experience of editing Thomas Carlyle's papers and shaken by the unfavorable reception of an outraged British public. Though it is important to analyze *The English in the West Indies* on its own terms as an important metropolitan position on the region, then, when the text is placed beside his letters to his family and friends during this trip or beside his reflections on the experience of being Carlyle's biographer, which he began to write about this time and eventually published as *My Relations with Carlyle,* the Caribbean becomes in some sense a setting for his anxieties about reticence and prestige.

I want to linger over this point for a moment before turning to *The English in the West Indies.* On the one hand, I have been indicating that the imperial context is key to understanding the "national," "English" character of a Victorian intellectual formation that would present itself as self-sufficient rather than dependent upon colonial matters for their clarification. This would suggest that a knowledge of Froude's travel writing is as crucial to understanding him as an intellectual as is a knowledge of his twelve-volume *History of England* or the controversial editions of Thomas and Jane Welsh Carlyle's papers. On the other hand, I am suggesting that Froude's text on the Caribbean does not tell us any more about his intellectual authority than do his texts on Australia, South Africa, or Ireland or any of his other texts and that *The English in the West Indies* was not as controversial in the context of his overall career as his Caribbean readers found it to be. Kingsley was more anxious about the reactions to his own text in the late 1860s than Froude was about reactions to his texts in the late 1880s, and this is indicative both of Kingsley's personal relationship to the Caribbean and of the specific discursive climate of the mid-1860s around matters of race and empire, a climate that affected both Kingsley and Froude.

Kingsley's visit to the Caribbean in 1869–70 was the culmination of a lifelong desire to visit the region, and he dreamt of it on his deathbed in 1874. The first words of *At Last* announce this desire: "At last the dream of forty years, please God, would be fulfilled, and I should see the West Indies and the Spanish Main" (1:1). We have seen that his meditations on the past and future of the Caribbean include an acknowledgment and even advocacy of interracial relationships: "How different might have been the history of Trinidad, if at that early period, while the Indians were still powerful, a little colony of English had joined them and intermarried with them" (1:108). Or he imagines English men who, as resident husbands of English women, provide "centers of civilization" for non-White labor. Froude, on the other hand, almost hysterically insists on the impossibility of racial combination of any kind: when he meets interracial couples, he stresses the absurdity of such unions. I am not arguing that Kingsley's positive representation of such unions entailed his own desire to live there or that his rendering of the Caribbean is any less hostile to the political aspirations of Caribbean inhabitants than is Froude's. But it is interesting that whereas Froude sees no future for Whites in the region, Kingsley textually ties the European male to the Caribbean.

I suggested in chapter 3 that Kingsley's utopian visions of Indian-White unions are a way of rhetorically erasing an unwanted Black presence in the region, and while not revoking this, I am further suggesting here that his imaginative if not necessarily political commitment to a future for Whites in the region is connected to his family's own Creole ties. In a limited sense we might recast the usual implications of *mother country,* which is usually understood as the colonial subject's ambivalent relationship to the metropole, and move the Caribbean from its typically imagined location at the margin of the imperial center to the center of the metropolitan subject's dream life.

What was in reality a first visit in 1869 seems to have been more of a homecoming, given the numerous references in *At Last* to the seashells in the cabinet of Kingsley's childhood household and to family stories of the region. Kingsley's mother was born in Barbados, and her family owned property there, as well as in Demerara, British Guiana. His description of his grandfather's calm response to a volcano—"he quieted his household and his Negros, lighted his candles, and went to his scientific books in that delight, mingled with an awe not the less deep because it is rational and self-possessed" (1:90)—indicates the Caribbean bequeathed to him by his mother: scientific, contemplative plantation owners taking giddy slaves in hand and restoring order to chaos. In the thirty years since the abolition of slavery his grandfather's "Negroes" had seemed quite different: unredeemable, untrainable, and unfit for the responsibilities of citizenship. The Morant Bay affair seemed to prove this to be the case.

The recall of Edward Eyre, the governor of Jamaica, for his brutal handling of the uprising in St. Thomas-in-the-east, Jamaica, in 1865–66 had a significant impact on intellectual life in London, bringing to a head issues of intellectual friendship, public discourse and silence, and race and ethnicity. Two committees of the most prominent intellectuals were formed around the issue. One group, headed by John Stuart Mill, protested Eyre's actions. The other, a conservative faction headed by Carlyle and including aristocrats with landowning interests in the Caribbean, felt that Eyre was being wrongly persecuted for what they saw as his attempt to save White lives. They pointed out that the concern over the slaughter in Jamaica was hypocritical since England's poor lived in much worse conditions than did Black Jamaicans. Catherine Hall's detailed analysis of the incident stresses that the public discourse generated by the affair became a way of defining the moral positions of these men and ultimately their particular conceptions of manhood and Englishness (*White, Male, and Middle Class,* 255–95).

The affair proved extremely embarrassing for Kingsley, who, to the dismay of colleagues such as Charles Darwin, gave public support to Eyre in the camp headed by Carlyle. At a Southampton dinner to welcome Eyre back to England in 1866 Kingsley suggested that Eyre should get a peerage for his role in the affair.[10] The radical press was contemptuous of his comments because of his earlier affiliation with the Christian Socialists and his novels on working-class life. His patriotic sentiments during the Crimean War had garnered him the attention of the court and resulted in his appointment as Regius Professor of Modern History at Cambridge in 1860, perhaps solidifying even more his altered political allegiances.

A negative liberal press discouraged Kingsley from further public comment on the Eyre affair, and this silence in turn earned him the displeasure of Carlyle and Ruskin in the pro-Eyre camp. In addition, he lost two of his friends from the Christian Socialist movement, Thomas Hughes and John Ludlow, who disliked his pro-Eyre statements. Both his forthrightness and his vacillation, therefore, angered his colleagues. He was viewed as cowardly in his reluctance to speak further by one faction and as a toady to the aristocrats by the radical press, who also attributed his support of Eyre to his brother Henry's defense of Eyre's activities in Australia years before his appointment in Jamaica (Eyre had been widely praised at that time as a "defender" of Australian aboriginal people) and to his mother's having been born in Barbados. One of Kingsley's biographers notes that when asked to make a financial contribution to the welfare of former slaves in the West Indies, he refused, saying that emancipation had "ruined" him, a reference to his family's plantation interests in the Caribbean having been adversely affected by the abolition of slavery (Martin, 258).

When Kingsley was preparing to write his travelogue on his visit to the Caribbean, in a letter to his publisher he indicated that he preferred to risk being criticized for his concentration on the descriptions on flora and fauna and his avoidance of political issues since he was afraid that the Anti-Slavery Society and Ludlow would condemn his discussion of West Indian people. He confessed to not wanting to "be dragged through the mire of controversy" and pledged to be "cautious and reticent."[11] What seems cryptic in his dedication of *At Last* to Arthur Hamilton Gordon—

"I could say more, but it is wisest to be silent on the very points on which one longs most to speak"—might therefore be read as a reference to his desire not to offend. Although William Herbert and other Caribbean readers might not have thought so, Kingsley, wary of further damage to his reputation, made a conscious decision to pay more attention to Trinidad's vegetation than to its humans.

The Eyre affair had repercussions for Froude as well. As one of those publicly identified with Carlyle, he was expected to demonstrate his loyalty to him. The following retrospective quotation indicates not only his reticence but also his sense of having failed in his duties: "I was myself one of the cowards. I pleaded that I did not understand the matter, that I was Editor of *Fraser*, and I should disturb the proprietors; mere paltry excuses to escape doing what I knew to be right. Ruskin was braver far, and spoke out like a man" (qtd. in Dunn, 2:315). While Ruskin publicly identified himself with Carlyle, then, Froude used his position as editor of a prominent periodical to argue that he could not afford to be publicly identified with a controversial cause. He rather miserably states that Ruskin "spoke out like a man," indicating the gendered distinction between "manly" individuals like Ruskin, who spoke out boldly and independently on an issue, and "cowards" like himself, who feared public censure and remained silent. Thus, the recall of Eyre had serious repercussions for both Froude's and Kingsley's reputations as forthright and (for Kingsley) liberal-minded intellectuals.

If Kingsley's embarrassment causes him to censor himself when he writes about the Caribbean in the early 1870s, however, Froude feels no such compunction in the 1870s and 1880s. During this period he made trips to South Africa, Australasia, Ireland, and the West Indies. These trips, as well as a trip to the United States, where he lectured on English rule in Ireland, brought him criticism for his views on the inability of colonial people to rule themselves and the necessity of the British government to maintain firm control of these territories. In *The English in the West Indies* he does not hesitate to make reference to the Eyre affair of 1865–66, declaring that despite his silence at the time, he thought that if Eyre had not been a "model" governor, he had been at least an "average" one who had been "unworthily sacrificed to public clamour" (229). As in Natal a few years after events in Jamaica, harsh punitive measures toward Blacks in response to the threat of conspiracies, even if these remained only threats, were always justified by the general lessons of history: "In England the massacre in Hayti is a half-forgotten story. Not one person in a thousand of those who clamoured for the prosecution of Governor Eyre had probably ever heard of it. In Jamaica it is ever present in the minds of the Europeans as a frightful evidence of what the negroes are capable when roused to frenzy" (227).

His late mentor provides the apposite analogy: "Carlyle used to say that it was as if, when a ship had been on fire, and the captain by skill and promptitude had put the fire out, his owner were to say to him, 'Sir, you poured too much water down the hold and damaged the cargo.' The captain would answer, 'Yes, sir, but I have saved your ship'" (225). About George William Gordon, the Colored member of the Jamaica Assembly who was executed for his involvement in the affair, Froude is no less frank. In one sense this is unsurprising given his views about Coloreds and Blacks, but in this case it is notable since the British public was particularly sympathetic to Gordon's plight, finding pathos in the letters that he wrote to his wife in his last hours (C. Hall, *White, Male, and Middle Class*, 278). Froude concedes that Gordon's hanging was extreme despite his dream "of regenerating the negro race by baptising them in the Jordan of English Radicalism." As he contemplates the scenery at Gordon's former estate at Cherry Gardens, where he goes to visit the current occupant, Froude expresses compassion for the executed man, who can no longer enjoy the landscape, though "one does not associate the sons of darkness with keen perceptions of the beautiful" (235).[12]

Clearly, then, in 1888 Froude was not troubled by the reaction of liberals as Kingsley had been in 1871. It was Froude's role as the Carlyles' biographer that haunted him during his Caribbean travels, though of course the one cannot be cleanly separated from the other. In death Carlyle hovered over everything, causing sleeplessness:

> The Carlyle worry comes back on me at night sometimes. . . . Bad Carlyle fit on me. What my connexion with Carlyle has cost me: my own prospects as a young man; later gave up *Fraser's* because Carlyle wanted it for Allingham, and my work on Charles V so as to be free to write Carlyle's biography; then the ten years of worry before the book was finished, and the worry for the rest of my life. By and by the world will thank me, but not in my own lifetime. I ought to shake the whole subject off me, but it is not easy to do. Tomorrow we shall be at Cuba in a strange scene altogether. (Dunn, 2:551)

Froude's publication of the Carlyles' papers in the 1880s raised a storm of controversy as Victorians discovered more than they would have preferred to know about the sage of Cheyne Row, his troubles with dyspepsia, and his treatment of his wife, including the whiff of an extramarital affair. As Trev Lynn Broughton has shown in a fascinating study, the incident raised questions about Froude's friendship and loyalty, as well as the place of discretion and reticence in literary life, and it also threatened to dissolve the precarious distinction between domestic life and the rugged, "masculine" heroic conception of the literary vocation, which Carlyle had helped to create.[13]

Reviewing a new edition of Jane Welsh Carlyle's papers in 1903, W. S. Lilly referred to Froude's desire to make his books on Carlyle "a pecuniary success," knowing that "nothing pays like a *succès de scandale*" (1006). Lilly declared all of Froude's work as a historian to be "not merely untrustworthy, but mendacious" (1007). Just as there were "kleptomaniacs," there were also "pseudomaniacs," and Froude was one of the latter (1009). To those of Froude's defenders who insisted on his "admirable English" Lilly (recalling Herbert's review of Kingsley, and Thomas's remarks on Donovan and Wenkstern) conceded that this was the case only in the sense of the "'easy vigour' and subtle grace" of newspaper editors ("leader writers"), who were "accomplished gentlemen" with "facile pens": "Surely, when the charge against him is that he has said the thing that is not, it is no defence to reply that he has said it in excellent English" (1008).

Froude's entire career had been plagued by controversy. Because of his exploration of a young man's loss of faith, published in *The Nemesis of Faith* in 1849, while he was still in his early twenties, he was asked to resign his fellowship at Exeter College, Oxford.[14] Having prepared for most of his life to take his place as a clergyman at the very apex of intellectual and spiritual life in England, he had jeopardized his prestige and his future by casting serious doubts on his moral and spiritual condition. As he later labored in the archives of Salamanca to produce his historical studies, he gained both prestige for his laborious transcriptions of original documents and notoriety for what many considered to be sloppy scholarship.

Traveling to the Caribbean in 1886, then, Froude was the prestigious historian who had edited a prominent periodical and who had been asked by Lord Carnarvon, the Colonial Secretary, for his impressions of the state of the British Empire, but he was also the "pseudomaniac" who had betrayed the Carlyles. Even as he was steaming toward the Caribbean, new editions of the Carlyle papers were being prepared to counter his publications. It is no wonder, then, that Froude experienced sleeplessness and a "bad Carlyle fit" as he pondered his reputation and his legacy: "By and by the world will thank me, but not in my own lifetime."

The English in the West Indies begins with an invocation of the Colonial Exhibition and Queen Victoria's jubilee celebration, occasions on which

British subjects across the world had reaffirmed their desire "to preserve unbroken the integrity of the British Empire" (1). Froude distinguishes here among colonies that are self-governing dependencies under the auspices of the British crown, such as Canada, New Zealand, Australia, and the Cape, whose "colonists are part of ourselves"; those "conquered countries" such as India and the West Indies, having large populations of "foreigners attached by force to our dominions . . . [who] will not always consent to rule themselves in accordance with our views or interests"; and territories such as Ireland, "neither one nor the other, where our own people . . . [ruled] an insubordinate population" (4). While Australia and other territories might flourish under self-government, the West Indies, because of its considerable Black population, presented the prospect of another Hayti if not checked.

This is particularly unfortunate, Froude argues, since the West Indies were "the earliest, and once the most prized of our distant possessions . . . the scene of our greatest naval glories" (5). The exploits of Drake, Hawkins, and Rodney, which had made England a great naval power—and which Froude proposed should be the subject of an epic poem, with the West Indies the theme of its most "brilliant cantos" (10)—were now lost to fainthearted politicians. Such politicians looked at the West Indies merely in terms of its market value and failed to honor the heroism of the past, as leaders of great nations ought to do. This was a sign of Britain's declining greatness, and these politicians, "spouting upon platforms," were to be contrasted with the "silent men [who] do the work," such as Rodney, who "struck a blow in the West Indies" for England's heroism when talkers in the House of Commons would have recalled him. Similarly, Warren Hastings won India for Britain while "the eloquent Burke [tried] to hang him for it." The orator cut down in a day the institutions that were "the slow growth of centuries," just as Demosthenes and Cicero had "misled their countrymen" with their words. People preferred leaders with fluent and facile tongues, persuasive speakers who contradicted themselves the next day.

The age cried out for the right candidate, the "true lord and master" to string Penelope Britannia's bow, presently unstrung, with the owner away and with evil suitors rivaling each other to "consume her substance" (14). This image of the nation as Penelope, the loyal wife in danger of being ravished by evil suitors, was suggested in the full title of his book: *The English in the West Indies, or the Bow of Ulysses.* "Only the true lord and master can string" the worm-eaten bow, "and in due time he comes" (14). Froude finds Gladstone to be generally repugnant in his condoning of dishonesty and his self-serving diagnosis of national progress. Gladstone and other political leaders, then, are "little men of talk" whose liberal policies at "home" reflect their failure to oversee the imperial scene of England's heroism: "Great warriors and statesmen built our Colonial Empire. Parliamentary oratory and the little men of talk are pulling it to pieces" (Dunn, 2:549).

As Froude travels through the Caribbean—he visits Barbados, St. Vincent, Grenada, Tobago, Trinidad, St. Lucia, Dominica, Jamaica, Haiti, and Cuba—he pronounces these territories to be in a bad or worse state based on the relative prosperity and numbers of Whites or Blacks. In Grenada, for instance, where much of the land is owned and tilled by Black "pure peasant proprietors," the inhabitants are as "litigious as Irish peasants" (49). "Black the island was and black it would remain," but Grenadians "knew their own deficiencies and would infinitely prefer a wise English ruler to any constitution which could be offered them" (50). There were two paths available to them—"either an English administration pure and simple, like the East Indian, or a falling eventually into a state like that of Hayti, where they eat the babies, and no white man can own a yard of land" (50)—and this held for the rest of the British Caribbean as well.

Froude insists on the impossibility of Whites', Coloreds', Blacks', and Indians' combining together, and these societies thus require wise White rule to hold them together. "The black does not love the mulatto, and despises the white man who consents to be his servant" (78), as he says about Trinidad. Furthermore, "The African and the Asiatic will not mix," Black women's desire that the "straight hair of Asia" replace their "unhappy wool" notwithstanding (65). This carries over into a repudiation of persons who represent the biological product of such combinations and, crucially, the social groups who violate boundaries by possessing characteristics that are unsuitable to their racial classification. There is a "small black boy" on the ship going out to the Caribbean, for instance, who, despite having "little more sense than a monkey, perhaps less," has been educated in Europe; "his parents must have been well-to-do" (22). He was therefore "spoilt as a black and could not be made into a white, and this I found afterwards was the invariable and dangerous consequence whenever a superior negro contrived to raise himself."

Similarly incongruous is the clamor for the franchise in Trinidad, where "certain busy gentlemen" have "discovered" that they are living under tyranny (75). Since Jamaica is getting reform—"no one knew why"—Trinidadians do not want to be left out. The demand for reform is "dressed up in the phrases borrowed from the great English masters of the art, about privileges of manhood, moral dignity, the elevating influence of the suffrage, etc., intended for home consumption among the believers in the orthodox Radical faith" (59). Even if, as we have seen, he despises those "at home," he does not question their comprehension of such words. They may be misguided, but they are not absurd.

Like Collens's students and Trollope's mimics, Trinidadians use big words that they do not really understand, the words of those at "home." Constitutional advocates at the franchise-reform meeting "imitate the fine phrases or the apostles of liberty in Europe, but they succeeded only in caricaturing their absurdities" (76). Invited to attend the meeting, Froude responds that he "knew too little of their affairs to make my presence of any value to them" (60) and notes that many of the thousands in attendance were more interested in seeing the governor batting in a cricket match nearby (76). The result of the meeting is "some petition or other" (76).[15] Such political gestures are dangerous and absurd, and they are particularly unsuited to the Caribbean: political agitation is the "commonplace [intruding] upon the imaginative," the enchantment of palm trees, starry skies, and long-winged bats disrupted by "an absurd awakening" (59).

Port of Spain's savanna, the scene of Kingsley's race-tracking, seems to repudiate Froude's preference for extremes rather than intermediates or hybrids. While its scenes are "beautiful"—"Tropical human beings, like tropical birds, are fond of fine colours, especially black human beings and the park was as brilliant as Kensington Gardens on a Sunday" (58)—or "pretty enough"—"Black coats and white trousers, bright-coloured dresses and pink parasols, look the same at a distance whether the wearer has a black face or a white one, and the broad meadow was covered over with sparkling groups" (75)—they may mask a potential danger. What might it mean that a white face looks the same as a black face from a distance? While Froude insists on a knowable and discernible difference, the savanna may mark his limit (as an outsider, that is; Trinidadians were ignorant of distinctions at their peril).

For those groups who do not violate their boundaries, Froude is willing to be more expansive. Having ordered the Black persons whom they find bathing in Trinidad's Blue Basin to leave so that they can swim there, he and his party concede the "conscious superiority" of one of their guides. The latter catches a crayfish when they are unable to catch anything, indicating the "knowledge in the head of a small nigger boy" (74). Everywhere he goes "the boundless happiness of the black race" is clear. Under English rule they experience "perfect felicity" and are much better off than they were in Africa (70). As he is informed by other guests on board on the journey out, "The curse is taken off from nature, and like Adam again they are under the covenant of innocence" (42–43). In Trinidad he finds that their food grows in abundance around them, thus requiring little, if any, labor to cultivate, and they are even immune to mosquitoes and snakes. Clothing is superfluous since they have no sense of shame, though because of European influence they have a "love of finery which would prevent a complete return to African simplicity" (69).

As we have seen, Froude is impressed by the women he meets in the market in Roseau, Dominica, who walk long distances with loads on their heads and yet are not "sullen." The region's coalers also recommend women's industry to him. In Jamaica "some hundreds of negroes, women and men, but women in four times the number, were hard at work" (174). While the men have it "comparatively easy," the women are "willing beasts of burden, for they had the care upon them of their children; the men disclaiming all responsibilities on that score, after the babies have been once brought into the world":

> The poor women are content with the arrangement, which they prefer to what they would regard as legal bondage. They earn at this coaling work seven or eight shillings a day. If they were wives, their husbands would take it from them and spend it in rum. The companion who is not a wife can refuse and keep her earnings for her little ones. If black suffrage is to be the rule in Jamaica, I would take it away from the men and would give it to the superior sex. The women are the working bees of the hive. They would make a tolerable nation of black amazons and the babies would not be offered to Jumbi. (175)

The Caribbean's laboring classes do actually labor, as it turns out, though it is the "poor women" who have the worst of it. Franchise-reform meetings notwithstanding, it is *women* who deserve the franchise—an indication of Froude's jocularity, since he would not grant the franchise to any Black constituencies, male or female, nor to nonelites or elite women in his own country.

THE APPEARANCE of Froude's book in early 1888 commanded significant and sustained attention from the region's newspaper readers. Philip Rostant's editorial in the *Public Opinion* of 28 February 1888 declared *The English in the West Indies* "grotesque" in its account of Trinidad's franchise-reform movement and faulted Froude for turning down an invitation to attend the franchise-reform meeting in 1886. Kingsley had accepted such invitations during his visit to Trinidad, the editorial noted. Furthermore, if Froude's book went into a second edition, there should be footnotes specifying his sources.

In June of that year Edgar Maresse-Smith and six other gentlemen visited Governor Robinson to ask that the first day of August be declared a public holiday. Since the pope's jubilee had been observed with a public holiday and celebrations the previous year and Queen Victoria's jubilee had been similarly celebrated in 1886, why not do the same to celebrate the abolition of slavery?[16] In a letter that infuriated the petitioners the governor refused to grant the holiday: "The freedom of the African Race was won not by your own efforts, not by your own orators, not by your warriors—it was fought for by white men and gained after fierce struggles against authority and power, and after unwearied sacrifices." "All English-men," Robinson continued, "are proud to be successors to those men who fought and won for you. . . . To the great Wilberforce are your and our thanks especially due." The governor stated that he could not comply with their request since Trinidad's population was "mixed": "We have Indians, Chinese, French, Spaniards, Portuguese and English amongst us and you are not a majority of the people." He hoped they would celebrate the day with a religious service in quiet reflection on the fact that "the African race" had not progressed sufficiently.

Maresse-Smith read the letter to a disgruntled public gathering on 25 June, making his disdain for the governor very clear. His speech was punctuated by comparisons of the governor to Froude, and in a letter to the *San Fernando Gazette* published on 30 June he called the governor's letter a "masterpiece of Froude-ism." Governor Robinson's "long Froudish tirade" missed the real reason for the insufficient progress of the African race since emancipation: a "long string of negro-hating Governors" who had "stunted" their "social growth." Under the exceptions to the rule, Lord Harris and Sir Arthur Hamilton Gordon, "we had fair play, and we proved ourselves capable of holding our own in an equal contest." The competitive examinations for entrance to the civil service, for instance, had been eliminated after Gordon's departure, and if they were to be reinstated at present, "how many nonentities of the Public Service would be dethroned to make room for darker, but more intelligent, men? We would be ready, at any time, without previous notice, to compete with all the present holders of important posts in the Government; and we would have no fear of failure." Maresse-Smith dismissed Governor Robinson's advice that the petitioners concentrate on improving the "social condition" of "those in a humbler state than ourselves" as an attempt to shirk his duties: "Can we grant Free Education, build a Reformatory?"

Another letter by Maresse-Smith, published in the same issue of the *Gazette*, condemned Rostant's account of the meeting in the *Public Opinion*. To refer to them as "a handful of boys" and to say that people would not join them unless "respectable men" supported them was to pretend that Rostant, the mayor, and others had not been invited and to avoid the issue of why the latter had not thought of jubilee celebrations. Rostant "cooked a story of your own which you have served hot to your readers," Maresse-Smith declared.

When it was resolved to organize jubilee celebrations despite the denial of the public holiday, a spate of letters ensued, many condemning the public criticism of the governor by "young upstarts." An alternative planning committee, chaired by the mayor of Port of Spain and attended by older public figures such as Rostant, planned a parallel celebration. They pleaded with the renegades to join in with them "in a large and liberal spirit without question of colour, creed, or party."[17]

Letters to the newspapers proposed erecting a monument to Wilberforce or using the occasion as an opportunity to thank the English nation, and a poem entitled "To Be or Not To Be" stated the latter position very forcefully:

> The slaves' descendants seem to want
> To keep this Jubilee
> Have they such cheerful memoirs of
> The days of slavery?
> If such a fête should e'er be kept
> 'Tshould be by English folk,
> For *they* it was that freed the slaves,
> And broke the blackman's yoke.
> But their descendants should *forget*
> Their ancestors' disgrace,
> When they had not the pluck to rise,
> And feared a whiteman's face
> 'Tis *we* should keep this jubilee,
> The honour is for *us*
> *They* have no thoughts to make them proud,
> Or e'en felicitous.[18]

By this account, Wilberforce and other British humanitarians had magnanimously bestowed freedom on British Caribbean colonies in 1834. Portrayed as inexperienced and irresponsible, members of Maresse-Smith's group received further condemnation when they scoffed at the suggestion that the day should be marked by religious services. Their response, that God had nothing to do with it, cast them as godless noisemakers in the eyes of the reading public.[19]

Members of the competing jubilee committees belonged to the Trinidad Literary Association in Port of Spain. In the midst of a June meeting debating "The Place of the American Civil War in History" and "Whether the Crusades were Beneficial to European Civilisation" a motion that the organization should plan for a suitable celebration of emancipation was rejected by Rostant, who chaired the meeting.[20] As the vice president of the association, he stated that the association was a "purely literary" one and that emancipation was a political issue. He admonished those who had proposed the motion for their youth and impetuousness, chiding them for not seeking the advice of influential, experienced members of the community and for alienating persons who would otherwise have participated.

Challenged by a younger generation that was invoking racial difference and questioning his distinction between the "political" and the "literary," Rostant sought to assert his authority as someone who had assumed the leadership role in various organizations for many years. The liberal, if not radical, leader of the constitutional-reform movement, he was now being cast as conservative in a movement in which a younger group of men defining themselves in explicitly racial terms were showing him that in political matters he could not always expect to take the lead. Indeed, he himself referred to the fact that he was old enough to be the grandfather of most of the Maresse-Smith faction—signifying wisdom and experience in one sense and irrelevance in another. On 1 August 1888, in addition to the celebrations taking place throughout Trinidad, two jubilee banquets were held in Port of Spain. One, led by the mayor and Rostant, was attended by the governor. The other was presided over by Maresse-Smith, who reportedly toasted the governor with his glass stem held disdainfully between thumb and forefinger (Hooker, 12).

As *Froudism* became a much-used term throughout 1888, Charles Spencer Salmon's book *The Caribbean Confederation,* published that year, countered Froude's by insisting that there was a healthy future for the British Caribbean because the Queen's Black subjects welcomed their subjecthood.[21] They might live in the Caribbean, but their vision and their loyalties were projected primarily, if not solely, toward England. Identified on the copyright page as "late President of Nevis, formerly colonial secretary and administrator of the government of the Gold Coast, Chief Commissioner of the Seychelles and a member of the Cobden Club," Salmon had served in the upper echelons of the British colonial administration in Africa and the Caribbean. His membership in the Cobden Club marked him as a liberal devoted to free trade, as opposed to the landowning interests of the West India Committee. Stating that "the black British subjects in the West Indies" ought to be allowed to share with Whites the "privileges of British subjects everywhere," Salmon urges the institution of local self-government throughout the British Caribbean and (anticipating a twentieth-century concern) the uniting of these colonies into a confederacy. Salmon links the past and future of Black people in the Caribbean to Africans: "It is impossible to dissociate the black British subjects in the West Indies from the kindred races of Africa; what one may be the other may be." He notes that the African continent is diverse, that it contains many examples of "useful political organisations," and that "European dominion has been often a curse and has never been of any service to the African people" (17–19). Froude, like Trollope before him, had not given the subject the care that it deserved, and thus "the history of the African races has yet to be written" (preface).

Salmon says that Froude dislikes every institution that would hinder "the undivided sway of Englishmen over every race and people they happen to be among" (31), and he fails to see that English colonists would be attracted to the Caribbean by a system in which both Whites and Blacks would have a political voice (41). Contrary to what Froude insists, the Caribbean is not ruined. Those who benefited from an "absentee proprietary holding nearly all the best lands, and a servile or semi-servile labouring class" (127) dislike the "new order," which is based on a large number of peasant proprietors.

Froude's negative views of the morality and capacity for civilization of Black Caribbean people are erroneous. While he would have his readers believe that the low incidence of marriage among Afro-Caribbean people is attributable to moral defects, Salmon counters that "our own base conduct and vile and unclean teaching in the past" is the real reason, considering that slaves were not permitted to marry during slavery (46). Froude's views on "Hayti" are exaggerated in their sensational tales of cannibalism and fail to make reference to the brutality of slavery. The chaos of continuous civil unrest, Salmon finds, is an obstacle to the solutions—education and Christianity: "The one remedy is missionary exertion, and the spread of education *with it*" (95, Salmon's emphasis).

"British black men" pay taxes, cultivate the land, and are "law-abiding" and "loyal to the Crown" (53). They appreciate what the English did for them when slavery was abolished and know that the English will do even more if their "efforts and position and loyal character entitle them" (54). Black people, Salmon asserts, must "struggle to merit that freedom" since Froude's text proves that naysayers are ready to "re-forge their chains" (54). "The leaders among the black men" should encourage their sons to be "men of action"—surveyors and scientists—instead of "lawyers and place-hunters" (54). Though Froude never mentions that "great Englishman," Wilberforce, his memory is cherished in the Caribbean, and this is why "the black man is so loyal and so true. He sees the greatness and generosity of England personified in a name dear to Englishmen and to the world" (58).

The Indians whom Froude and Kingsley find to be the key to the region's future are "weaklings" compared with the "herculean" African and represent an "effete" and "bygone" civilization (133). Black Caribbean people are "open to civilising influences" (89) and can be "moulded more easily" than other races (146). Owing nothing to "the islands of their birth," they are "loyal and devoted to the throne" and "owe everything" to England (133). Thus, British Caribbean territories do not want self-government that is "inconsistent with British supremacy" (124).

Nicholas Darnell Davis was a Grenadian-born senior official in British Guiana's colonial service. His response to Froude, "Mr. Froude's Negrophobia, or Don Quixote as a Cook's Tourist," was published in British Guiana in 1888.[22] Davis declares early on his interest in challenging Froude's "rampant Negrophobia" (85), and we have seen that his use of the terms *froudacity* (99, 117) and *froudacious* (109) landed Thomas in controversy when *Froudacity* was published the following year.

Juxtaposing two models of heroism, Davis says that Froude "would pass himself off as the Ulysses of the Empire" but that "stripped of his mask, he is discovered to be but the Don Quixote of Colonial and Imperial Politics" (125). Froude is "in quest of Wind Mills, not of Sugar Mills" (104), an absurd Quixote obsessed with past glories, and a "Cook's Tourist," like the nineteenth-century travel agent rapidly touring many places. He uses Froude's distinction between talkers and doers to cast Froude as someone who "does" places by driving around in a carriage. Froude is "the Great Mr. Wordy" (125), "a man of books rather than a man of the world" (90), and Carlyle, "whom Mr. Froude served as worshipper and iconoclast in turn," would have detested this. Echoing Herbert's criticism of Kingsley and Lilly's of Froude, he declares that Froude writes a book for the purpose of creating "sensation."

"Imagination" is Froude's forte, and thus Froude's Trinidad "was alternately Spanish and French," according to Froude, when in actuality

France never possessed Trinidad. Similarly, Froude "tries to set the Barbadians right as to the origin of the name of their Island" by determining that it must mean bearded Caribs, instead of referring to a species of banyan trees. However, the full name given to the island by the Europeans who conquered and named it was "Los Arboles Barbados, the Bearded Trees." Noting the documentation of Froude's inaccuracies in the region's newspapers, Davis concludes that Froude's book "is a mere piece of Bookmaking, containing no real study of the past History, and still less of the present life, of the English and African Races in the West Indies" (86–87).

Froude's "Negrophobia" is demonstrated, for instance, by his positing of Grenada—"this now flourishing little colony, which the Black Man, by industry, is turning into a garden"—"not as an example, but as a warning" (88). Sir George Strahan, a former governor of the Windward Islands, had thought Grenada was "a little Paradise," but then with him "the Black Man was somebody, whereas with Mr. Froude the Black Man is nobody in the political system." For Davis and Strahan, then, paradise was marked by industry and black resourcefulness, in the context of English rule.

Froude missed good opportunities to study the region's people and their political aspirations, Davis notes, and thus he turned down the invitation to attend the meeting on constitutional reform in Trinidad. He preferred the company of the "dominant colonists," and his encounter with the women at the Roseau market in Dominica shows his occasional willingness to interact with the "labouring classes." But "not a single instance can be recalled of any attempt on our author's part to make himself acquainted with those intermediate classes who, *willy nilly,* are the coming people of the West Indies. He was not unaware of their existence, but he studiously ignored it when he might have made acquaintance with it. The main burden of his book is, however, a fulmination against the growing importance of those classes" (95). If he had visited the plantations, he would have learned "what men of African and of mixed Races are doing" and that "not a single white man" had any part in managing some of these enterprises (102–3). Focused on white planters and emancipated slaves, Froude pronounces the mixed-race constituency to be disliked by both and says that they will die out. Instead, Davis asserts, "the future of the West Indies belongs to the Mixed Race" (113).

On Froude's invocation of Haiti, Davis notes that even if it were as bad as Froude claims, there is no comparison to "British Africans" (121–22) since Haiti was founded by "revolted slaves, many of them pure barbarians." Present-day Haitians for the most part "have not enjoyed the leavening power of European influence" (122), though if Froude took the trouble to speak to the intermediates, "for the most part mulattoes," he would get a different perspective. While superstitions still exist in the British Caribbean, the "Black Man's" progress toward "a more civilised view of Religion" has been striking, and most "West Indian Africans" have emerged from "Religious Bondage": "A much more powerful Medicine Man now roams at large. This is the Schoolmaster. Working hand in hand with him are the Ministers of Religion" (119). In the British Caribbean, "English influence and control" have been constant, and "second and third generations of freemen," rather than the "emancipated slaves" that Froude insists on terming them, have paid for their land with their industry rather than the violence used by Haytians. Their industry has made agricultural land more valuable (123).

Davis concludes by appealing to the authority of a man of action, a doer who is in marked contrast to Froude. Henry Norman, the governor of Jamaica, whose role in the inquiry of the 1884 Hosay massacre in Trinidad I noted earlier, is Davis's model of a hero. Froude meets Norman briefly in Jamaica and speaks highly of him in *The English in the West Indies,* but though he says that Norman is an eminent man, he has not really spent time with him. Not wishing to follow Froude's tendency to unsubstantiated assertions, Davis outlines Norman's career, including his 1857 service in Lucknow, where his heroism was demonstrated by the fact that his horse was shot under him. "Mr. Froude admires men of action. He cannot but admit that Sir Henry Norman is a man of action." For Norman, Davis notes, Jamaica has good prospects because of Black and Brown people, prospects which Froude denies. In addition, Norman is supportive of representative government.

Davis ends his article with a final tribute to the wisdom of British statesmen serving in colonial territories. With their guidance, "the English African cannot but be the gainer by the continuance of English authority" (129). Even when such ties are "loosened" after a "prolonged Apprenticeship to the business of Representative Government," the English language, the "great deeds" of English soldiers and sailors, and English political institutions would be the legacy.

For both Salmon and Davis, then, Black people in the Caribbean are demonstrating their potential for civilization, and the intermediate classes, particularly "mixed races" for Davis, are capable of sharing representative government with Whites. For Salmon, loyalty to England seems to displace loyalty to the Caribbean. For both, Black prospects for improvement are placed solidly within the context of British rule and guidance.

Thomas was residing in Grenada when Froude's book appeared in 1888. As he participated in Grenada's plans for the jubilee celebrations, he questioned a general tendency to focus on Wilberforce's contributions to the abolition of slavery.[23] In two letters entitled "The Pioneers and Champions of Negro Emancipation," he noted that long before Wilberforce, the Quakers had been hostile to slavery, as had Granville Sharpe, Thomas Clarkson, and a host of others. Just as these men had battled the lies of those who "flourished" by slavery's atrocities, those in the present day battled the "scoundrelism" of Froude, that "spokesman of the pro-slavery survivals."[24] Thomas interrupted what appeared to be the beginning of a projected series on abolitionists to begin reviewing Froude's book in the articles that he would eventually publish in London as *Froudacity*.

In a letter to the *Grenada People* on 12 July 1888 Thomas expressed disappointment at the news from Trinidad that people were objecting to the "fair complexion" of those who were planning the emancipation celebration and at reports that some persons of African descent objected to the celebration because it would commemorate slavery's "degradations." During slavery, Thomas pointed out, "no colour was exempt either from owning or becoming slaves," and so it made perfect sense that "even the whitest" would participate in the commemoration of its abolition. On the second point, the Jews observed Passover, Americans Independence Day, and the British Guy Fawkes Day to commemorate not the "degradation" of their oppressors' tyranny but the efforts of their ancestors in securing freedom. Such misconceptions made it essential that "enlightened" West Indians, "and especially those of African origin," spread knowledge of West Indian history through "books and other instrumentalities." *Froudacity* can be read as an effort in this direction.

Froudacity begins with an explanation of why the book was necessary. Froude's attempt to "thwart political aspiration in the Antilles," an attempt "thinly draped with rhetorical flowers," required a response (51). To Froude's insistence on perpetual hostility between Blacks and Whites because of the history of slavery Thomas counters that all "well-thinking West Indian Whites" remembered slavery only with "regret" and "Negroes" had only "precarious tradition or scarcely accessible documents" in regard to the suffering of their ancestors; death and time had intervened to make it impossible for "mutual hatred" to survive. Froude's "White-master and Black-slave theory" ignored the historical fact that any free persons could own slaves, and therefore not only Whites but also Blacks and "half-breeds" did, "dusky" planters enjoying the same privileges as "pure-blooded Caucasian" planters (55).

In addition, Froude's constant recourse to Haiti as a standard against which to measure the rest of the Caribbean "because of our oneness with its inhabitants in origin and complexion [was] perversity gone wild in the manufacture of analogies" since it was common knowledge that Haitians, having "gloriously conquered their merited freedom," were "free, but perfectly illiterate barbarians," and Mulattoes had abandoned Blacks instead of standing in solidarity with them. Liberia would have been the better analogy for "a coloured population starting a national life, really and truly equipped with the requisites and essentials of civilised existence" (54).

Froude's fallacies required a response, and "Mr. C. Salmon" had provided a "luminous and effective vindication of us," for which Thomas thanked him on behalf of the "entire coloured population of the West Indies." A high-ranking European, Salmon did not, like Froude, view Negroes from balconies "or the seats of moving carriages." Salmon's vindication as someone not of our race, spurred Thomas to "self-help." The "best writers of our race" had contributed "masterly refutations" of Froude's text to the region's newspapers, in addition to which many newspapers and periodicals in Great Britain and the United States had published commentaries on Froude's text. But this forum was not conducive to future reference, and thus these responses would prove "ephemeral" compared with the permanence that Froude's book would enjoy.

A permanent, book-form response by one of "Her Majesty's Ethiopic West Indian subjects" (56) was needed, and despite his illness Thomas volunteered. The delays in *Froudacity*'s publication, caused by his unfamiliarity with "English publishing usages" and the "hindrances" leading to "frequent and sometimes long suspension of my labour" had prompted suggestions in some quarters that there would be no interest in the text since there was little interest in Caribbean affairs and it had already been a year since the publication of Froude's text. Thomas hoped that some of Froude's readers would still be interested in *Froudacity,* particularly when "a member of that very same race" that Froude had vilified had written it. Since an Australian had recently responded to Froude's *Oceana,* published before *The English in the West Indies,* Thomas hoped that his own text's delay would not affect the interest in his vindication. At any rate, the interest of Caribbean people had been confirmed by "a numerous and influential body of my fellow West Indians, men of various races, but united in detestation of falsehood and injustice" (60).

We can only guess at Thomas's reference here to "frequent and sometimes long suspension of my labour." We have seen that he had to secure funding for the project. In addition, he refers to twelve years of "bodily and mental obstacles that have beset and clouded my career" (56). He connects this physical and mental infirmity to his inability to write "easily," echoing his comparison of Otto Wenkstern and William Donovan. For Alexander Pope, Thomas reminds his readers, "True ease in writing comes from Art, not Chance / As those move easiest who have learnt to dance." It turns out that only "Art," connoting the conscious practice and labor of craft, can produce "ease." "Bodily sickness and mental tribulation" deny Thomas that "regularity of practice in composition which alone can ensure" Pope's "true ease" (58). Here, then, it is not lack of aristocratic leisure that is offered as the obstacle to "ease," as in Donovan's case, but illness.

Those who are practiced at dancing, such as Froude, ought to show good judgment, says Thomas. Froude is a "master in that craft" of "artistic phrase-weaving," acknowledged "even among the foremost of his literary countrymen," and Thomas knows that he cannot compete with him in matters of style (58). However, Froude sacrifices "all obstacles," including "verity," in order to "secure an artistic perfection of style" (63). In an interesting turn of phrase, Thomas pronounces Froude a "bond-slave of his own phrases" (63). Furthermore, "his injurious statements against the hapless Blacks" are so erratic that Thomas's own style suffers, since in responding to him he is forced to meet Froude's points "exactly how, when, and where I found them," resulting in "irregular" sequence (58).

However, "literary competency" is not the issue here, and to judge Thomas's work solely on that "purely artificial" score would be wrong since this text, indeed the whole body of his work, clearly indicates that this is not his priority. "The judges to whom I do submit our case are those Englishmen and others whose conscience blends with their judgment, and who determine such questions as this on their essential rightness which has claim to the first and decisive consideration" (58). Thomas's preferred audience, then, might well take aesthetics into account but would be more swayed by considerations of truth and "conscience." Notably, this audience consists of "Englishmen and others," indicating their importance, though of course it does not mean that they constitute his only audience.

In fact, Thomas notes that another audience for the work is sure to get him into trouble. In the course of repudiating Froude he will criticize colonial officials in the Caribbean, and he knows what this will mean, considering that "such criticism has on many occasions been much more severe than my own strictures." Since *Froudacity* is in book form, he anticipates consequences but "cheerfully" accepts them "in the interests of public justice" (59).

Froude's bias leads him "to see much that is, and always has been invisible to mortal eye," as when he notes that the waters of the Grenada Carenage have a violet tint because of the surrounding trees, when "every one familiar with that locality knows that there are no forest trees within two miles of the object which they are so ingeniously made to colour" (65). He also mishears, as when he asserts that Anglo-Barbadians speak "pure English, the voices without the smallest transatlantic intonation." Noting that no Barbadian could avoid the fate of "Peter of Galilee when skulking from the peril of a detected nationality: 'Thy speech betrayeth thee!'" Thomas refers to two metropolitan travel writers whose "auditory powers" are better than Froude's. Both G. J. Chester (in *Transatlantic Sketches*) and Trollope confirm that both Black and White Barbadians have a "drawl" that is unique.

It is interesting that Trollope is used to counter Froude's faults here, considering Salmon's reservations about Trollope. Like Thomas, Darnell Davis cites Trollope approvingly when, at the outset of his critique of Froude, he says that Trollope's travel narrative "may be classed with the brightest of his Novels" (85). For Davis and Thomas, at least, Trollope is preferable to Froude. The references to the Grenadian landscape and to Barbadian accents in the passage above indicate Thomas's keen aware-ness of regional differences, and this leads him to counter Froude's asser-tion that "the characteristics of the people are the same in all the Antilles, and could be studied elsewhere." The Caribbean's "Negro inhabitants" are distinguished not only by differences in "local surroundings and influ-ences," Thomas notes, but also by "the great diversity of their African ancestry. We might as well be told that because the nations of Europe are generally white and descended from Japhet, they could be studied one by the light derived from acquaintance with another." On the contrary, "unless a common education from youth has been shared by them, the Hamitic inhabitants of one island have very little in common with those of another, beyond the dusky skin and woolly hair. In speech, character, and deportment, a coloured native of Trinidad differs as much from one of Barbados as a North American black does from either, in all of the above respects" (74).

Homogeneity such as Froude's stems from an unwillingness to take Black aspirations seriously. Far from being the "half-civilised, out-of-the-way region under British sway, and inhabited chiefly by a horde of semi-barbarian ignoramuses of African descent," that Froude makes Grenada out to be, for instance, "all of its chief intellectual business" is conducted by "men of colour," and this is why Grenadians have done so well (75).

Thomas's response to Froude's description of the Black youth on board ship who was "spoilt as a black and could not be made into a white" and who, "being lifted above his own people . . . had been taught to despise them," is rooted in a commentary on social mobility in the Caribbean as well as in Europe. It is "reckless" and even "unpatriotic" for Froude, a European, to suggest that a European education would lead its pupils to despise their own people. Furthermore, the relationship between "educated black men" and their "unenlightened fellow-blacks" has nothing of the "cynicism" of Englishmen towards "their less favoured countrymen" (67–68). Only a "worship of the skin" could lead to the conclusion that education would "spoil" someone: "The Ethiopian of whatever shade of colour who is not satisfied with being such was never intended to be more than a mere living figure," and no sympathy should be wasted on such a person. While Froude states that the family of such a person would "feel their blood as a degradation," the "poor Irish peasant who toils and starves" so that the eldest son can enter the priesthood feels anything but humiliation when that son secures a congregation.

Caribbean households are similarly "elevated" and "ennobled" by children who have excelled, as are the friends of the family, since "the African race" is as "self-loving," "sympathetic," and "tender" as anyone else. Thus one could expect, Thomas notes, that the families of the late M. M. Philip and Conrad Reeves, chief justice of Barbados—and he might have added himself—would rejoice at these men's success.

Thomas then addresses Froude's assertion that "sinister" social relations are produced by the fact that educated Black children do not want to marry other Blacks and that Whites refuse to marry Blacks. Thomas asserts that women from "high" White families may not marry Black men, but they form "base private connections even with menials of that race" (69). Similarly, during slavery there was less "skin-distinction" than at the present time since "all planters, black and white alike," had common interests, so that expatriate Whites who wanted to consolidate their "position" and "influence" would make "advantageous Creole marriages" (69–70). But "sheer uncalculating love" of "dusky" women also prompted White men to risk "exclusion from 'Society'" if rich, or "dismissal from employment" if poor. Even the enforcers of these "penalties" had "Ethiopic" "house-keepers." As he states at the outset of the text, then, color prejudice in the Caribbean is overstated since historically plantation owners and other members of the upper echelons have come from all races. It was only after "administrative power passed entirely into the hands of British officials," Thomas notes, that "skin-discrimination" commenced. For Thomas, then, "the blending of the races" is not the urgent question that Froude makes it out to be.

Thomas echoes neither Froude's hysteria about race mixing, then, nor Darnell Davis's assertion that "the future of the West Indies belongs to the Mixed Race." Indeed, Thomas's comments here counter Froude by denying the existence of tensions. No "cynicisms" (class tensions? elitism?) mark relations between "educated" and "unenlightened" Afro-Caribbean people, and there is no color prejudice—or at least he downplays it—because class interests cut across race. Since so many of Thomas's interactions with his society over the course of his career seem to have been rooted in such prejudices, we might join late-twentieth-century commentators in wondering if he is "out of touch with reality" (see Brereton, "John Jacob Thomas," 32). We can assume with such commentators that he was motivated by his advocacy of constitutional reform. Still, Thomas does not blindly celebrate the existence of a happy band of White, Colored, and Black slave owners. Elsewhere in the text he refers to the wealthy "Ethiopic accomplices of the oppressors of their own race" (116). Froude's appeal to racial tension in the Caribbean is in the interest of denying the possibility of political power, and by showing that there is in fact a long tradition of collaboration across racial lines, Thomas undercuts Froude's logic.

Thomas's reference to the days before the influence of British officials shows him to be appealing to a reading of the Caribbean that is in line with elite francophone Trinidadian conceptions of the "good old days" and that perhaps contradicts his own references to the roach's struggle in the face of the bird in the *Creole Grammar*. Furthermore, there is an interesting appeal in the passage to the charms of "Ethiopic damsels" (as well as, presumably, those "Ethiopic" men with whom Whites form "base private connections"). Sexual liaisons, Thomas implies, equalize powerful Blacks, Browns, and Whites, and this erases the possibility of discrimination, which would manifest itself, presumably, if only powerful Whites were involved. Thomas exoticizes "Ethiopic damsels" and their male counterparts and draws attention away from the racial and class inequities of such liaisons.

Thomas indicates that Froude himself would have been susceptible to the "piquant charms that proved irresistible to so many of his brother-Europeans" (70), noting the positive references in Froude's text to Black women: whereas the women of Barbados are "perfectly upright," like "Greek and Etruscan women," and "might serve for sculptors' models," their male counterparts are "active enough, driving carts, wheeling barrows, and selling flying-fish." Thomas highlights the word *enough* since it proves that Froude could not deny that Black people, and men in particular, actually worked instead of sitting around lazily, though he admits it only grudgingly. If Froude had been willing to make even these limited concessions to the industry of Black people elsewhere in his text, Thomas notes, his unfair references to men might have been overlooked, since they are more than compensated by his "chivalrous appreciation of our womankind" (72).

Turning to constitutional reform, Thomas's comparison of "good" and "bad" colonial officials indicates that crown colony administration places colonial subjects at the mercy of the "moulder of men's destinies": governors who either accepted this responsibility or showed themselves to be "tools" of this or that interest (82). Thomas lists these governors by name, reminding us of his prefatory reference to the possible consequences of angering public officials. While some governors failed because they allowed themselves to be overwhelmed by corruption or because they lacked the initiative to overcome their "clerk-like dread" or "constitutional timidity" and act aggressively, others were afflicted by "vulgar colonial prejudices" leading to corrupt management, denial of official appointments to "Creoles in general, and to coloured Creoles in particular," and efforts to reduce the ability of "boys of African descent" to attend Queen's Royal College (84–86).

Good governors include his own patron, A. H. Gordon, in the late 1860s, who earned fierce opposition because of his refusal to pander to special interests. "Statesmanlike" Gordon united warring factions of English and Creole, Catholic and Protestant, and installed "an educational system that opened (to even the humblest) a free pathway to knowledge, to distinction, and, if the objects of its beneficence were worthy of the boon, to serviceableness to their native country" (83). Thomas's euphoric account of the "free pathway to knowledge" and "distinction" in a context where, as we have seen, so few managed to trod it and his uncomplicated linkage of service and "worthiness" are not endorsed by Donovan's obituary of Thomas, though it echoes Maresse-Smith's comments at the 1888 public meeting.

After the 1870 departure of Gordon, this "true king in Israel" (88), Thomas continues, Trinidadians were subjected to some good but mostly bad governors, including a timid one who was "an old woman, garbed in male attire" (89). William Robinson, Trinidad's governor at the time Thomas was writing, was, interestingly enough, one of Thomas's "good" governors, "a ruler operating as a safeguard to the people's interests" (82). It is reasonable to assume that Maresse-Smith would not have agreed with Thomas's assessment of Robinson. Thomas ends his exposé of Trinidad's governors by stating that Froude's slurs against the leaders of the constitutional-reform movement who throw around half-understood phrases about the "dignity of manhood," his refusal of the invitation to attend the franchise-reform meeting during his trip, and his "slanderous" suggestion that the reform leaders have a personal interest in the governors' salaries show him to be void of the "dignity of manhood" himself, "however masculine his name" (92).

Thomas counters Froude's "roseate picture of Arcadian blissfulness," his statement that Black people live "under the beneficent despotism of the English Government, which knows no difference of colour and permits no oppression" (95), by giving examples of the suffering of Trinidad's working class at the hands of an incompetent magistracy. A Barbadian immigrant "of the better sort" is maltreated by one of the "Barbadian rowdies" in the police force, and the court fails to support her. Similarly, a "member of one of those brawling sisterhoods that frequently disturbed the peace of the town of Port of Spain" is unfairly thrown into jail, while the court upholds the theft of an Indian immigrant's cart.

The "bloody catastrophe" at the 1884 Hosay festival in San Fernando similarly shows the actions of an incompetent magistrate but also those of the governor at that time. When the festival's participants acted in good faith, submitting petitions and accepting responsibility for fines or imprisonment, they were met with "violent death or a life-long mutilation." Furthermore, anyone who had condemned the massacre was arrested, proof to Thomas that "the poorer and more ignorant classes can be handled with greater impunity than those who are intelligent and have the means of self-defence" (107). These inefficient magistrates are contrasted to others who are "ideally upright, just, and impartial dispensers of justice" (109).

Clearly, Thomas has followed these cases closely over the years, perhaps because he acted as a magistrate at some points in his career or because his tenure at the San Fernando Boy's School coincided with the events of the 1884 massacre. He is concerned about all who fail to secure proper justice before the law, even when, as in the case of the jamette, he might disapprove of their behavior in general. These incidents prove that Trinidad's poor are far from the "sleek and contented" people Froude makes them out to be and justify Thomas's own concern for the welfare of this constituency and his impatience with the expatriate officials who serve them so poorly.

Tackling Froude's views on the prospects of Black rule, Thomas compares Blacks' participation in political life in the anglophone Caribbean with their participation elsewhere in the region, as well as in North America. "Scores of brilliant coloured officials" are allowed to participate in political life in French and Spanish territories. Though "Ethiopic accomplices of the oppressors of their own race" enjoy the privileges of wealthy planters in the British Caribbean, in the United States "no 'nigger,' however alabaster fair, was ever allowed the privileges of common citizenship" (116). Despite their hardships, these Americans, after the Emancipation Proclamation in 1863, prove the lie to Froude's characterization of Frederick Douglass as an "exception." Black public officers are "as thick as blackberries" there, while Froude can only point to the example of Conrad Reeves, the chief justice of Barbados. Thus, the "strong-minded" Americans have achieved in twenty-five years, however expediently, what "British policy . . . hostile to the advancement of the Ethiopians" has failed to do in fifty. While Thomas refers to the "blunders of the Reconstructionists" elsewhere in the text (183), he clearly believes that the erasure of these gains in the United States is a temporary setback.

Since Froude uses Barbados's Reeves and North America's Douglass to concede that "individual blacks of exceptional quality" have the potential to conquer their "natural tendencies" with "higher instincts" and should thus receive "opportunities to rise," Thomas painstakingly sorts out the hypocrisy of this sort of appeal to White beneficence and Black exceptionality by referring to the differences between "opportunities" in the Caribbean and those in the United States and between "pure" and "mixed blood" categories (124–25). On the latter point, whereas Froude refers to Douglass and Reeves as "individual *blacks,*" both are "of mixed blood." Though neither of these "eminent descendants of Ham" cares about what are ultimately "trivial" matters, Froude's "crusade is against the Negro—by which we understand the *undiluted* African descendant, the *pure* Negro," and both Douglass and Reeves would concede that not only are they far from being "exceptional," as Froude terms them, but there are "scores of genuine black men" in the Caribbean and the United States who are their equals. Interestingly, then, Thomas is at pains to vindicate "pure Negroes" who risk being slighted in Froude's privileging of the "mixed blood" Reeves and Douglass, though Froude shows himself to be oblivious to such distinctions.

While the United States provides Douglass and others with "opportunities [that] are really free and open to all," in the British Caribbean "parasitical non-workers are to be found, eager to eat bread, but in the sweat of other people's brows" (125). Thomas gives a rather starry-eyed account of North American democracy as a foil to parasitical expatriate Whites in the Caribbean who feed off of the labor of others. *These,* it would seem, are the pumpkin eaters in an inefficient crown colony system. Yet for Froude to imply that Douglass and Reeves "should be offered" opportunities is to hypocritically ignore the extent to which such opportunities have been actively withheld, as well as the efforts of both men and others to assert themselves despite their obstacles. In the United States, Douglass "regained his freedom" by fleeing from the South to the equally "maniacal" North. "Conquering his way into the Temple of Knowledge," he gained fame abroad until "America, like a repentant mother [helped] him to stand forward and erect, in the dignity of untrammeled manhood" (127).

Reeves had opportunities that Douglass did not, and his brilliant legal and political career in Barbados since that time was unquestioned, though the very "Anglo-West Indians" on whose behalf Froude lobbies in his text persisted in providing him with obstacles. Though Reeves holds the highest legal office in Barbados, then, and though it is illegal in "English jurisprudence" to discriminate "on the ground of race and colour," Thomas "shudders to think of" the "petty cabals, the underbred indignities, direct and indirect," that Reeves endures at the hands of British colonial officials (129).

Countering Froude's claim that Black voters would only vote for Black public officials, Thomas notes that the "demand for Reform in the Crown Colonies—a demand which our author deliberately misrepresents—is made neither by nor for the Negro, Mulatto, White, Chinese, nor East Indian. It is a petition put forward by prominent responsible colonists— the majority of whom are Whites, and mostly Britons besides" (131). Again, it seems curious that Thomas would challenge Froude's insistence on the impossibility of interracial alliances by indicating that it is Whites who lead the movement for constitutional reform. Yet we should place beside his insistence that there are no demands that "Negroes *as a body*" should have political privileges—Froude having claimed that this was the case—the assertion, further on, that "there is not a single black man— though there should have been many—among the leaders of the movement for Reform" (135). Froude knows that "sturdy Britons are at the head of the agitation," Thomas states, but he insists that constitutional reform has as its goal "negro domination" (135). That Thomas stresses White-only leadership, then, means neither that he approves this situation nor that he resents Whites per se, who are perfectly acceptable as long as they are not "pro-slavery" spokespersons like Froude.

That Froude dares to be an apologist for slavery—as when he notes of courteous Black Jamaicans that though slavery was horrible, "there must have *been something human and kindly* about it, too, when it left upon the *character the marks of courtesy and good breeding*"—is an outrage to Thomas, who reflects on the "ages of outrage, misery, and slaughter" (134, his emphasis). Besides justifying slavery, the passage discounts the origin of Black "courtesy and breeding," since "African explorers, from Mungo Park to Livingstone and Stanley, have all borne sufficient testimony to the world regarding the natural friendliness of the Negro in his ancestral home, when not under the influence of suspicion, anger, or dread" (134).

Countering Froude's assertion that those sold into slavery were "slaves already to worse masters," Thomas praises White abolitionists in North America and Britain but also specifies the role of White traders: "the factory dealers did not wait at their seaboard mart, as our author would have us suppose, for the human merchandise to be brought down to them" (143). They actively sought out their captives and delivered them to a journey and a lifetime of "atrocities." Thomas also appeals to the authority of his own experience, "since early childhood," with the variety of ethnic groups brought to the Caribbean from West Africa.

Turning to religion, Thomas rebukes Froude for daring to philosophize about the spiritual condition of Caribbean Black people, when he himself lacks a "solid faith" (164). Because of the influence of the Catholic and Dissenting Churches, Thomas notes, Black people have been teachers and preachers, "bearing glorious testimony to the humanising effects [of] the religion of charity" (167). The North Americans Josiah Henson and Sojourner Truth are standards "of spiritual excellence" that the race has produced. But Thomas also submits a longer list of Christians whose attention to the mitigation of "the tremendous trinity of Ignorance, Vice, and Poverty" highlights the "criminality" of persons such as Froude, who "waste their brief threescore and ten years in abstract speculations" (171–72). Paul the Apostle and Vincent de Paul are joined in the contemporary period by David Livingstone and Charles Gordon, "the martyr-soldier of Khartoum, in trusting faith a very child, but in heroism more notable than any mere man of whom history contains a record." The "heathen of Africa, the man-hunting Arab, the Egyptian, the Turk," and "the exulting children of Britain" are all "glorified by his life and history"

(174). So opposed to the spirit of such Christians is Froude's text, which "scoffs at humanitarian feeling" and upsets the "equilibrium of feeling between good men of different races" (176), that it is much worse than the cannibalism that Froude invokes so constantly, which is at least limited by public outrage and the death penalty. Froude's work "[strikes] at the root of national manliness by eulogising brute force directed against weaker folk . . . [denying] the possibility of a Divine Power" (176) and thus invoking hell on earth.

As we saw in chapter 2, Thomas ends *Froudacity* by listing some of the names of the great Black vindicators. They are charged with the rehabilitation of African people both within the continent and dispersed globally, since the "intra-African Negro" is besieged by the "violence and unholy greed" that are targeted at the continent. It is to such urgent political questions, instead of to his "bastard philosophizing" on the overriding importance of the "possession of a white skin" (179), that Froude ought to have directed his attention. The great civilizations of the world having "got their turn" "on the world's stage," it would one day be the turn of the African race, asserts Thomas, echoing a common theme of nineteenth-century Black leaders. The hardiness of the race is attested to by its survival of the experiences of slavery, and the American Civil War had witnessed both the "eager" participation of Black soldiers in the northern army and the "loyalty and good faith" of Black slaves left to guard southern plantation households when the White owners went off to fight.

Networks of kinship had helped enslaved communities to survive, since those traveling on the same ship in the Middle Passage had continued to regard each other with the "sanctity of blood-relationship," and their descendants had continued this (183). In Catholic territories the church "had stood open and ready to welcome them," and the planter class had maintained ties that were "more solemn than the naturalties of secular parentage" (184). Thus, "higher motives than mere greed of gain or the pride of racial power" eased the burdens of slavery. Planters established connections "with such of the slave-women as attracted their sympathy, through personal comeliness or aptitude in domestic affairs, or, usually, both combined," and relatives of the female slaves, as well as their "Mulatto" children, enjoyed extended benefits because of these relationships (184–85). By contrast, for the Puritan in North America, "whenever he condescended thereto, familiarity with even the loveliest of the subject people was regarded as a mighty self-unbending for which the object should be correspondingly grateful. So there could, in the beginning, be no frequent instances of the romantic chivalry that gilded the quasi-marital relations of the more fervid and humane members of the Latin stock" (186).

Here, Thomas reproduces the francophone Creole account of the institution of slavery writ large: warm, humane Catholics with extended, interracial family networks and cold, racist Anglo-Saxons. In the Caribbean context, the English influence, including the stereotyping of Blacks as lazy that originated with the "overseer class," had the effect of erasing a tradition of patronage that had allowed "the coloured influence" to penetrate positions in the public service. Even "personages no less exalted than Governors," Thomas states, had "[relaxed] in the society of some fascinating daughter of the sun from the tension and wear of official duty" (188). This strengthened the tradition of godparents and sponsors: "For the god-children of Governors there were places in the public service, and so from the highest to the lowest the humanitarian intercourse of the classes was confirmed" (188–89).

Here, either Thomas is oblivious to the fact that such patronage would have excluded many persons of working-class origin, such as himself, or he feels that his own ability to benefit from personal interaction with prominent persons at various points in his career underscores the value of such networks. In any case, in Thomas's account the British planter class that assumed ascendancy in Trinidad proceeded to retard Blacks' progress in the wake of emancipation by attempting to monopolize their labor and keep down wages. However, it was too late to place permanent obstacles in their way since "according to the Negroes' own phrase, people of colour had by that time already 'passed the lock-jaw stage'" (190), a Creole phrase indicating the survival of an infant beyond the critical initial days.

Thomas stressed Blacks' continuing advancement, as well as the value of interracial solidarity. Trinidad's education system brought together "children of all races and ranks" and facilitated the "intercommunion between all the intelligent of the inhabitants." Thus "there is no possibility of maintaining distinctions based on mere colour, as advocated by Mr. Froude" (191). The recent Emancipation Jubilee had shown that there was a "strong desire for intercommunion and intercomprehension amongst the more distinguished of our people" (193). The African race had survived hardships and would continue to do so. Much had been done in a short time, and "Providence, time, and circumstances" would facilitate the "comprehensive racial enterprises" that the future held.

THOMAS'S LENGTHY discussions of the history of slavery, the impact of the slave trade on the African continent, comparative social relations in

the Caribbean and North America, the Caribbean judiciary, and the role
of the church indicate that in responding to Froude he gave himself the
opportunity to discuss a range of subjects that he had obviously been
thinking about for a long time. Some of his assertions echo his comments
elsewhere, while some seem to contradict them. The beneficial role of the
Roman Catholic Church, for instance, is elsewhere disputed by his and
others' condemnation of its backwardness and discrimination. His response
to Father Violette comes to mind here, as does his implicit critique of the
Catholic Church's relevance to the working-class when he notes that one
reason for his interest in a Creole grammar is that the Mass is delivered in
French. Strategically, in *Froudacity* francophone, Catholic realities are
shown to be more humane to Caribbean people than Protestant, Anglo-
Saxon ones.

Thomas shows himself to be a keen student of the American Civil War
and the progress of prominent African Americans. In his discussion of
Reeves and Douglass we see him weighing the potential benefits to Black
people of what he sees as an expedient and efficient American democracy,
on the one hand, and a discriminatory imperial British policy that falls
short of the ideals of the humanitarian principles that allowed it to lead the
world in abolishing slavery, on the other. In assessing British imperialism
he clearly demarcates "good" Englishmen—colonial governors, explorers
of the African continent, and so on—from those who, like Froude, fail to
live up to British ideals.

Thomas believes in the capacity of education and religion to civilize
the world and looks forward to helping to expand opportunities for his
race to harness these so that they can participate fully in the affairs of
respectable people throughout the world. Froude and others have misused
their own access to education and religion to try to deny the Black people
of the Caribbean their rightful place in the political decision making that
is the responsibility of all respectable people.

Registering an impatience with Black self-hatred, Thomas also insists
that since many Blacks have shared power with Whites for generations in
the region, for good or ill, it is a misreading of history to impose artificial
limits on the ability of Black people to join with Whites in charting the
future of the Caribbean. Finally, his impatience with Froude's dismissal of
"intermediates" does not displace Thomas's close and sustained interest
in the hardships of the laboring classes.

To explain "West Indian fables," then—the phrase is part of the subtitle
of *Froudacity*—is to counter Froude's "jumby stories." Though Thomas
denied a rumor that he was publishing *Froudacity* "wholly and solely" to

support Trinidad's constitutional-reform movement, the text certainly responds to this political imperative.[25] Just before leaving Grenada for England in 1888, he noted that illness prevented him from writing his own proposed book on the history of emancipation. *Froudacity* therefore emerges out of the urgency of responding to Froude but also out of a regional need for a history of slavery and emancipation, made more pressing by the plans for the celebration of the jubilee anniversary. A permanent rather than "ephemeral" response to Froude, *Froudacity* is also pressed into service as the history that illness has prevented him from writing, his version of the historical novel that others critique him for shirking.

Afterword

IN A POWERFUL account of her intellectual production, Marlene Nourbese Philip describes the two reading communities that haunt her early cultural production—at her shoulder the "white, Oxford-educated, and male" and on her left "an old wizened and 'wisened' black woman." She gradually manages to push "the reader to the right further into the shadows, and the reader over my left shoulder has emerged more clearly from the shadows into the light" (295). No doubt Thomas and his contemporaries would have bristled at the male and female "intermediates" who are missing from this paradigm, but Philip's suggestive formulation reminds us that each generation of writers configures its own relationship to both its influences and its audience. Jamaica Kincaid's declaration that she never aspired to be a writer "because I didn't know that any such thing existed" accords with the opposition between a female, African-derived, oral folk tradition and a male, lettered, English-derived upper-class tradition that characterizes current discussions of Caribbean women writers (Cudjoe, "Jamaica Kincaid," 218).

In the 1960s, at a nationalist moment that is as canonically definitive in Caribbean literature as the late 1980s has proved to be for women writers in the region, C. L. R. James traces two lines of intellectual descent through his parents. He delineates a passionate and unruly "mother-line" in the private realm that facilitates the development of a pleasurable intellectual life and a public, vigorous, and philistine patrilineal side defined in a more obvious way by rules and obligations. Both lines are respectable and marked off from the noisy masses (F. Smith, "Coming Home," 911–13).

If James is unflinchingly honest about the extent to which he was more dazzled by metropolitan infallibility and virtue than was his friend Learie Constantine—"You have it all wrong. You believe all that you read in those books. They are no better than we"—he is nevertheless insistent on his debt to "Western civilization": "I didn't learn literature from the mango-tree, or bathing on the shore and getting the sun of the colonial countries; I set out to master the literature, philosophy and ideas of Western civilisation" (*Beyond a Boundary*, 116; "Discovering Literature," 238). And in specifying the impact of Thackeray's *Vanity Fair* on his Marxist sensibilities this reader is loudly silent about the caricatured portraits of Sambo, the butler, and the heiress from St. Kitts, Miss Schwartz.

When James reads *Froudacity* in the 1960s, he links Thomas's attentiveness to history and the African diaspora, as well as his command of the English language and his familiarity with British political and cultural institutions more generally, to his own formation in the early twentieth century.[1] But in embracing Thomas genealogically in this way James is silent about their differences. Highly conscious of what distinguished him, as a scholarship boy, from the upper-class students, and rebellious of the limitations of the curriculum, James still occupied an insider position in relation to Queen's Royal College. If the twentieth-century student labored to escape his classical curriculum by improving his cricket skills, Thomas labored to escape the stigma of not having had formal access to the classics. Furthermore, as the grandson of Barbadian immigrants who were already in the lower echelons of the middle class in the late nineteenth century, James and others in the northwestern Tunapuna-Arima corridor were well positioned to avail themselves of the opportunities and rewards of a solidly Anglophile trajectory if they wished to do so.

James is also silent about the Indo-Trinidadians who attended Queen's Royal College with him. In noting that figures such as Rudranath Capildeo and V. S. Naipaul attended that institution, I do not mean to impose easy, interracial alliances onto a historical record that is much more complex. But discussions of writers such as James and Naipaul often occur in separate spheres, just as other writers are discussed without reference to educational socialization altogether.

How might the actual or perceived alignment of institutions along ethnic and gender lines in the early twentieth century—Naparima College and Naparima Girls High School for male and female Indo-Trinidadians, Bishop Anstey High for the female counterparts of those attending Queen's Royal College, St. Mary's College of the Immaculate Conception, and St. Joseph's Convent for French Creole male and female constituencies, respectively—shed light on the work of various intellectuals? (Campbell, *Young Colonials*, 170–71). What might a July 1925 debate between the (Black) San Fernando Literary and Debating Society and the (Indian) Southern East Indian Debating Association on the topic "Is western civilization a failure?" tell us about the texture of intellectual life in the 1920s? (The San Fernando society argued against, while the Southern East Indian association argued affirmatively.)

Naipaul's frequent insistence on his separation from Caribbean figures and institutions and his denial that he comes out of a rich, longstanding cultural and intellectual Caribbean milieu is at odds with the details of his formation. His admiring letter to James after reading *Beyond a Boundary* suggests their mutual investment in being read by particular audiences in specific ways: "I have only read half of the book so far but I want to let you know at once I am extremely glad because it lets these English people know who and what we West Indians are" (James, "Discovering Literature," 243).

To ignore this similarity because of their ideological differences is also to discount the way in which Kamau Brathwaite's admiration for Naipaul's *House for Mr. Biswas* at the same moment in the 1960s is routed through English nineteenth-century writers: "To write really well about a living society [one] has simply to be an 'old-fashioned' writer like Hardy, Dickens, George Eliot, or Jane Austen. This is what Naipaul is." Brathwaite contends that the "black West Indian cannot really expect novels like *Biswas* until he has a strong enough framework of social convention from which to operate and until his own technique is flexible and subtle enough to take advantage of it" (Brathwaite, "Roots," 53–54). It is not that Naipaul, Hardy, and Austen undercut Brathwaite's elaboration of an Afrocentric aesthetics in the Caribbean but that Englishness must be understood as helping to define such an aesthetic (Edmondson).

Jean Rhys's response to an English nineteenth-century writer, *Wide Sargasso Sea*, can be read as her insertion of White Creole identities into the Caribbean landscape at a moment in the nationalist 1960s when such identities are either demonized or dismissed as inauthentic. She responds to Brontë's anglophone Jamaican Bertha Mason with a heroine from the eastern Caribbean whose heritage echoes Thomas's and others' representations of francophone cultures as conflictual yet sensitive, passionate, and marked by powerful interracial affinities (see Brontë, Gregg, and Hulme).

If Thomas is tied, then—complexly rather than simply—to these twentieth-century figures, his preoccupations can shed light on many other figures. When Edwin Ball Harper recalls Thomas's promotion of the Creole language at the moment of Trinidad's independence in 1962, he names Eugene Chen as one of Thomas's students in San Fernando. As solicitors in Port of Spain, Chen's and C. P. David's knowledge of classical and oral French "did not [prevent] them from taking daily exercise in their native tongue—the creole" nor from reaching "the greatest heights in English prose or verse."[2] Chen eventually migrated to England, and from there to China, where he became the foreign minister in Sun Yat-sen's government. His participation in the construction of national narratives in China therefore had its origins in his participation in discourses of creolization in Trinidad.

Ball Harper himself was offering the people of Trinidad the Creole language as their national inheritance at a moment when it was fast disappearing. One of his notebooks is entitled "Harper's Creole Patois Grammar," and it includes Creole-to-English translations of days of the week, proverbs, recipes, excerpts from the speeches of Trinidadian politicians, extracts from Eric Williams's *History of the People of Trinidad and Tobago,* and the national anthem.[3]

Countering such appeals to the past, Ramabai Espinet stresses that the "dhows of Naipaul's yearnings" are not hers, separating herself from the preoccupations of a previous generation. She claims a separate tradition that does not rely on nostalgic accounts of communal, national, or intellectual histories. Indeed, the novel of manners that Rostant called for in the 1880s, and Brathwaite in the 1960s, is being transformed by diasporic figurations as well as by a questioning of the anticolonial, masculinist, and heterosexual narratives that scripted independence.

Yet the women writers and younger male writers at the helm of this new dispensation are as likely to lay claim to nostalgic readings of the past as they are to question them. Sometimes the place to look for the most conservative recitations is in the most technologically advanced venue, as dislocated subjects scramble for cover from the same global realignments that they celebrate (Smith, "You Know You're West Indian If"; Edmondson and Smith). Current recitations of what makes "us" authentically "West Indian" in e-mail messages and other forums enthusiastically spurn the very technological modes and international journeys that are facilitating new readings of Caribbean identities.

Notes

Preface

1. *San Fernando Gazette*, 9 February 1884.
2. *St. George's Chronicle and Gazette*, 28 July 1888.
3. *Trinidad Echo*, 16 August 1876.
4. I follow Harris here and throughout in the spelling of *vodun*.
5. "From Toussaint L'Ouverture to Fidel Castro" is the title of the 1962 appendix to James's *Black Jacobins*, first published in 1938.
6. *New Era*, 25 October 1889.
7. *San Fernando Gazette*, 29 November 1884.

Introduction

1. Louis de Verteuil puts the population at 109,638 in 1871 and 153,128 in 1881 (157).
2. For a comprehensive social portrait of nineteenth-century Trinidad see Brereton, "Social Organisation"; and Brereton, *Race Relations.*
3. Here as elsewhere I use *Colored* to denote the category of mixed-race Trinidadians otherwise designated *free people of color.* When Thomas uses the term it denotes all persons of African descent.
4. For a rich reading of the meanings of the term *Creole* see Allen, "Creole Then and Now" and "What's in a Name."
5. *Froudacity,* 142. An obituary furnished by C. P. David states that Thomas's parents "on both sides" came from Africa (*Academy* [London] 36 [1889]: 203).
6. Benítez-Rojo, 10. I thank Flavia Vidal for bringing this passage to my attention.
7. The two descriptions of Froude are from "The West Indian Intellectual," C. L. R. James's introduction to the 1969 New Beacon Press edition of *Froudacity* (27) and from the back cover of the same edition, respectively.
8. See Viswanathan's study of the teaching of English literature in India, *Masks of Conquest.*

9. Viswanathan, "Raymond Williams," 49. Other discussions of Englishness and imperialism include Schwarz; Said, "Jane Austen"; and Gikandi.

10. *San Fernando Gazette,* 19 July 1892.

11. See Brereton, *Race Relations,* 88. I have not located these pamphlets.

12. For St. Joseph's Convent see Campbell, *Young Colonials.*

13. "Police News," *Trinidad Chronicle,* 10 October 1876. I have found no other reference to this incident.

14. 6 February 1866, Stanmore Papers, BL, Add. MSS 49,271.

15. See Reddock; and Niranjana. On women's wages see also Rodney, 42.

16. Morton, *John Morton of Trinidad,* 342–43, quoted in Reddock, 42–43. For an extended treatment of the relationship between Canadian Presbyterians and Indians in Trinidad see Moore.

17. Niranjana, 9–10. Niranjana also cites Chatterjee, 121, 127, on 9.

18. Dickens, *Letters,* 459. Patrick Brantlinger reads Dickens's "half-Negro and half-Indian" character, the treacherous "Sambo" Christian George King, as Dickens's fictional response to events in India, though in this story the character is Amerindian and the events take place off the coast of Belize. The story, "The Perils of Certain English Prisoners," appeared in the Christmas 1857 issue of Dickens's journal, *Household Words.*

19. I thank Natasha Barnes for this reference.

1. "Writing Was Easy to Him"

1. Editorials in Donovan's *Grenada People* on 26 September 1884 and 23 December 1885 lamented the lack of education for girls in Grenada. On 13 July 1887 the paper noted that it was not unusual in Trinidad to see a black girl sent to England to be educated, whereas in Grenada it was a novelty "which we hope will be imitated by those who can afford to."

2. *San Fernando Gazette,* 29 November 1884; *Grenada People,* 28 March 1884.

3. *San Fernando Gazette,* 2 and 9 August 1884. See also Brereton, *Race Relations,* 39–40.

4. Brereton, "Reform Movement." The question whether the reform meeting was significant, inconsequential, or dangerous would be taken up by Froude and his critics.

5. *New Era,* 25 October 1889.

6. *San Fernando Gazette,* 25 October 1884.

7. See the letter from Edgar Maresse-Smith to the *San Fernando Gazette,* 24 May 1890.

8. Gerard Besson, personal conversation with author, June 2001. On Caribbean Freemasonry, see Rich.

9. Moi, 68–72. The quotation is from Beauvoir, 422.

10. Calhoun, 70. For Bourdieu's inattention to the possibility of transformation see Garnham and Williams.

11. I thank Angelia Poon for this point.

12. Campbell, "John Jacob Thomas," 5; *Port of Spain Gazette,* 30 June 1855.

13. *Academy* 36 (1889): 203, information provided by C. P. David.

14. Campbell, "John Jacob Thomas," 8–10, emphasis added. Campbell quotes PRO, CO 299/10, Annual Report of the Inspector for Schools [Alexander Anderson] for the Year 1858, dated 1 March 1859.

15. Campbell, "John Jacob Thomas," 8, quoting from *Port of Spain Gazette,* 23 November 1859, Anderson's report for the quarter ending March 1859, enclosure: Report of Sugars [the headmaster].

16. Campbell, "John Jacob Thomas," 9, quoting from Wood, "John Jacob Thomas," 10; and *Port of Spain Gazette,* 4 April 1860, report of Anderson for quarter ending December 1859.

17. Campbell, *Young Colonials,* 22–23; PRO, CO 295/196, Keate to Labrouchere, 6 September 1857, enclosure: printed speech of Warner.

18. Thomas's emphasis. *New Era,* 14 September 1874, reported that Tronchin's essay was available for sale at Messrs. Tench & Co.

19. *Public Opinion,* 13 September 1887.

20. Ibid., 17 and 24 July 1888.

21. *Trinidad Chronicle,* 30 November 1869.

22. Ibid., 20 July 1870.

23. *Trinidad Chronicle,* 23, 31 October 1876, 1 December 1880; *New Era,* 31 January 1881. Apart from a series of translations in 1883 issues of the *Trinidadian Review,* it is not clear that Thomas's translation was ever published.

24. See also Brereton's "John Jacob Thomas," 19, 30.

25. *Port of Spain Gazette,* 10 December 1870; *New Era,* 19 December 1870, 22 June 1874.

26. J. H. Collens, the English headmaster of Woodbrook in 1886, described Guppy as the "energetic" inspector of schools and a prominent geologist and conchologist: "His valuable collection of specimens is probably the best in the West Indies" (204).

27. *Trinidad Chronicle,* 16 June 1871.

28. *Trinidad Telegraph,* 31 July 1871, 31 July 1872.

29. *San Fernando Gazette,* 17 October 1874. Dated 7 October, and the letter was sent from Port of Spain.

30. *San Fernando Gazette,* 12, 19 January 1884.

31. Ibid., 26 January 1884.

32. Ibid., 9 February 1884.

33. Ibid., 14 March 1885. I thank Michael Anthony for bringing this incident to my attention.

34. Ibid., 20 December 1884.

35. Ibid., 28 March 1885.

36. Letter signed "A Parent," ibid., 6 December 1884.

37. *San Fernando Gazette,* 11 July 1885; see also 26 September 1885.

38. From *Rowdy Dowdy,* quoted in the editorial of *Public Opinion,* 26 May 1886. See also *San Fernando Gazette,* 29 May 1886.

39. *Public Opinion,* 26 May 1886.

40. *Grenada People,* 27 July, 22 September, 24 November 1887.

41. Ibid., 29 September 1887.

42. *St. George's Chronicle and Gazette,* 28 July 1888. Hallam's and Julien's tributes are referred to as English translations of the Spanish originals, as are Thomas's replies.

43. *Public Opinion,* 19 February 1889; Mathurin, 11–12. I have found no other references to Unwin's position.

44. *New Era,* 12 July 1889. Thomas wrote the letter to T. W. Carr, of the Trinidad Public Library.

45. Davis's review appeared in *Timehri,* published in Demarara by the presses of the *Argosy* for the Royal Agricultural and Commercial Society of Demarara.

46. The *New Era* may not have known of *Timehri* or Darnell Davis's review of Froude, but the *Colonial Standard and Jamaica Despatch* reviewed it favorably in its 31 August 1888 issue.

47. *New Era,* 30 August 1889.

48. *Port of Spain Gazette,* 18 September 1889.

49. The reviews in the *Christian Leader,* the *Star,* and the *Echo* were reprinted in the *New Era* on 13 September 1889.

50. *Grenada People,* 17 October 1889.

51. *San Fernando Gazette,* 25 January 1890. The article refers to a report in the *Dominica Dial.*

2. "Her Majesty's Ethiopic Subjects"

1. *European Mail,* 3 October 1889, reprinted in *New Era,* 18 October 1889.

2. The phrase "Undiluted African descent" is from a description of Thomas in the *Port of Spain Gazette,* 10 October 1874.

3. This quotation, as well as those in the following paragraph, is from *Anthropological Review* 1 (1863): 386–89.

4. On William and Ellen Craft see Craft; Blackett, "Fugitive Slaves"; and McCaskill.

5. These minutes are housed at the University of London. Thomas read his paper on 7 November, and he was enrolled as a member on 21 November. Every prospective member had to be recommended by at least three members of the society, one of whom had to know the candidate personally. Beside Thomas's name in the list of candidates proposed for admission is the parenthetical notation: "by W. Furnivall from personal knowledge." Frederic Furnivall, the honorable secretary of the Philological Society during that period, had corresponded with Thomas after the *Creole Grammar*'s publication in 1869. I have found no mention of Thomas in Furnivall's papers.

6. The second edition of the *Oxford English Dictionary* (Oxford: Clarendon

Press, 1989) includes as a definition of *lion* "Things of note, celebrity, or curiosity . . . sights worth seeing [as in] 'to see, or show the lions'" and "A person of note or celebrity who is much sought after." Two examples of usage include "1850 Thackeray *Contrib to Punch Wks* 1886 XXIV, 251. 'What is a lion? A lion is a man or woman one must have at one's parties'" and "1889 T. A. Trollope *What I Remember* III, 131. 'Longfellow . . . largely paid the poet's penalty of being made the lion of all the drawing rooms.'"

7. Kingsley, *Charles Kingsley,* 2:240. For Jane Welsh Carlyle's reference to her own visit with the queen see Froude, *Letters and Memorials of Jane Welsh Carlyle,* 3:289–90.

8. For a discussion of Sarah Bartmann, spectacle, and race, see Sharpley-Whiting, 18.

9. *Saturday Review,* 13 October 1866. 446, quoted in Lorimer, *Colour, Class,* 178.

10. Jacobs; Brown, 221–23; Lorimer, *Colour, Class,* 49–50; A. Smith, 149. After leaving England, Smith spent two years in India.

11. I am indebted to Joan Bryant for this information.

12. Martin Delaney, from the appendix to his 1852 *Condition, Elevation, Emigration, and Destiny of the Colored People of the United States,* quoted in Moses, 121.

13. I take the term *transnation* from Charles Carnegie's discussion of Marcus Garvey's simultaneous linking and delinking of race, nation, territory.

14. Here Thomas is quoting the words of "Rev. P. H. Douglin, Rector of St. Clement's, Trinidad, a brilliant star among the sons of Ham" (*Froudacity,* 191).

15. *New Era,* 9 September 1872. The letter, dated 22 May 1872, presumably was first published in the *Negro* in Freetown. The *New Era* notes that the letter had been sent to it for publication but does not say by whom.

16. Ibid., 23 September 1872. Dated 13 September, the letter was sent from Cedros.

17. *Public Opinion,* 10 April 1885. For a history of this denomination, see C. Smith. For international missions more specifically, see Berry; and Dodson.

18. *San Fernando Gazette,* 25 April 1885.

19. Ibid., 4 April 1885.

20. The two passages are taken from, respectively, "The Condition *Sine Qua Non* of the Complete Elevation of the Negro Race" and "Truths to Be Remembered," *Jamaica Advocate,* 6 April and 14 September 1895, quoted in Bryan, *Jamaican People,* 233.

3. Can Anything Good Come out of Cedros?

1. *Port of Spain Gazette,* 10 August 1887. The 25 August 1887 *Grenada People* also refers to a "second edition shortly to be published." However, Thomas was understood to be working on a second, revised edition of the *Creole Grammar*

when he traveled to England shortly before his death to conduct further research. The *Grenada People* of 27 June 1889 announces that Thomas's *Gramme Creyol,* a "corrected and enlarged" edition, is ready for the press. A short list of the contents includes "Specimens of Creole as spoken (and written) in Trinidad, Martinique, Hayti, New Orleans, Mauritius," which suggests that a second edition was published.

2. One could travel by steamship from Port of Spain to Cedros on Mondays, Thursdays, and Saturdays, leaving Port of Spain at 7:00 A.M. and arriving at Cedros at 2:00 P.M. "There is also a land communication, partly along the beach and partly through the forest, over some of the points which project into the sea; this road is a mere bridle-path, and the traveller must always time his journey with the ebb of the tide, unless he should prefer being exposed to be drenched by the waves at the flow, or even prevented altogether from proceeding." The population was 3,802 in 1871 (L. de Verteuil, 322). J. H. Collens notes that Cedros was one-third Indian (meaning Asian) in the 1880s (174).

3. Another instance of non-Creole-speaking Barbadians in Trinidad is to be found in the tension between immigrant Barbadian policemen and members of the Creole-speaking working class (see Trotman, 97. On elite education in Barbados, see Sandiford and Stoddart).

4. I am thinking here of Wilson Harris's contention that limbo, vodun, Carib bush-baby omens, and other nonsanctioned discourses still remain to be acknowledged in the process of unearthing new perspectives of Caribbean history and society.

5. Patrick Keenan's 1869 *Report Upon the State of Education* notes nineteen "sworn interpreters" of French, nine of Spanish, one of German, and one of "Hindoostanee." The 1895 *Trinidad and Tobago Official and Commercial Register and Almanack* lists interpreters for that year in French, Spanish, Portuguese, Tamil, Chinese, and "Hindustani." Those listed for "French" include Sylvester Devenish, Edgar Maresse-Smith, and Philip Rostant. The lack of a distinction here between French and Creole explains Thomas's concern that even "our best interpreters" approached the Creole language as "mispronounced French."

6. During the three years prior to the publication of the *Grammar* Thomas was in both Cedros and Port of Spain; in 1867 he got a job in the civil service and moved to the capital.

7. Aub-Buscher, xiii, xiv. She points out that *French Creole* is a misleading term since while French and Creole are similar in vocabulary, in its "grammatical structure" Creole shares more with "Creoles which have resulted from the contact between other European and African languages, than with Standard French" (xvi n. 2).

8. Here the bird is the White oppressor, and the cockroach is the Negro. There is another usage for *cockroach* in the eastern Caribbean that refers to Whites or near-Whites: "albino cockroach," for example, or "whitey cockroach." See, e.g., Jean Rhys's *Wide Sargasso Sea,* where *cockroach* refers to victimized White Creoles.

9. The rendering of biblical material in Creole for the purpose of instructing Creole-speaking converts in Surinam had caused a furor four decades earlier, when the British and Foreign Bible Society published the Moravian New Testament in Sranan Creole (also called Negro-English, Taki-Taki, and Bouriki) in London. A reviewer in the December 1829 *Edinburgh Christian Instructor* had objected to the debasement of the Scriptures (see also Greenfield; and *Fife Herald,* 24 June 1830. On translations of the British and Foreign Bible Society generally, see Zemka).

10. The *Spectator* review was reprinted as "A Negro Grammarian" in *Trinidad Chronicle,* 28 September 1869.

11. See Warner-Lewis, *Trinidad Yoruba,* chap. 9, which argues that the erasure of African languages in the Caribbean was overstated.

12. Van Name, 127. Van Name's work has been described as the "beginning of the scientific study of creole languages, [the] first comparative study of creoles from all four lexical bases found in the Caribbean" (Holm, 24).

13. Thomas, "Creole Philology." The article was reprinted in the *Trinidad Chronicle* on 22 November 1870, along with a note saying that Thomas had been asked to write it by an eminent philologist in London.

14. If Thomas, following the philological procedures of his day, had used the traditional historical-comparative mode, he would have proceeded along two axes. First, the structural (lexical and morphophonological) character of Creole would have been explained according to its systematic correspondence to European languages (French in the case of Trinidadian Creole), just as Latin was a lexifier for French. Second, African languages would have been identified as substrates in the genesis of Creole, just as French had Gaulish and other Celtic substrates in its genesis from French. Here, second-language acquisition by adult speakers whose first languages were African would have been identified as the source of the African elements of Creole languages. Taken together, Thomas's statements on the "origins" of Creole veer inconsistently between indicating that French was *the* "source" of Trinidadian Creole and indicating that African languages (or a single African language) were *the* source of Caribbean Creoles.

On the "Afrogenesis" theory—that historically an African "Ur-Creole" was the source of all Caribbean Creole languages, in the same way that Latin is said to be the source of Indo-European languages—see DeGraff, "Origin of Creoles," 79–84. While DeGraff agrees that African languages are key to understanding the development and character of Caribbean Creole languages, he disagrees with all attempts to classify Creoles that assume that Creoles have developed in ways that are distinct from the "normal" processes that apply to other languages. He thus discounts Afrogenesis, historical-comparative, and any other methods of classifying Creoles that assume their "exceptionality."

15. It should be noted, however, that the earliest written texts in Creole languages in the region were not francophone but those produced under the auspices of the Moravian Church in St. Thomas and Surinam. Missionaries who learned "Negerhollands" in St. Thomas produced dictionaries and sermons, and their

enslaved converts produced letters dating from the 1740s. These are housed in the Moravian archives in Saxony (Holm).

16. A French priest, Abbé Goux, "published the first systematic treatment of a French-based creole in 1842 [attached] to a *Catéchisme en langue créole*" (Holm, 23).

17. "A Negro Grammarian." Thomas includes Marbot's text in the 1870 *Trübner* essay.

18. *Anti-Slavery Reporter* (London), 31 December 1869, reprinted in *Trinidad Chronicle*, 15 February 1870.

19. Pierre Larousse, *Grand dictionnaire universel du XIXe siècle* (1869), quoted in English in DeGraff, *Morphology in Creole Genesis*, 94. For Maria Nugent (later Lady Nugent), the American wife of a governor of Jamaica, Creole spoken by White women in that colony was decidedly *not* sweet: "Many of the ladies, who have not been educated in England, speak a sort of broken English, with an indolent drawling out of their words, that is very tiresome if not disgusting. I stood next to a lady one night, near a window, and, by way of saying something, remarked that the air was much cooler than usual; to which she answered, 'Yes, ma-am, *him rail-ly too fra-ish*'" (132).

20. See Allsopp; Warner-Lewis, *Guinea's Other Suns*, 190; and esp. Rohlehr, *Calypso and Society*, 11–23. *Calenda*, for instance, is often glossed as the dance and music accompanying stick fights, but Rohlehr notes that meanings changed over time. He also notes that the *calenda, jouba*, and *bellair* are dances named by Borde in the second volume of his *Histoire*.

21. *Trinidad Chronicle*, 4 January 1870.

22. *San Fernando Gazette*, 10 March 1875.

23. *Trinidad Chronicle*, 30 July 1869.

24. *Port of Spain Gazette*, 30 November 1869.

25. *Trinidad Chronicle*, 4 February 1870.

26. Journal entry, 4 November 1866, Stanmore Papers, BL, Add. MSS 49,271.

27. For a rich reading of this passage see Adams.

28. Mrs. Arthur Hamilton Gordon, 23 February 1869, Stanmore Papers, BL, Add. MSS 49,271.

29. See F. Smith, "Beautiful Indians"; and Adams's discussion of English men and Indian women generally in Kingsley's texts.

30. Charles Kingsley, "The Legend of La Brea," *Macmillan's Magazine* 22 (June 1870): 106–10, reprinted in *Trinidad Chronicle*, 26 July 1870. This poem appeared after his return to England and before the publication of *At Last* in 1871.

31. *Star of the West*, 23 February 1870.

32. Almost two decades later critics would compare Kingsley favorably with Froude, noting the latter's unwillingness to accept invitations to political events during his trip.

33. *Star of the West,* 20 January 1870.

34. Newman led the Tractarians, a group based at Oxford (and including James Anthony Froude's brother, Richard Hurrell) that stressed the Roman Catholic character of the Church of England. Newman shocked followers and foes alike when he converted to Catholicism in 1845. He was subsequently ordained to the Catholic priesthood. Reviewing James Anthony Froude's *History of England* in the January 1864 issue of *Macmillan's Magazine,* Kingsley declared that Catholic clergy were untruthful. Newman's famous response, *Apologia pro Vita Sua,* appeared in 1864, earning him sympathy and Kingsley criticism.

35. Cudjoe, preface, 8.

36. William Herbert, "Review of New Books," *Trinidad Telegraph,* 2 August 1871, reprinted in *Chronicle and Gazette* (Grenada), 12 August 1871. This article is unsigned; Herbert was the editor of the *Telegraph.*

37. I thank Burton for sharing this with me.

38. The tribute and Herbert's reply to it appeared in the *Trinidad Telegraph* on 16 September 1871.

39. John Jacob Thomas, "Words, Sentiments and Behaviour," *Trinidad Chronicle,* 11 August 1871. Although the letter is headed "No. 1," and ends by promising a follow-up letter that will examine more fully "the opinions and sentiments [these terms] engender and promote, and the kind of conduct and intercourse sanctioned by such opinions and sentiments," I have been unable to find a subsequent letter from Thomas on this topic.

40. "The Trial of N. W. Brunton and others," Port of Spain, 1870, CO 295/256, no. 341, quoted in Trotman, 88, 310.

41. "Siam naygar hai" is "incorrect" because *Sir, hum naygar hai* (Thomas probably collapses *Sir, hum* into "Siam") means literally "Sir, *we is* naygar," and she ought therefore to have said, "Sir *mai* naygar *hoon.*" I thank Sujata Moorti for clarifying this for me.

42. According to Peggy Mohan, "Few recognize [Bhojpuri] as a language distinct from, rather than derivative of, Standard Hindi, with the result that the language is generally held to be a 'broken' variety of Standard Hindi that evolved spontaneously on the Trinidadian sugar estates. . . . long before Bhojpuri ever came to Trinidad it was already the junior partner in a diglossic relationship with a lexically similar but grammatically very different language [i.e., Hindi], of which it outwardly appeared to be merely a simpler dialect. Moreover, the diglossic relationship ensured that Hindi lexicon could always find its way into Bhojpuri and be accepted, while Bhojpuri usage would always be stigmatized in Hindi" (25).

4. West Indian Fables Explained

1. *Quashie,* related to *Kwasi,* the Twi name for a male child born on Sunday, is often used disparagingly in the Caribbean to refer to a Black person who is unsophisticated. It is possible that the term does not have this meaning in all territories or, more significantly, across different time periods. Donovan's use of it here

may indicate a middle-class term for working-class people that was implicitly rather than explicitly pejorative, or not necessarily so.

2. Letter from "A Friend of Grenada," *San Fernando Gazette,* 2 October 1875, and letter from "B," ibid., 13 November 1875 (both referring to a lecture on Grenada by Thomas on 20 September 1875 at the Wesleyan Chapel in San Fernando); "Notes on a Trip to Grenada in 1873 by an Invalid," *Trinidad Review,* 22, 29 November, 6, 13, 20 December 1883.

3. *Trinidad Review,* 9 August 1883. In glossing "the peculiar music of their Quelbays" Gordon Rohlehr cites J. D. Elder, *Folk Song and Folk Life in Charlotteville,* which notes that "Quelbay" songs and dances were performed at wakes in Tobago, accompanied by the "marlidoundoun" steel drums played by women (36), though Rohlehr is cautious about the connection, given the fact that songs and dances which were very different from each other had the same names in different islands.

4. "Public Immorality," *Port of Spain Gazette,* 2 February 1889, quoted in Rohlehr, 37, 539.

5. "The All-Engrossing Topic," *San Fernando Gazette,* 8 November 1884.

6. *Jumby,* or *jumbie,* is a regional term for the false, the comical, or the dangerous. Jumbies are evil spirits who are to be exorcised, reflecting a typically Caribbean preoccupation with only the negative aspects of God/Devil (Allsopp gives the Congo-Mbangala *insambi/ndsumbi*) African cosmologies (see Allsopp, 317).

7. *San Fernando Gazette,* 6 August 1887. On Douglin see Brereton, *Race Relations,* 93.

8. *Psalms and Church Hymnary,* 116. My thanks to Rev. Ashley Smith and Mrs. Winifred Smith for identifying the reference.

9. *Grenada People,* 7 June 1888. The arrival of King Ja-Ja and his son Sunday attracted large crowds at the docks of Grenada, where it was first reported that he would disembark, and then at Kingstown, St. Vincent. A "little man" King Ja-Ja may have been to the British authorities who exiled him, but not to the masses of St. Vincent, who continued to follow him in the streets during his residence in Kingstown. The *New Era* reported on 22 July 1891 that he was in the Canary Islands, on the way back to West Africa, where he would be reinstated as monarch of Opobo.

10. My discussion of Kingsley is based on the accounts in Bernard Semmel, 92–101; Lorimer, *Colour, Class;* Chitty; Martin; and Kingsley, *Charles Kingsley,* vol. 2.

11. Kingsley to Macmillan and Co., October 1870, BL, Add. MSS 54911, 203–4.

12. The Jamaica *Colonial Standard and Despatch* of 15 February 1888 noted that Froude had identified the wrong house as Gordon's and that contrary to Froude's statement, Gordon had not been arrested in his or anyone else's house, but had given himself up voluntarily.

13. See also Gilbert. Froude edited *Reminiscences by Thomas Carlyle, Thomas Carlyle: A History of the First Forty Years of His Life, 1795–1835,* and *Letters*

and Memorials of Jane Welsh Carlyle. He wrote a biography of Carlyle, and also a meditation on their relationship, *My Relations with Carlyle.*

14. In fact, the senior tutor at Exeter burned the novel publicly.

15. This meeting was one organized by Rostant in 1886.

16. *Port of Spain Gazette,* 23 and 27 June, 6 July, 1888; *San Fernando Gazette,* 30 June, 11 August 1888; *Truth,* 30 June 1888; *Public Opinion,* 6 July 1888. See also Brereton, "Birthday of our Race."

17. *Public Opinion,* 20 July 1888; *Daily Commercial Budget,* 19 July 1888.

18. *Public Opinion,* 10 July 1888. The poem is signed "Idalia."

19. Ibid., 6 July 1888.

20. Ibid.

21. The book's full title is *The Caribbean Confederation: A Plan for the union of the Fifteen British West Indian colonies, preceded by an account of the past and present condition of the Europeans and the African races inhabiting them, with a true explanation of the Haytian mystery, in which is embodied a refutation of the chief statements made by Mr. Froude in his recent work, "The English in the West Indies."*

22. The article was reprinted as a separate document in Demerara that year.

23. *Grenada People,* 28 June, 5 July 1888. The 28 June issue lists Thomas as a participant in a public meeting in St. George's to plan for a jubilee celebration.

24. Ibid., 12 May 1888.

25. *Grenada People,* 27 June 1889.

Afterword

1. James, "West Indian Intellectual" and "Discovering Literature in Trinidad." The latter first appeared in the *Journal of Commonwealth Literature* in July 1969.

2. Edwin Ball Harper Papers, Belmont Library, Port of Spain. These are type-written notes, as well as scrapbooks containing clippings, including some from the *Trinidad Sunday Guardian* of 26 August 1962. For Chen see also Chen.

3. Williams's own account of his intellectual formation, and his assessment of British historians, are well known (*British Historians; Inward Hunger*).

Works Cited

Adams, James Eli. *Dandies and Desert Saints: Styles of Victorian Masculinity.* Ithaca, N.Y.: Cornell University Press, 1995.

Adderly, Rosanne Marion. "'Africans,' 'Americans,' and 'Creole Negroes': Migration and Black Population Diversity in Nineteenth-Century Trinidad." In *Marginal Migrations: The Circulation of Cultures within the Caribbean,* ed. Shalini Puri. Warwick University Caribbean Studies. London: Macmillan Caribbean, 2002, forthcoming.

Akenson, D. H. *The Irish National Experiment: The National System of Education in the Nineteenth Century.* London: Routledge & Kegan Paul, 1970.

Allen, Carolyn. "Creole Then and Now: The Problem of Definition." *Caribbean Quarterly* 44, nos. 1–2 (1998): 33–49.

———. "What's in a Name: Defining Caribbean Creoleness." Paper presented at the annual meeting of the Caribbean Studies Association, Barranquilla, Colombia, 26–30 May 1997.

Alleyne, Mervyn. *Comparative Afro-American.* Ann Arbor: Karoma, 1980.

Allsopp, Richard, ed. *Dictionary of Caribbean English Usage.* Oxford: Oxford University Press, 1996.

Anderson, Benedict. *Imagined Communities.* London: Verso, 1983.

Anthony, Michael. "J. J. Thomas." In *The Book of Trinidad,* ed. Gerard Besson and Bridget Brereton, 327–28. Newtown, Port of Spain: Paria Press, 1992.

Appiah, Kwame. *In My Father's House.* New York: Oxford University Press, 1992.

Asiegbu, Johnson. *Slavery and the Politics of Liberation, 1787–1861.* London: Longman, 1969.

Aub-Buscher, Gertrude. "John Jacob Thomas." In *Theory and Practice of Creole Grammar,* by John Jacob Thomas, v–xvii. London: New Beacon Books, 1969.

Bair, Barbara. "Pan-Africanism as Process: Adelaide Casely Hayford, Garveyism, and the Cultural Roots of Nationalism." In *Imagining Home: Class, Culture, and Nationalism in the African Diaspora,* ed. Sidney Lemelle and Robin D. G. Kelley, 120–34. London: Verso, 1994.

Barnes, Natasha. "Black Atlantic—Black America." *Research in African Literatures* 27, no. 4 (1996): 106–7.

Barros, Juanita de. "'Race' and Culture in the Writings of J. J. Thomas." *Journal of Caribbean History* 27, no. 1 (1993): 36–53.

Beauvoir, Simone de. *The Prime of Life.* Trans. Peter Green. Harmondsworth: Penguin, 1988.

Beenie Man. "Heights of Great Men." *Art and Life.* Virgin Records America compact disk 49093.

Belgrave, Valerie. *Ti Marie.* London: Heinemann, 1988.

Bell, Caryn Cossé. *Revolution, Romanticism, and the Afro-Creole Protest Tradition in Louisiana, 1718–1868.* Baton Rouge: Louisiana State University Press, 1997.

Benítez-Rojo, Antonio. *The Repeating Island: The Caribbean and the Postmodern Perspective.* Trans. James Maraniss. Durham, N.C.: Duke University Press, 1992.

Benn, Dennis. *The Growth and Development of Political Ideas in the Caribbean, 1774–1983.* Kingston: Institute of Social and Economic Research, 1987.

Bernabé, Jean, Patrick Chamoiseau, and Raphaël Confiant. "In Praise of Creoleness." Trans. Mohamad Khyar. *Callaloo* 13, no. 4 (1990): 886–909. First published as *Eloge de la créolité* (Paris: Editions Gallimard, 1989).

Berry, L. L. *A Century of Missions of the African Methodist Episcopal Church, 1840–1940.* New York: Gutenberg, 1942.

Besson, Gerard. *A Photograph Album of Trinidad at the Turn of the Nineteenth Century.* Newtown, Port of Spain: Paria Press, 1985.

Bhabha, Homi. "The Third Space." In *Identity: Community, Culture, Difference,* ed. Jonathan Rutherford, 207–21. London: Lawrence & Wishart, 1990.

Bickerton, Derek. Introduction to *The Ethnography of Variation: Selected Writings on Pidgins and Creoles by Hugo Schuchardt.* Trans. T. L. Markey. Ann Arbor: Karoma, 1979.

Blackett, R. J. M. "Fugitive Slaves in Britain: The Odyssey of William and Ellen Craft." *Journal of American Studies* 12 (1978): 41–62.

———. "The Hamic Connection: African-Americans and the Caribbean, 1820–65." In *Before and After 1865: Education, Politics, and Regionalism in the Caribbean,* ed. Brian Moore and Swithin Wilmot, 317–29. Kingston: Ian Randle, 1998.

Bleek, W. H. I. "Grimm's Law in South Africa; or, Phonetic Changes in the South African Bantu Languages." 1. In the South-Eastern Branch." *Transactions of the Philological Society,* 1873–74, 186–200.

Blyden, Edward Wilmot. *Selected Letters of Edward Wilmot Blyden.* Ed. Hollis Lynch. Milwood, N.Y.: KTO Press, 1978.

Bolland, O. Nigel. "Creolization and Creole Societies: A Cultural Nationalist View of Caribbean Social History." In *Intellectuals in the Twentieth-Century*

Caribbean. Vol. 1, *Spectre of the New Class: The Commonwealth Caribbean,* ed. Alistair Hennessy, 50–79. London: Macmillan, 1992.

Borde, Pierre-Gustave-Louis. *The History of Trinidad under the Spanish Government.* 2 vols. Trans. James Alva Bain (vol. 1, 1932) and A. S. Mavrogordato (vol. 2, 1961), preface and notes in both volumes translated by Sister Marie Thérèse Rétour. Reprint, 2 vols. in 1, Newtown, Port of Spain: Paria Press, 1982. Originally published as *Histoire de l'ile de la Trinidad sous le gouvernement espagnol,* 2 vols. (Paris: Maisonneuve et Cie, 1876–82).

Bourdieu, Pierre. *Distinction: A Social Critique of the Judgement of Taste.* 1979. Trans. Richard Nice. Cambridge: Harvard University Press, 1984.

———. *Language and Symbolic Power.* Trans. Gino Raymond and Matthew Adamson. Cambridge: Harvard University Press, 1991.

Brantlinger, Patrick. *Rule of Darkness: British Literature and Imperialism, 1830–1914.* Ithaca, N.Y.: Cornell University Press, 1988.

Brassey, Lady A. *In the Trades, the Tropics and the Roaring Forties.* London: Longmans & Green, 1885.

Brathwaite, Edward Kamau. *The Arrivants: A New World Trilogy.* Oxford: Oxford University Press, 1973.

———. *The Development of Creole Society in Jamaica, 1770–1820.* Oxford: Clarendon, 1971.

———. *History of the Voice: The Development of Nation Language in Anglophone Caribbean Poetry.* London: New Beacon Books, 1984.

———. "Roots." In *Roots.* Havana: Casa de las Americas, 1985.

Brereton, Bridget. "The Birthday of Our Race: A Social History of Emancipation Day in Trinidad, 1838–1888." In *Trade, Government, and Society in Caribbean History, 1700–1920,* ed. Barry Higman, 69–83. Kingston: Heinemann, 1983.

———. "The Experience of Indentureship, 1845–1917." In *From Calcutta to Caroni,* ed. John La Guerre. St. Augustine, Trinidad: UWI Extra Mural Studies Unit, 1985.

———. "The Historiography of Trinidad and Tobago and Guyana: The Last Thirty Years." Paper presented at the annual meeting of the Association of Caribbean Historians, Suriname, April 1998.

———. *A History of Modern Trinidad, 1783–1962.* Kingston: Heinemann, 1981.

———. "John Jacob Thomas: An Estimate." *Journal of Caribbean History* 9 (May 1977): 22–42.

———. "The Liberal Press of Trinidad, 1869–1985." Paper presented at the annual meeting of the Association of Caribbean Historians, Barbados, April 1977.

———. "Michael Maxwell Philip (1829–1888): Servant of the Centurion." *Antilla: Journal of the Faculty of Arts* (University of the West Indies) 1, no. 3 (1988): 6–20.

———. *Race Relations in Colonial Trinidad, 1870–1900.* London: Cambridge University Press, 1979.

————. "The Reform Movement in Trinidad in the Later Nineteenth Century." Paper presented at the annual meeting of the Association of Caribbean Historians, St. Augustine, Trinidad, April 1973.

————. "Social Organisation and Class, Racial, and Cultural Conflict in Nineteenth-Century Trinidad." In *Trinidad Ethnicity*, ed. Kevin A. Yelvington, 33–55. London: Macmillan, 1993.

————. "The White Elite of Trinidad, 1838–1950." In *The White Minority in the Caribbean*, ed. Howard Johnson and Karl Watson, 32–67. Kingston: Ian Randle, 1998.

Bridges, Yseult. *Child of the Tropics: Victorian Memoirs*. Ed. and comp. Nicholas Guppy. Port of Spain: Aquarella, 1988.

Brody, Jennifer DeVere. *Impossible Purities: Blackness, Femininity, and Victorian Culture*. Durham, N.C.: Duke University Press, 1998.

Brontë, Charlotte. *Jane Eyre*. New ed. New York: Penguin, 1982.

Broughton, Trev Lynn. *Men of Letters, Writing Lives: Masculinity and Literary Auto/Biography in the Late Victorian Period*. London: Routledge, 1999.

Brown, William Wells. *The American Fugitive in Europe: Sketches of Places and People Abroad: The Travels of William Wells Brown*. 1855. Reprint, New York: Markus Wiener, 1991.

Bryan, Patrick. "Black Perspectives in Late Nineteenth-Century Jamaica." In *Garvey: His Work and Impact*, ed. Rupert Lewis and Patrick Bryan, 47–63. Trenton, N.J.: Africa World Press, 1991.

————. *The Jamaican People, 1880–1902: Race, Class, and Social Control*. London: Macmillan, 1991.

Burton, Antoinette. "Tongues Untied: Lord Salisbury's 'Black Man' and the Boundaries of Imperial Democracy." Typescript.

Cain, William E. "Introduction: *Emmanuel Appadocca* in Its American Context." In *Emmanuel Appadocca: Or, Blighted Life, A Tale of the Boucaneers*, by Michel Maxwell Philip. New ed. Amherst: University of Massachusetts Press, 1997.

Calhoun, Craig. "Habitus, Field, and Capital: The Question of Historical Specificity." In *Bourdieu: Critical Perspectives*, ed. Craig Calhoun, Edward LiPuma, and Moishe Postone, 61–88. Chicago: University of Chicago Press, 1993.

Cameron, Norman Eustace. *The Evolution of the Negro*. 2 vols. Georgetown: Argosy, 1929–34.

Campbell, Carl. "The Development of Education in Trinidad, 1834–1870." Ph.D. diss., University of the West Indies, 1973.

————. "Jean-Baptiste Philippe, Man from the Naparimas." In *Free Mulatto*, by Jean-Baptiste Philippe, x–xxix. Newtown, Port of Spain: Paria Press, 1987. Reprint of document printed for private circulation by the author in 1824 as *An address to the Right Hon. Earl Bathurst His Majesty's Principal Secretary of State for the Colonies, relative to the claims which the coloured population of Trinidad have to the same civil and political privileges with their white fellow subjects. By a Free Mulatto of the Island.*

———. "John Jacob Thomas of Trinidad: The Early Career of a Black Teacher and Scholar, 1855–70." *African Studies Association of the West Indies Bulletin* 8 (1976): 4–17.

———. *The Young Colonials: A Social History of Education in Trinidad and Tobago, 1834–1939.* Kingston: The Press, University of the West Indies, 1996.

Carlyle, Thomas. *Latterday Pamphlets.* London: Chapman & Hall, 1869.

———. "Occasional Discourse on the Nigger Question." In *English and Other Critical Essays by Thomas Carlyle,* ed. Ernest Rhys, 303–33. London: J. M. Dent; New York: E. P. Dutton, 1915.

Carlyle, Thomas, and Jane Welsh Carlyle. *The Collected Letters of Thomas and Jane Welsh Carlyle.* Ed. Charles Richard Sanders. Vol. 3. Durham, N.C.: Duke University Press, 1970.

Carnegie, Charles V. "Garvey and the Black Transnation." *Small Axe* 5 (1999): 48–71.

Cave, Roderick. "History of Printing in Trinidad." 1975. Archives of the John Carter Brown Library, Brown University, Providence, R.I.

Cesareo, Mario. "When the Subaltern Travels: Slave Narrative and Testimonial Erasure in the Contact Zone." In *Women at Sea: Travel Writing and the Margins of Caribbean Discourse,* ed. Lizabeth Paravisini-Gebert and Ivette Romero-Cesareo, 99–134. New York: Palgrave, 2001.

Chamoiseau, Patrick. *School Days.* Trans. Linda Coverdale. Lincoln: University of Nebraska Press, 1997.

Chatterjee, Partha. *The Nation and Its Fragments: Colonial and Postcolonial Histories.* Princeton: Princeton University Press, 1993.

Chen, Percy. *China Called Me: My Life inside the Chinese Revolution.* Boston: Little, Brown, 1979.

Chester, G[reville] J[ohn]. *Translatlantic Sketches in the West Indies, South America, Canada, and the United States.* London: Smith, Elder, 1869.

Chitty, Susan. *The Beast and the Monk: A Life of Charles Kingsley.* New York: Mason Charter, 1975.

Christ, Carol. "The Hero as Man of Letters: Masculinity and Victorian Nonfiction Prose." In *Victorian Sages and Cultural Discourse: Renegotiating Gender and Power,* ed. Thaïs E. Morgan, 19–31. New Brunswick: Rutgers University Press, 1990.

Clarke, Norma. "Strenuous Idleness: Thomas Carlyle and the Man of Letters as Hero." In *Manful Assertions: Masculinities in Britain since 1800,* ed. Michael Roper and John Tosh, 25–43. London: Routledge, 1991.

Cobham, Rhonda. "Revisioning Our Kumblas: Transforming Feminist and Nationalist Agendas in Three Caribbean Women's Texts." *Callaloo* 16, no. 1 (1993): 44–64.

Coleridge, Henry Nelson. *Six Months in the West Indies.* London: Thomas Tegg, 1841.

Collens, J. H. *A Guide to Trinidad: A Handbook for the Use of Visitors.* 2nd ed. London: E. Stock, 1888.

Condé, Maryse. "On the Apparent Carnivalization of Literature from the French Caribbean." In *Representations of Blackness and the Performance of Identities,* ed. Jean Muteba Rahier, 91–97. Westport, Conn.: Bergin & Garvey, 1999.

Craft, William. *Running a Thousand Miles for Freedom: or, the Escape of William and Ellen Craft from Slavery.* 1860. Reprint, Salem, Mass.: Ayer, 1991.

Crowther, Samuel, and Rev. John Christopher Taylor. *The Gospel on the Banks of the Niger: Journals and Notices of the Native Missionaries Accompanying the Niger Expedition of 1857–1859.* 1859. Reprint, London: Dawsons of Pall Mall, 1968.

Cudjoe, Selwyn. "The Audacity of It All: C. L. R. James's Trinidadian Background." In *C. L. R. James's Caribbean,* ed. Paget Henry and Paul Buhle, 39–55. Durham, N.C.: Duke University Press, 1992.

———. Introduction to *Free Mulatto,* by Jean-Baptiste Philippe, v–xxi. Wellesley, Mass.: Calaloux, 1996.

———. "Jamaica Kincaid and the Modernist Project." In *Caribbean Women Writers: Essays from the First International Conference,* ed. Selwyn Cudjoe, 215–32. Wellesley, Mass.: Calaloux, 1990.

———. Preface to *Emmanuel Appadocca: Or, Blighted Life, a Tale of the Boucaneers,* by Michel Maxwell Philip. New ed. Amherst: University of Massachusetts Press, 1997.

———. *Speaking Truth to Power, or Why We Need an Association for the Empowerment of Afro-Trinbagonians.* Wellesley, Mass.: Calaloux, 1998.

Dash, Michael. *Literature and Ideology in Haiti, 1915–1961.* Totowa, N.J.: Barnes & Noble Books, 1981.

———. *The Other America: Caribbean Literature in a New World Context.* Charlottesville: University Press of Virginia, 1998.

Davies, Carole Boyce. *Black Women, Writing, and Identity: Migrations of the Subject.* London: Routledge, 1994.

Davis, N. Darnell. *The Cavaliers and Roundheads of Barbados, 1650–1652.* Georgetown: Argosy, 1887.

———. "Mr. Froude's Negrophobia, or Don Quixote as a Cook's Tourist." *Timehri, Journal of the Royal Agricultural and Commercial Society of British Guiana,* n.s., 2 (1888): 85–129.

DeGraff, Michel. "Morphology in Creole Genesis: Linguistics and Ideology." In *Ken Hale: A Life in Language,* ed. Michael Kenstowicz, 53–121. Cambridge: MIT Press, 2001.

———. "On the Origin of Creoles: A Cartesian Critique of 'Neo'- Darwinian Linguistics." Typescript.

de Verteuil, Fr. Anthony. *Sylvester Devenish and the Irish in Nineteenth Century Trinidad.* Newtown, Port of Spain: Paria Press, 1986.

————. *The Years of Revolt: Trinidad, 1881–1888.* Newtown, Port of Spain: Paria Press, 1974.

de Verteuil, Louis A. A. *Trinidad: Its Geography, Natural Resources, Administration, Present Condition, and Prospects.* London: Cassell, 1884.

Devonish, Hubert. *Language and Liberation: Creole Language Politics in the Caribbean.* London: Karia, 1976.

Dickens, Charles. *Great Expectations.* Oxford: Clarendon Press, 1983.

————. *The Letters of Charles Dickens.* Vol. 8. Ed. Graham Storey and Kathleen Tillotson. Oxford: Clarendon, 1995.

————. "The Niger Expedition." In *The Works of Charles Dickens: Miscellaneous Papers, Plays and Poems,* 1:43–61. National Edition, 35. London: Chapman & Hall, 1908.

————. "The Perils of Certain English Prisoners." In *The Works of Charles Dickens: Christmas Stories,* 1:50–71. National Edition, 26. London: Chapman & Hall, 1907.

Dodson, Jualynne E. "Encounters in the African Atlantic World: The African Methodist Episcopal Church in Cuba." In *Between Race and Empire: African-Americans and Cubans before the Cuban Revolution,* ed. Lisa Brock and Digna Castañeda Fuertes, 85–103. Philadelphia: Temple University Press, 1998.

Douglass, Frederick. *Narrative of the Life of Frederick Douglass, an American Slave.* 1845. Harmondsworth: Penguin, 1982.

Drabble, Margaret, ed. *Oxford Companion to English Literature.* London: Oxford University Press, 1985.

Drayton, Arthur. "Francis Williams." In *Fifty Caribbean Writers,* ed. Daryl Cumber Dance, 493–97. Westport, Conn.: Greenwood, 1986.

Dunn, Waldo. *James Anthony Froude.* 2 vols. Oxford: Clarendon, 1963.

Dyde, Brian. *Caribbean Companion: The A–Z Reference.* London: Macmillan Caribbean, 1992.

Edmondson, Belinda. *Making Men: Gender, Literary Authority, and Women's Writing in Caribbean Narrative.* Durham, N.C.: Duke University Press, 1999.

Edmondson, Belinda, and Faith Smith. "Anxieties of Influence: The Caribbean Digital Diaspora." Paper presented at the annual meeting of the Modern Language Association, New Orleans, December 2001.

Edwards, Norval. "Roots, and Some Routes Not Taken: A Caribcentric Reading of *The Black Atlantic.*" *Found Object* 4 (1994): 27–35.

Espinet, Ramabai. "Hosay Night." In *Nuclear Seasons,* 10. Toronto: Sister Vision, 1991.

Ferguson, Moira. Introduction to *The History of Mary Prince, A West Indian Slave, Related by Herself.* 1831. Reprint, Ann Arbor: University of Michigan Press, 1993.

Firmin, Anténor. *De l'égalité des races humaines.* Paris: F. Picton, 1885.

Foster, Frances Smith. Introduction to *A Brighter Coming Day: A Frances Ellen*

Watkins Harper Reader, ed. Frances Smith Foster. New York: Feminist Press at the City University of New York, 1990.

Froude, James Anthony. *The English in the West Indies, or the Bow of Ulysses.* London: Longmans, Green, 1888.

——. *My Relations with Carlyle.* London: Longmans, Green, 1903.

——. *Nemesis of Faith.* London: J. Chapman, 1849.

——, ed. *Letters and Memorials of Jane Welsh Carlyle.* 3 vols. London: Longmans, Green, 1883.

——. *Thomas Carlyle: A History of the First Forty Years of His Life, 1795–1835.* 2 vols. London: Longmans, Green, 1882.

——. *Thomas Carlyle: A History of His Life in London, 1834–1881.* 2 vols. London: Longmans, Green, 1884.

Galván, Manuel de Jesús. *Enriquillo: Leyenda histórica dominicana 1503–1533.* Mexico City: Editorial Porrúa, 1976.

Gamble, W. H. *Trinidad: Historical and Descriptive.* London, 1866.

Garnham, Nicholas, and Raymond Williams. "Pierre Bourdieu and the Sociology of Culture: An Introduction." *Media, Culture, and Society* 2 (1980): 209–23.

Gates, Henry Louis. *Race, Writing, and Difference.* Chicago: University of Chicago Press, 1985.

Gell, Simeran Man Singh. "The Inner and the Outer: Dalip Singh as an Eastern Stereotype in Victorian England." In *The Victorians and Race,* ed. Shearer West, 68–83. Aldershot, Hants: Scolar Press; Brookfield, Vt.: Ashgate, 1996.

Gikandi, Simon. *Maps of Englishness.* New York: Columbia University Press, 1998.

Gilbert, Elliot. "Rescuing Reality: Carlyle, Froude, and Biographical Truth-Telling." *Victorian Studies* 34, no. 3 (1991): 295–314.

Gilroy, Paul. *The Black Atlantic: Modernity and Double Consciousness.* Cambridge: Harvard University Press, 1992.

——. "Cultural Studies and Ethnic Absolutism." In *Cultural Studies,* ed. Lawrence Grossberg, Cary Nelson, and Paula A. Treichler, 187–98. New York: Routledge, 1992.

——. *There Ain't No Black in the Union Jack: The Cultural Politics of Race and Nation.* Chicago: University of Chicago Press, 1991.

Goveia, Elsa V. *A Study on the Historiography of the British West Indies to the End of the Nineteenth Century.* 1956. Reprint, Washington, D.C.: Howard University Press, 1980.

Greenfield, William. *A Defence of the Surinam Negro-English Version of the New Testament: Founded on the History of the Negro-English Version, a View of the Situation, Population, and History of Surinam, a Philological Analysis of the Language, and a Careful Examination of the Version; In Reply to the Animadversions of an Anonymous Writer in the Edinburgh Christian Instructor.* London: Samuel Bagster, 1830.

Gregg, Veronica Marie. *Jean Rhys's Historical Imagination: Reading and Writing the Creole.* Chapel Hill: University of North Carolina Press, 1995.

Hall, Catherine. "'From Greenland's Icy Mountains . . . to Afric's Golden Sand': Ethnicity, Race, and Nation in Mid-Nineteenth Century England." *Gender and History* 5, no. 2 (1993): 212–30.

———. *White, Male, and Middle Class.* Cambridge: Polity Press, 1992.

Hall, Stuart. "Culture, Community, Nation." *Cultural Studies* 7 (1993): 349–63.

Haller, John S., Jr. *Outcasts from Evolution: Scientific Attitudes of Racial Inferiority, 1859–1900.* Urbana: University of Illinois Press, 1971.

Hamilton, R. C. G., earl of Kimberley. "Hamilton Report into the Carnival Disturbances." *Port of Spain Gazette,* 22 October 1881.

Harries, Elizabeth. "'Out in Left Field': Charlotte Smith's Prefaces, Bourdieu's Categories, and the Public Sphere." *Modern Language Quarterly* 58, no. 4 (1997): 457–73.

Harris, Wilson. *History, Fable, and Myth in the Caribbean and Guianas.* Georgetown: National History and Arts Council, Ministry of Information and Culture, 1970.

Helg, Aline. *Our Rightful Share: The Afro-Cuban Struggle for Equality, 1886–1912.* Chapel Hill: University of North Carolina Press, 1995.

Heuman, Gad. *The Killing Time: The Morant Bay Rebellion in Jamaica.* Knoxville: University of Tennessee Press, 1994.

Higman, B. W. *Writing West Indian Histories.* London: Macmillan, 1999.

Hill, Robert, ed. *The Marcus Garvey and Universal Negro Improvement Association Papers.* Berkeley: University of California Press, 1983.

Holm, John. *Pidgins and Creoles.* Vol. 1, *Theory and Structure.* Cambridge: Cambridge University Press, 1988.

Holt, Thomas. *The Problem of Freedom: Race, Labor, and Politics in Jamaica and Britain, 1832–1938.* Baltimore: Johns Hopkins University Press, 1992.

Hooker, J. R. *Henry Sylvester Williams: Imperial Pan-Africanist.* London: Rex Collings, 1975.

Howard, Philip A. *Changing History: Afro-Cuban Cabildos and Societies of Color in the Nineteenth Century.* Baton Rouge: Louisiana State University Press, 1998.

Hoyos, F. A. *Barbados: A History from the Amerindians to Independence.* London: Macmillan, 1978.

Hulme, Peter. "The Locked Heart: The Creole Family Romance of *Wide Sargasso Sea.*" In *Colonial Discourse / Postcolonial Theory,* ed. Francis Barker, Peter Hulme, and Margaret Iversen, 72–88. Manchester: Manchester University Press, 1994.

Hume, David. "Of National Characters." In *Essays Literary, Moral, and Political,* 116–27. New ed. London: Ward, Lock & Bowden, 1875.

Hutchinson, Lionel. "Conrad Reeves: A Kind of Perfection." *New World* 3, nos. 1–2 (1966): 62–67.

Irving, Washington. *The Sketch Book of Geoffrey Crayon.* London: J. Murray, 1824.

Jacobs, Harriet A. *Incidents in the Life of a Slave Girl, Written By Herself.* New ed. Cambridge: Harvard University Press, 1987.

James, C. L. R. *Beyond a Boundary.* Kingston: Sangster's Book Stores, 1963.

——. *The Black Jacobins: Toussaint L'Ouverture and the San Domingo Revolution.* 1938. Reprint, New York: Vintage, 1963.

——. "Discovering Literature in Trinidad in the 1930s." In *Spheres of Existence,* 237–44. Westport, Conn.: Lawrence Hill, 1980.

——. "Michel Maxwell Philip: 1829–1888." In *From Trinidad: An Anthology of Early West Indian Writing,* ed. Reinhard Sander, 253–68. New York: Africana, 1978. Originally published in *Beacon* 1, no. 6 (1931).

——. "The West Indian Intellectual." In *Froudacity: West Indian Fables by J. A. Froude,* by John Jacob Thomas, 23–49. London: New Beacon Books, 1969.

Jha, J. C. "The Indian Mutiny-cum-Revolt of 1857 and Trinidad." Archives of the Special Collections, University of the West Indies, St. Augustine, Trinidad.

Johnson, Howard. "Barbadian Immigrants in Trinidad, 1870–1897." *Caribbean Studies* 13, no. 3 (1973): 5–30.

Kale, Mahdavi. "Projecting Identities: Empire and Indentured Labor Migration from India to Trinidad and British Guiana, 1836–1885." In *Nation and Migration: The Politics of Space in the South Asian Diaspora,* ed. Peter van der Veer, 73–92. Philadelphia: University of Pennsylvania Press, 1995.

Keenan, Patrick. *Report Upon the State of Education in the Island of Trinidad.* Dublin: Alexander Thom, 1869.

Kincaid, Jamaica. *Lucy.* 1990. New York: Plume, 1991.

Kingsley, Charles. *At Last: A Christmas in the West Indies.* 2 vols. London: Macmillan, 1871.

——. *Charles Kingsley: His Letters and Memories of His Life.* Ed. Fanny Kingsley. 2 vols. London: Henry King, 1877.

Labat, Jean Baptiste. *Nouveau voyage aux isles de l'Amérique.* 1742. Paris: Edition du Père Labat: Nicolas Bridoux Reprints, 1992.

Laurence, K. O. *A Question of Labour: Indentured Immigration into Trinidad and British Guiana, 1875–1917.* Kingston: Ian Randle, 1994.

——. "The Settlement of Free Negroes in Trinidad before Emancipation." *Caribbean Quarterly* 9, nos. 1–2 (1963): 26–52.

Lebow, Richard Ned. *White Britain and Black Ireland: The Influence of Stereotypes on Colonial Policy.* Philadelphia: Institute for the Study of Human Issues, 1976.

Lewis, Gordon. *Main Currents in Caribbean Thought.* Baltimore: Johns Hopkins University Press, 1983.

Lewis, Rupert. "John Jacob Thomas and Political Thought in the Caribbean." *Caribbean Quarterly* 36, nos. 1–2 (1990): 46–58.

Lilly, William S. "New Light on the Carlyle Controversy." *Fortnightly Review* 79 (1903): 1000–1009.

Lindo, Locksley. "Francis Williams: A 'Free' Negro in a Slave World." *Savacou* 1 (1970): 75–80.

Longfellow, Henry Wadsworth. "The Ladder of St. Augustine." In *Birds of Passage*, 20–21. Boston: Houghton Mifflin, 1886.

Lorimer, Douglas A. *Colour, Class, and the Victorians.* Leicester: Leicester University Press; New York: Holmes & Meier, 1978.

———. "Race, Science, and Culture: Historical Continuities and Discontinuities, 1850–1914." In *The Victorians and Race,* ed. Shearer West, 12–33. Aldershot, Hants: Scolar Press; Brookfield, Vt.: Ashgate, 1996.

Lovelace, Earl. *The Dragon Can't Dance.* Burnt Mill, Harlow, Essex: Longman, 1979.

Lynch, Hollis. *Edward Wilmot Blyden: Pan-Negro Patriot, 1832– 1912.* New York: Oxford University Press, 1967.

Martin, Robert. *The Dust of Combat: A Life of Charles Kingsley.* London: Faber & Faber, 1959.

Márquez, Roberto. "Nationalism, Nation, and Ideology: Trends in the Emergence of a Caribbean Literature." In *The Modern Caribbean,* ed. Franklin W. Knight and Colin A. Palmer, 293–340. Chapel Hill: University of North Carolina Press, 1989.

Mathurin, Owen. *Henry Sylvester Williams and the Origins of the Pan-African Movement, 1896–1911.* Westport, Conn.: Greenwood Press, 1976.

McCaskill, Barbara. "'Yours Very Truly': Ellen Craft—The Fugitive as Text and Artifact." *African American Review* 28, no. 4 (1994): 509–29.

McDaniel, Lorna. "The Philips: A 'Free Mulatto' Family of Grenada." *Journal of Caribbean History* 24, no. 2 (1990): 178–94.

Mighty Sparrow. *Dan Is the Man in the Van.* Port of Spain: National Recording Co., 1958.

Miller, Errol. *Marginalization of the Black Man: Insights from the Development of the Teaching Profession.* 2nd ed. Kingston: Canoe Press, 1994.

———. *Men At Risk.* Kingston: Jamaica Publishing House, 1991.

Minturn, Robert B. *From New York to Delhi by way of Rio de Janeiro, Australia, and China.* 2 vols. New York: D. Appleton, 1858.

Mohan, Peggy. "The Rise and Fall of Trinidad Bhojpuri." *International Journal of the Sociology of Language* 85 (1990): 21–30.

Moi, Toril. *Simone de Beauvoir: The Making of an Intellectual Woman.* Cambridge: Blackwell, 1994.

Moodie, Sylvia. "The Spanish Language as Spoken in Trinidad." *Caribbean Studies* 13, no. 1 (1973): 88–94.

Moodie-Kubalsingh, Sylvia Maria. *The Cocoa Panyols of Trinidad: An Oral Record.* London: British Academic Press, 1994.

Moore, Dennison. *Origins and Development of Racial Ideology in Trinidad: The Black View of the East Indian.* Tunapuna, Trinidad: Chakra, 1995.

Morton, Sarah E., ed. *John Morton of Trinidad.* Toronto: Westminster, 1916.

Moses, Wilson Jeremiah. *Alexander Crummell: A Study of Civilization and Discontent.* New York: Oxford University Press, 1989.

Naipaul, V. S. "A Flag on the Island." In *A Flag on the Island,* 124–214. 1967. Reprint, London: Penguin, 1969.

———. *A House for Mr. Biswas.* New York: Knopf, 1961.

———. *The Middle Passage.* London: Andre Deutsch, 1962.

———. *Miguel Street.* 1959. Oxford: Heinemann, 1974.

Niranjana, Tejaswini. "'Left to the Imagination': Indian Nationalisms and Female Sexuality in Trinidad." *Small Axe* 2 (1997): 1–18.

Nixon, Rob. *London Calling: V. S. Naipaul, Postcolonial Mandarin.* New York: Oxford University Press, 1992.

Norman, H. W. Letter to Daly. 13 January 1885. In *"Correspondence respecting the recent Coolie disturbances in Trinidad at the Mohurrum Festival,* the report thereon by Sir H. W. Norman, K.C.B., C.I.E, March 1885," 39–40. Library of the Institute of Commonwealth Studies, London.

Nugent, Lady Maria. *Lady Nugent's Journal.* 1839. Ed. F. Cundall. London: West India Committee for the Institute of Jamaica, 1939.

Oxaal, Ivar. *Black Intellectuals and the Dilemmas of Race and Class in Trinidad.* Cambridge, Mass: Schenkman Books, 1982.

Parmasad, Kenneth. "Resisting the Recruiter's Net: The Attitude of India's Poor to Indentureship Recruitment Practices." Paper presented at the annual meeting of the Association of Caribbean Historians, Suriname, April 1998.

Paton, William Agnew. *Down the Islands: A Voyage to the Caribbees.* London: Kegan Paul, Trench, 1888.

Philip, Marlene Nourbese. "Managing the Unmanageable." In *Caribbean Women Writers: Essays from the First International Conference,* ed. Selwyn Cudjoe, 295–300. Wellesley, Mass.: Calaloux, 1990.

Philip, Michel Maxwell. *Emmanuel Appadocca; or Blighted Life. A Tale of the Boucaneers.* New ed. Amherst: University of Massachusetts Press, 1997.

Philippe, Jean-Baptiste. *Free Mulatto.* Newtown, Port of Spain: Paria Press, 1987. Reprint of document printed for private circulation by the author in 1824 as *An address to the Right Hon. Earl Bathurst His Majesty's Principal Secretary of State for the Colonies, relative to the claims which the coloured population of Trinidad have to the same civil and political privileges with their white fellow subjects. By a Free Mulatto of the Island.*

Plummer, Brenda Gayle. "Firmin and Martí at the Intersection of Pan-Americanism and Pan-Africanism." In *José Martí's "Our America": From National to Hemispheric Cultural Studies,* ed. Jeffrey Belnap and Raúl Fernández, 210–27. Durham, N.C.: Duke University Press, 1998.

Pope, Alexander. *The Complete Poetical Works.* Boston: Houghton Mifflin, 1931.

Pouchet Pacquet, Sandra. "The Enigma of Arrival: *The Wonderful Adventures of Mrs. Seacole in Many Lands.*" *African American Review* 26, no. 4 (1992): 651–63.

———. "The Heartbeat of a West Indian Slave: *The History of Mary Prince.*" *African American Review* 26, no. 1 (1992): 131–46.

Pratt, Mary. *Imperial Eyes: Travel Writing and Transculturation.* New York: Routledge, 1992.

Prince, Mary. *The History of Mary Prince, A West Indian Slave, Related by Herself.* New ed. Ann Arbor: University of Michigan Press, 1993.

Psalms and Church Hymnary. London: Oxford University Press, 1927.

Rainger, Ronald. "Race, Politics, and Science: The Anthropological Society of London in the 1860s." *Victorian Studies* 22 (1978): 51–70.

Reddock, Rhoda. *Women, Labour, and Politics in Trinidad and Tobago: A History.* London: Zed Books, 1994.

Reynolds, Harry. *Minstrel Memories: The Story of Burnt Cork Minstrelsy in Great Britain from 1836 to 1927.* London: Alston Rivers, 1928.

Rhys, Jean. *Wide Sargasso Sea.* New ed. New York: Norton, 1999.

Rich, Paul. "Transmutations of Caribbean Freemasonry." Paper delivered at the annual meeting of the Caribbean Studies Association, Mérida, Mexico, May 1984.

Richmond, M. A. *Bid the Vassal Soar.* Washington, D.C.: Howard University Press, 1974.

Rodney, Walter. *A History of the Guyanese Working People, 1881–1905.* Baltimore: Johns Hopkins University Press, 1981.

Rohlehr, Gordon. *Calypso and Society in Pre-Independence Trinidad.* Port of Spain: G. Rohlehr, 1990.

———. "Froudacity: A Re-examination." *New World* 7, nos. 1–2 (1971): 17–20, 35–38.

Said, Edward. "Jane Austen and Empire." *Culture and Imperialism.* New York: Vintage, 1993.

———. *Orientalism.* New York: Vintage, 1979.

Salmon, Charles S. *The Caribbean Confederation.* 1888. Reprint, New York: Negro Universities Press, 1969.

Samaroo, Brinsley. "Cyrus Prudhomme David: A Case Study in the Emergence of the Black Man in Trinidad Politics." *Journal of Caribbean History* 3 (November 1971): 73–89.

Sander, Reinhard, ed. *From Trinidad: An Anthology of Early West Indian Writing.* New York: Africana, 1978.

———. *The Trinidad Awakening: West Indian Literature of the Nineteen-Thirties.* Westport, Conn.: Three Continents Press, 1988.

Sandiford, Keith A. P. *Measuring the Moment: Strategies of Protest in Eighteenth-Century Afro-English Writing.* Selinsgrove, Pa.: Susquehanna University Press, 1988.

Sandiford, Keith A. P., and Brian Stoddart. "The Elite Schools and Cricket in Barbados: A Study in Colonial Continuity." In *Liberation Cricket: West Indies Cricket Culture,* ed. Hilary McD. Beckles and Brian Stoddart, 44–60. Manchester: Manchester University Press, 1995.

Scholes, Theophilus E. S. *Glimpses of the Ages, or the "Superior" and "Inferior" Races So-Called, Discussed in the Light of Science and History.* 2 vols. London: John Long, 1905–7.

Schuchardt, Hugo. *Pidgin and Creole Languages.* Trans. Glenn Gilbert. London: Cambridge University Press, 1980.

Schwarz, Bill. "Englishness and the Paradox of Modernity." *New Formations* 1 (1987): 147–53.

Seacole, Mary. *Wonderful Adventures of Mrs. Seacole in Many Lands.* 1857. New ed. Bristol: Falling Wall, 1984.

Segal, Daniel A. "'Race' and 'Colour' in Pre-Independence Trinidad and Tobago." In *Trinidad Ethnicity,* ed. Kevin A. Yelvington, 81–115. London: Macmillan, 1993.

Semmel, Bernard. *Jamaican Blood and Victorian Conscience: the Governor Eyre Controversy.* New York: Houghton Mifflin, 1963.

Sharpley-Whiting, T. Denean. *Black Venus: Sexualized Savages, Primal Fears, and Primitive Narratives in French.* Durham, N.C.: Duke University Press, 1999.

Singh, Kelvin. *Bloodstained Tombs: The Muharram Massacre, 1884.* London: Macmillan, 1988.

Smith, Amanda. *Amanda Smith: The King's Daughter.* Hanley, Staffs: M.O.V.E. Press; Greencastle, Ind.: Harta-Flame, 1977.

Smith, Charles S. *A History of the African Methodist Episcopal Church.* Philadelphia: Book Concern of the AME Church, 1922.

Smith, Faith. "Beautiful Indians, Troublesome Negroes, and Nice White Men: Caribbean Romances and the Invention of Trinidad." In *Caribbean Romances: The Politics of Representation,* ed. Belinda Edmondson, 163–82. Charlottesville: University Press of Virginia, 1999.

———. "Coming Home to the Real Thing: Gender and Intellectual Life in the Anglophone Caribbean." *South Atlantic Quarterly* 93, no. 4 (1994): 895–924.

———. "John Jacob Thomas and Caribbean Intellectual Life in the Nineteenth Century." Ph.D. diss., Duke University, 1995.

———. "A Man Who Knows His Roots: J. J. Thomas and Current Discourses of Black Nationalism." *Small Axe* 5 (March 1999): 1–13.

———. "You Know You're West Indian If: Codes of Authenticity in Colin Channer's *Waiting in Vain.*" *Small Axe* 10 (2001): 41–59.

Sommer, Doris. *Foundational Fictions: The National Romances of Latin America.* Berkeley: University of California Press, 1991.

Stepan, Nancy. *The Idea of Race in Science.* London: Macmillan; Hamden, Conn.: Archon Books, 1982.

Stewart, Robert J. "Reporting Morant Bay: The 1865 Jamaican Insurrection as Reported and Interpreted in the *New York Herald, Daily Tribune,* and *Times.*" In *Before and After 1865: Education, Politics, and Regionalism in the Caribbean,* ed. Brian Moore and Swithin Wilmot, 330–42. Kingston: Ian Randle, 1998.

Stocking, George. "What's in a Name? The Origins of the Royal Anthropological Institute, 1837–1871." *Man: The Journal of the Royal Anthropological Institute* 6 (1971): 369–90.

Stuckey, Sterling. *Slave Culture: Nationalist Theory and the Foundations of Black America.* New York: Oxford University Press, 1987.

Thackeray, William. *Vanity Fair.* New ed. New York: Random House, 1958.

Thomas, John Jacob. "Creole Philology: Extracts from an Essay on the Philology of the Creole Dialect, by the Author of the Creole Grammar." *Trübner's American and Oriental Literary Record,* 31 December 1870, 57–58.

———. *Froudacity: West Indian Fables by J. A. Froude.* 1889. Reprint, London: New Beacon Books, 1969.

———. *The Theory and Practice of Creole Grammar.* 1869. Reprint, London: New Beacon Books, 1969.

Thomas-Bailey, Melisse. "Samuel Carter and the *San Fernando Gazette.*" Paper presented at the Conference on Henry Sylvester Williams and Pan-Africanism, University of the West Indies, St. Augustine, Trinidad, January 2001.

Tinker, Hugh. *A New System of Slavery: The Export of Indian Labour Overseas, 1830–1920.* London: Oxford University Press for the Institute of Race Relations, 1974.

Tracy, Robert Archer. *The Sword of Nemesis.* 1919. Reprint, New York: AMS Press, 1975.

Trollope, Anthony. *The West Indies and the Spanish Main.* 1860. Reprint, New York: Carroll & Graf, 1999.

Trotman, David. *Crime in Trinidad.* Knoxville: University of Tennessee Press, 1986.

Trouillot, Michel-Rolph. "Culture on the Edges: Creolization in the Plantation Context." *Plantation Society in the Americas* 5, no. 1 (1998): 8–28.

———. "From Planter's Journals to Academia: The Haitian Revolution as Unthinkable History." *Journal of Caribbean History* 25, nos. 1–2 (1991): 81–99.

Van Name, Addison. "Contributions to Creole Grammar." *Transactions of the American Philological Association* 1 (1869–70): 123–67.

Vaughan, H. A. "Samuel Prescod: The Birth of a Hero." *New World* 3, nos. 1–2 (1966): 55–60.

Viswanathan, Gauri. "Currying Favor: The Politics of British Educational and Cultural Policy in India, 1813–54." *Social Text* 19–20 (fall 1988): 85–104.

———. *The Masks of Conquest.* New York: Columbia University Press, 1991.

———. "Raymond Williams and British Colonialism." *Yale Journal of Criticism* 4, no. 2 (1991): 47–66.

Walcott, Derek. "Tarpon." In *Collected Poems, 1948–1984,* 61. London: Faber & Faber, 1992.

Ward, Samuel Ringgold. *Autobiography of a Fugitive Slave.* 1855. Reprint, New York: Arno Press and the New York Times, 1968.

Warner, Maureen. *Language in Trinidad with Special Reference to English.* Ph.D. diss. University of York, 1967.

Warner-Lewis, Maureen. *Guinea's Other Suns: The African Dynamic in Trinidad Culture.* Dover, Mass.: Majority, 1991.

———. *Trinidad Yoruba: From Mother-Tongue to Memory.* Tuscaloosa: University of Alabama Press, 1996.

———. "Trinidad Yoruba: Its Theoretical Implications for Creolisation Processes." *Caribbean Quarterly,* 44, nos. 1–2 (1998): 50–61.

Williams, Eric. *British Historians and the West Indies.* 1964. Reprint, Brooklyn: A&B Books, 1994.

———. *History of the People of Trinidad and Tobago.* New York: Praeger, 1964.

———. *Inward Hunger: The Education of a Prime Minister.* London: Andre Deutsch, 1969.

Williams, Raymond. *Keywords: A Vocabulary of Culture and Society.* 1976. New York: Oxford University Press, 1985.

Wood, Donald. "John Jacob Thomas." In *Froudacity: West Indian Fables by J. A. Froude,* by John Jacob Thomas, 9–22. London: New Beacon Books, 1969.

———. *Trinidad in Transition: The Years after Slavery.* Oxford: Oxford University Press, 1968.

Woodward, Servanne. "The Head of the Crafty Serpent: Missionary Grammars and Bilingual Dictionaries in African and Caribbean Countries." *Diogenes* 152 (1990): 50–72.

Wynter, Sylvia. "Lady Nugent's Jamaica Journal." *Jamaica Journal* 1, no. 1 (1967): 23–34.

Zemka, Sue. "The Holy Books of Empire: Translations of the British and Foreign Bible Society." In *Macropolitics of Nineteenth-Century Literature,* ed. Jonathan Arac and Harriet Ritvo, 102–37. Durham, N.C.: Duke University Press, 1995.

Index

New World Studies

New World Studies publishes interdisciplinary research that seeks to redefine the cultural map of the Americas and to propose particularly stimulating points of departure for an emerging field. Encompassing the Caribbean as well as continental North, Central, and South America, books in this series examine cultural processes within the hemisphere, taking into account the economic, demographic, and historical phenomena that shape them. Given the increasing diversity and richness of the linguistic and cultural traditions in the Americas, the need for research that privileges neither the English-speaking United States nor Spanish-speaking Latin America has never been greater. The series is designed to bring the best of this new research into an identifiable forum and to channel its results to the rapidly evolving audience for cultural studies.

Vera M. Kutzinski
Sugar's Secrets: Race and the Erotics of Cuban Nationalism

Richard D. E. Burton and Fred Reno, editors
French and West Indian: Martinique, Guadeloupe, and French Guiana Today

A. James Arnold, editor
Monsters, Tricksters, and Sacred Cows: Animal Tales and American Identities

J. Michael Dash
The Other America: Caribbean Literature in a New World Context

Isabel Alvarez Borland
Cuban-American Literature of Exile: From Person to Persona

Belinda J. Edmondson, editor
Caribbean Romances: The Politics of Regional Representation

Steven V. Hunsaker
Autobiography and National Identity in the Americas

Celia M. Britton
Edouard Glissant and Postcolonial Theory: Strategies of Language and Resistance

Mary Peabody Mann
Juanita: A Romance of Real Life in Cuba Fifty Years Ago
Edited and with an introduction by Patricia M. Ard

George B. Handley
Postslavery Literatures in the Americas: Family Portraits in Black and White

Faith Smith
Creole Recitations: John Jacob Thomas and Colonial Formation in the Late Nineteenth-Century Caribbean